"The medical community must demonstrate high reliability as part of its social contract with society. K. Scott Griffith's work, manifest through *The Leader's Guide to Managing Risk*, offers an easy-to-understand approach that aligns nicely to that contract and the osteopathic profession's focus on interconnectedness, holism, and prevention."

—ROBERT A. CAIN, DO, FACOI, FAODME,
president and chief executive officer at the
American Association of Colleges of Osteopathic Medicine

"Healthcare delivery is complex, serving multiple values in an everchanging environment. Griffith makes the sequence of reliability understandable and achievable with everyday examples."

—PEGGY DUGGAN, MD,
executive vice president and chief medical officer at Tampa General Hospital

T0265839

What People Are Saying About
The Leader's Guide to Managing Risk

"When did you last learn something so novel, so brilliant, and so helpful that y
could hardly wait to share it with others? *The Leader's Guide to Managing Risk*
book that has given me new eyes, providing clarity to a pattern for understand
and seeing things that now seem so obvious."

—DAVID BO
manager of human performance improvem
Battelle Energy Alliance / Idaho National Labora

"A must-read for those in healthcare safety and performance improvement.

—JACK CO
senior vice president / chief quality c
Providence St. Joseph Health and former Air Force flight

"I thoroughly enjoyed the book! *The Leader's Guide to Managing Risk* sh
required reading of anyone desiring to understand modern safety princ

—JOHN
vice president and chief safety officer at JetBl

"This is one of those books you can't put down . . . a must-read for all av
high consequence industry safety professionals."

—NICK
associate administrator for regulation and
at the Federal Aviation Administra

"This book takes the spaghetti diagram of complex thinking about ris
and makes it accessible to the reader on the first pass. The use of
stories to accentuate the points really works and makes the book
interesting read."

—JEFF
senior vice president of human resources at American

"Today's leaders must be prepared to navigate through levels of u
industries. In this remarkable book, K. Scott Griffith will challer
aspiring and current leaders to enhance their risk skills."

—CHIEF C
Department of Justice (retired), court-
author, and police

THE LEADER'S GUIDE

TO MANAGING RISK

A PROVEN METHOD TO BUILD

RESILIENCE AND RELIABILITY

K. Scott Griffith

HarperCollins
Leadership

An Imprint of HarperCollins

Published by HarperCollins Leadership, an imprint of HarperCollins Focus LLC.

Any internet addresses, phone numbers, or company or product information printed in this book are offered as a resource and are not intended in any way to be or to imply an endorsement by HarperCollins Leadership, nor does HarperCollins Leadership vouch for the existence, content, or services of these sites, phone numbers, companies, or products beyond the life of this book.

ISBN 978-1-4002-4379-2 (eBook)

ISBN 978-1-4002-4378-5 (HC)

Library of Congress Cataloging-in-Publication Data

Library of Congress Cataloging-in-Publication application has been submitted.

Printed in the United States of America

23 24 25 26 27 LBC 5 4 3 2 1

To Sean, Sam, Sophie, Farhin, Joey, and Omar

CONTENTS

BLIND SPOTS

HIDING IN PLAIN SIGHT

We see and understand the world through the lens of our experiences. We have unique pathways in life. How we interpret our experiences depends on our biology, our ancestors' DNA ingrained in our consciousness,[1] our environment and culture, and the specific circumstances of a situation.

Sometimes our interpretations help us survive, such as avoiding predators, learning to hunt and gather, mastering fire, or winning a war. Understandably, we celebrate our successes: profitable financial results, good grades in school, getting to work on time, meeting our obligations, and enjoying our personal lives. We work with colleagues who share our mission, vision, and values. We strive to produce results that last by focusing on what we do well.

But sometimes we learn the *wrong* lessons from our successful outcomes. Our risky systems and behaviors produce dividends until they don't, and we pay for our miscalculations with our fortunes, our lives, and sometimes the lives of others.

There's a hidden pattern to how bad things unfold and a sequence to preventing them. This book will illuminate that science and show us how to apply it in our business and everyday life.

Leading a business is typically about focusing on what we do well—serving marketplace needs through the efficient delivery of products and services.

In fact, many top leaders are hired or promoted because of their operational experience and expertise—being good at serving the mission. But how many are experts outside the core business?

A founder and CEO may understand that IT support is essential to product delivery and revenue, but the expertise to ward off a cyberattack likely lies beyond her direct experience. After all, the thrill and gratification of starting a new company comes from managing our successes—not from thinking about the negative consequences of running the business.

The unexpected outcome might be from forces beyond our control, such as a pandemic, natural disaster, economic downturn, or supply chain disruption. Or sometimes harm comes from our own hand, doing what we're good at doing, only this time with a different result, such as a breach of customer privacy. Either way, it's the menace lurking below the surface that doesn't go away, despite our past successes.

It's the harm that takes place in any organization—a result of unintended consequences. Sometimes the harm is catastrophic, a seminal event such as an industrial accident. It could be the ongoing cost of injuries or damages to employees or clients—a problem that simply won't go away. It can be seen as the cost of doing business, although no one in the organization wants that to be the case. Despite our best efforts, the numbers aren't getting better, and we're beginning to wonder if the problem can be solved. We've benchmarked against our competitors, and no one seems to have found the magic bullet. Even organizations with some success admit the problem is far from solved. It keeps us awake at night thinking about what would happen if things got worse, or if people start wondering if a change in leadership might produce better results.

In a dangerous world, blind spots are everywhere. Many of the things you and I do in our everyday lives—drive to the store, send our kids to school, fly in an airplane, get treated at a hospital, manage a business—come with inherent risks. Another driver could swerve in front of us, our child could fail a final exam, the nurse could give us the wrong medication, or we could lose a contract with a major client and declare bankruptcy. There are also global risks we didn't anticipate, such as the COVID-19 pandemic.

And who knows what else lies ahead as our world becomes more complex and potentially dangerous?

Similarly, the homeowner standing on the top rung of the ladder reaching too far to clean the gutters or the teenage driver weaving in and out of traffic aren't thinking about falling or colliding with another car. Most of us are wired for success, until we fail. What we all have in common is that our optimism and direct experience often outweigh our risk intelligence—the ability to perceive and calculate situational danger. Humans are driven by aspirations and consequences, and if we've never experienced a bad outcome, we believe it won't happen to us. Until it does.

We're human, you might say, and accidents will happen. But wouldn't it be better if we could understand the causes of these unintended outcomes and keep them from happening?

The best strategy highly reliable organizations use is to not focus exclusively on what the organization does well, but to devote equal attention to what the organization lacks: expertise in preventing the potential negative consequences of running the business.

Certain high-consequence activities, such as military combat operations and the nuclear power industry, are steeped in principles of catastrophic risk management and are typically funded appropriately to meet the level of risk. But most businesses are not similarly resourced. Sometimes the cost of running a business isn't recognized until it's too late, then our attention turns to loss control and mitigation rather than prevention. Insurance can cover part of these liabilities, of course, but the costs can be enormous. Healthcare, aviation, manufacturing, and finance are examples of industries that at times struggle with preventing harm to customers and employees. In the past, the strategies organizations employed in these sectors were based on reactive response. But that's changing.

A BETTER WAY

The trick is to see, understand, and manage *socio-technical* risk—the everyday systems and human interactions in the world around us—in a specific order.

In this book I will reveal the Sequence of Reliability and how I developed it. This secret to managing risk and preventing catastrophe is a simple, straightforward strategy that works for any endeavor—from crashes and pandemics to avoiding medical mistakes, to improving workforce morale, to achieving better results in our everyday lives.

How is this done? It's simple but not always easy or intuitive. These concepts and the skills to apply them are within our grasp. This book will illuminate the secret to that success. Anyone can learn it, from CEOs to frontline workers to parents and students. It's governed by the laws of physics—but instead of atoms and molecules, it's the science of how people and systems interact to produce results. This sequence of managing risk is essential to keeping our households, our businesses, and our public institutions safer and more productive.

We'll start by looking at a plane crash I witnessed years ago, and the lessons I learned from it. I'll explain how this accident shifted my perspective on how bad things happen in our everyday world. We'll explore the quirky path that led me to devote my professional life to organizational improvement, and I'll share a few stories along the way to help anchor the principles in everyday experience.

We'll learn from common occurrences—waking up on time and getting to work, driving to the store, helping with homework, managing our diet and exercise regimens—and from examining catastrophes of *Titanic* proportions. From these, a strategy to help us improve will emerge.

If we're running a business, this strategy will help us navigate the turbulent waters of competition, weather the changing external environment, and perhaps most important, to see, understand, and respond to the risk of employee burnout every organization faces today.

We'll build on these experiences together and learn the Sequence of Reliability in successive chapters. Each one builds to the final chapter, where I will describe how I developed the Aviation Safety Action Program, a transformational approach adopted in the airline industry that led to a 95 percent reduction in the fatal accident rate. This program, which has been replicated more than 767 times, transformed an entire industry through collaboration among businesses, labor associations, and their regulators.

We'll learn how to see and understand risk through different lenses, manage systems and people more effectively, and improve organizational performance. We'll discuss ways to identify the environmental and organizational contributors to employee burnout and a collaborative strategy to respond accordingly. We'll learn how to improve company morale and reduce turnover, resulting in enhanced customer service and satisfaction.

Finally, we'll explore the world's first independently audited high reliability standard known as Collaborative High Reliability®—a program I developed as a culmination of the experiences and lessons presented throughout the book. We'll examine how this standard can be replicated and is available to any business aspiring to sustain high-reliability performance.

But first, we must recognize that what we see ahead may disguise the dangers below the surface. We must flip the iceberg.

FLIGHT 191

ROCKED BY THE INVISIBLE

On August 2, 1985, I began a routine walk-around inspection of a Boeing B-727 airliner, preparing to fly from Dallas/Fort Worth International to New York's LaGuardia Airport. As a young pilot about to complete my first year with American Airlines, everything in life seemed to be falling into place. I had grown up with family and friends around me, I worked hard, and now I had the dream job I always wanted. The world made sense to me.

In the cockpit of a modern airliner, a pilot might fly at any time with pilots who live somewhere else. So all pilots must be trained until they are proficient in system and human performance standards, such as using checklists and following procedures. This focus on standardization makes aviation very reliable.

Or so I thought.

As the flight engineer on this flight, it was my job to check the outside of the plane before the captain and first officer arrived. Starting at the nose and walking around the fuselage, I repeated the inspection exactly as I was taught. The process was second nature. As I made my way around, my mind began to wander, thinking about what I would do later that evening when I arrived in New York, one of my favorite cities in the world. *Where should I eat?* I thought as I inspected the nose gear inside the wheel well, looking for potential hydraulic leaks and debris. Continuing down the starboard side, I glanced up to make sure the pitot tubes and static ports were free and clear, providing accurate inputs on airspeed, altitude, and barometric pressure. *Maybe I'll try to get tickets to a play*, I thought as I walked in front of the right wing.

The smell of jet fuel filled my nostrils. A quarter of the way into my walk-around, I was next to the fuel truck that was filling our plane. Jet fuel is mostly kerosene, engineered for its combustion properties. The B-727 I was flying that day would contain more than fifty thousand pounds of explosive power.

Our aircraft was parked at the northeastern terminal. Standing under the tip of the right wing, I could see that clouds had moved just north of the airport. The weather patterns in north Texas generally move from west to east, along the southern edge of a corridor known as tornado alley. But these clouds didn't look tornadic. It was a typical summer day in north Texas—billowing clouds and threatening rain, but easy to see and avoid when flying a modern airliner. *I wonder if these clouds will bring rain to the area*, I thought. *We could sure use it.*

Then something caught my eye. State Highway 114, just north of the airport, was thick with afternoon rush hour traffic. *It was the road I had taken to work today*, I thought. The southern edge of a developing storm cell, with a column of rain pouring from the dark clouds, appeared to be almost touching the highway. Suddenly, a wide-body jet burst through the clouds. But this plane wasn't flying normally.

I had never seen an aircraft so low on final approach, at least not that far from the runway. Something was wrong. For a moment, the plane appeared to be sinking in the nose-up attitude I knew indicated the start of a stall. I heard the plane's power surge, engines roaring over the din of the airport vehicles around me.

I could see the plane was a Delta Air Lines Lockheed L-1011, a wide-body workhorse. The L-1011 can carry more than 250 passengers, 90,000 pounds of cargo, and 200,000 pounds of fuel. But at this moment, the L-1011 wasn't just an airplane with technical specifications—it was a colossal machine in distress, and 163 people's lives were depending on it.[1]

My eyes were riveted on the descending plane. It plummeted out of my sight and, I later learned, slammed onto a car on Highway 114, killing the unsuspecting driver instantly. The plane then bounced back into view. Stunned, I slowly realized what was happening. *This plane is about to crash.*

The pilots were steering the plane toward the runway, although the flight path was still erratic. *They might make it,* I thought, stuck in my tracks. The plane appeared to be gaining momentum. Without being conscious of the process, my brain automatically estimated the projected flight path: energy, lift, drag, thrust. And the final, most unforgiving force of all: gravity.

At this moment, I was losing proportion among time, experience, and visual interpretation. What I was seeing wasn't familiar. I couldn't process it in the normal way we live our daily lives. I was performing a familiar task, but what I saw didn't make sense. I could perceive what was happening, but I had no data bank of experience to prepare me for the emotional and psychological impact of what came next.

The flight turned catastrophic. The left wing struck a water tank northeast of the runway's centerline, cartwheeling the plane into a second water tank, breaking the fuselage into pieces. Violent impacts continued as inertia carried the plane forward. Then came ignition—explosions and fires erupting in the fuselage, beginning at the fuel tanks and spreading rapidly throughout the cabin and surrounding areas. Except for the aft fuselage and tail section, the entire plane disintegrated.

The human experience was horrific. Inside the airplane, 163 passengers and crew felt g-forces that few people have ever encountered. Many were ejected from the plane, still belted in their seats. Some died from blunt trauma, internal organs colliding with skeletal barriers. Others died from explosions, fire, and smoke inhalation. The smell of kerosene, hydraulic fluids, cleaning solutions, and other caustic liquids permeated the air. By the time emergency crews arrived, most passengers were dead.

Less than half a mile away, where I was conducting my inspection, there was relative calm. Few people could see what had happened, and the storm seemed unremarkable unless you were in its path. Many of the airport workers outside were wearing ear protection and didn't hear the impact. People inside the terminal could have confused the explosions with thunderclaps. The busy drone of airport activity continued. The fueler was finishing filling my plane. Workers were loading bags onto the conveyor belt that glided luggage into the cargo holds. People in the terminal were ambling to their gates and checking departure and arrival times.

I was caught between two worlds: one that made sense, with people and systems moving according to plan, and another I had never seen, where things go unexpectedly, catastrophically wrong.

Aviation was familiar, a logical framework I had come to understand through experience. *Sure, there was risk involved*, I thought, *but human aspiration and engineering had taken us to the moon and back. Flying is the safest mode of transportation in the world. It's my chosen profession.* The thought of a plane crashing was something I instinctively suppressed. Our brains have evolved to learn most effectively from direct experience. And what I had just seen was beyond my comprehension.

Suddenly, the air pressure where I was standing dropped. The downburst of wind that only moments before brought down the L-1011 now rumbled over me. A violent gust knocked my hat off and slammed me to the concrete. My flashlight rolled away. Looking up, I could see fear on the fueler's face. He had just disconnected from the plane's tank and ground supply but had not reeled in the hose. Picking myself up, I could see him trying to recoil it. But before I could move, a torrent of rain engulfed me. The plane began rocking violently. *The passengers must be boarding*, I realized.

Though it was hard to see in the rain, I ran over to the jet bridge and up the stairs, fumbling for my keys, without my hat and flashlight. As I stumbled onto the plane's entryway, I could see the flight attendant's look of disbelief. "What's happening?" she screamed.

Without answering, I ran onto the plane and down the aisle to see how many people were aboard. The plane was more than half full and thick with tension. When people are packed inside a confined space, and one person believes lives are threatened, panic grows exponentially. At first, people were alarmed that violent winds were rocking the plane. Then a passenger looked out the starboard window and saw the aftermath of what I had just witnessed. He shouted: "There's been a plane crash!"

The viral panic was overwhelming. People were rushing to the emergency exits. I knew if I didn't act quickly, passengers would eject right into the forces of wind and rain that had just brought down the Delta L-1011. And I knew anytime people evacuate by the emergency exits, injuries are bound to happen, even in the best conditions.

I grabbed the passenger address system handset: "This is your pilot. We're experiencing a sudden rainstorm. *Do not*, I repeat, *do not* move toward the emergency exits. The safest place to be right now is on this airplane."

But people were shouting at me, asking questions I couldn't answer. The captain had not yet arrived. I was shaking.

Then, as quickly as they had begun, the rain and violent winds subsided. The plane was no longer rocking, but conditions inside were anything but calm. Outside, the airport alarm had sounded, and within seconds firefighters were speeding across the tarmac. The gate agent ran down the jet bridge and asked me what I wanted to do.

"Let's get these passengers off the airplane through the jet bridge. This plane isn't going anywhere right now," I said.

But my mind was racing.

What had just happened? How could this occur? My brain was having difficulty processing what I had just witnessed. I was soaking wet and numbed by the experience.

Accidents don't just happen randomly, I thought. *Or do they? There must be an explanation.*

Slowly at first, then with greater clarity as time went by, the answers began to appear—not just in this plane crash, but in other catastrophes around the world, past and present. Over the ensuing decades, I searched for a pattern in the chaos, seeking to understand how best to prevent accidents, both organizational and individual. This is the story of that picture, how it came into focus, and how seeing, understanding, and applying it in sequence can help all of us in our everyday lives.

It's the hidden science of reliability.

THE REPORT[2]

The National Transportation Safety Board summarized the fatal crash of Delta Air Lines Flight 191 (see figure P.1).

NATIONAL TRANSPORTATION SAFETY BOARD
WASHINGTON, D.C.

AIRCRAFT ACCIDENT REPORT

Adopted: August 15, 1986

DELTA AIR LINES, INC.
LOCKHEED L-1011-385-1, N726DA,
DALLAS/FORT WORTH INTERNATIONAL AIRPORT, TEXAS
AUGUST 2, 1985

SYNOPSIS

On August 2, 1985, at 1805:52 central daylight time, Delta Air Lines flight 191, a Lockheed L-1011-385-1, N726DA, crashed while approaching to land on runway 17L at the Dallas/Fort Worth International Airport, Texas. While passing through the rain shaft beneath a thunderstorm, flight 191 entered a microburst which the pilot was unable to traverse successfully. The airplane struck the ground about 6,300 feet north of the approach end of runway 17L, hit a car on a highway north of the runway killing the driver, struck two water tanks on the airport, and broke apart. Except for a section of the airplane containing the aft fuselage and empennage, the remainder of the airplane disintegrated during the impact sequence, and a severe fire erupted during the impact sequence. Of the 163 persons aboard, 134 passengers and crewmembers were killed; 26 passengers and 3 cabin attendants survived.

The National Transportation Safety Board determines that the probable causes of the accident were the flightcrew's decision to initiate and continue the approach into a cumulonimbus cloud which they observed to contain visible lightning; the lack of specific guidelines, procedures, and training for avoiding and escaping from low-altitude wind shear; and the lack of definitive, real-time wind shear hazard information. This resulted in the aircraft's encounter at low altitude with a microburst-induced, severe wind shear from a rapidly developing thunderstorm located on the final approach course.

Figure P.1

The crew members on the flight deck, including Captain Edward Connors, First Officer Rudy Price Jr., and flight engineer N. Nassick, could see the thunderstorm clouds moving from right to left out the first officer's side window. The weather radar was on and functioning properly, and the precipitation returns showed rain wouldn't be a factor on their approach and landing. They referred to the precipitation as "a little rain shower"[3] ahead, and "we're gonna get our airplane washed."

As the plane was configured for landing—flaps, gear, spoiler handle, airspeed, and glide path—it began its final descent. Imperceptibly at first, then rapidly, then catastrophically, the plane lost momentum. On the cockpit voice recorder recovered after the crash, the captain is heard discussing the loss of airspeed and telling the flying pilot, First Officer Price, to "push it up" just before impact, instructing the copilot to advance the engine throttles.

Astonishingly, the recorded conversation revealed the pilots were correcting course to continue the approach and landing. There was no discussion about an escape maneuver known as a "go-around." Why is that important? Because it tells us the pilots didn't fully "see" the microburst they encountered and didn't recognize they were about to crash until it was too late.

THE SYSTEM

Aviation is at its core an engineering endeavor. Leonardo da Vinci, in his visionary design of a flying machine, once noted:[4]

A bird is an instrument working according to mathematical law, an instrument which is within the capacity of man to reproduce with all its movements.

So, the quest to soar like a bird began in earnest. In subsequent years, artists, scientists, and mechanics combined their skills to advance the physics of flight. The Smithsonian National Air and Space Museum says the "first powered, heavier-than-air machine to achieve controlled, sustained flight with a pilot aboard" was at Kitty Hawk, North Carolina, on December 17, 1903.[5] But the Wright brothers' success was just the beginning. Over the next century, aviation evolved both incrementally and dramatically, and the advances were applied to recreation, commercial enterprise, warfare, and space exploration.

As technologies improved, so, too, did the system of delivery—that is, the *reliability* of flying machines. What may have begun as an attempt to emulate birds evolved into an ongoing exercise in engineering. Artistry and an understanding of theoretical aerodynamic principles were necessary to envision the possibilities of flight, but aviation advanced only if the aircraft and its occupants didn't crash—and that required engineering.

So the technology improved, and by the late twentieth century, jet airliners became marvels of science, fine-tuned by computer-aided design and refined through decades of data collection, analysis, and redesign. Air traffic and mission control facilities were established, directing flights while monitoring real-time progress. Weather reporting and maintenance repair stations were built to avoid environmental threats and improve mechanical reliability.

All these improvements advanced aviation. But despite the industry's engineering expertise and advancements in technology, one aspect of the system remained critical to flight performance: the unpredictable, quirky component known as the human being.

THE HUMAN COMPONENT

Flying is a process of trial and error. Pilots learn the principles of flight early in their training, including the forces of lift, weight, thrust, and drag, all in the dispassionate presence of gravity. Gravity isn't something humans can see, but it unwaveringly influences everything pilots experience about flying. They learn how an airplane stalls, and how it can overspeed. They practice flying up to the various edges of the "envelope," the performance limits imposed by physical laws.

Every pilot learns about these limits through experience. You want the plane to fly straight and level, but it drifts off, so you correct. Moving the flight controls, and gauging the plane's response, involves your whole body—including hands, feet, eyes, ears, nose, even the "seat of your pants." Sometimes all at once.

The interaction among human, machine, and the environment provides immediate feedback. When the plane veers uncommanded left, the pilot steers right and the plane responds. The pilot readjusts as needed. This process repeats itself over and over, tens or even hundreds of thousands of times on a typical flight. The balancing act becomes automatic, and the proficiencies pilots attain come from experience.

And so it is, too, with pilot judgment. In the early days of aviation, the collective pool of experience was shallow. Learning came at a high price, and deaths were common. But with each death came an opportunity to improve—to learn from tragedies and store those lessons in a collective consciousness. In the United States, the National Transportation Safety Board became the world's leading investigative agency, a forensic organization conducting autopsies on fatal plane crashes. Pilots—along with scientists, engineers, politicians, and the public—learned from those experiences.

The human brain is a fascinating instrument, capable of collecting and interpreting data and forming conclusions. Curiously, our interpretations are not strictly logical. They're also shaped by experiences and colored by biases that alter our abilities to learn, adapt, and improve.

Pilots, like all of us, have evolved to learn through experience. But sometimes those experiences teach us the wrong lesson.

THE WEATHER

The same year Flight 191 crashed, meteorologist Theodore Fujita coined the term *microburst* in his book *The Downburst*.[6] A microburst—a small but high-velocity downdraft of wind at low altitude—can form from the convective air movement in a thunderstorm, or even milder weather such as a rain shower. Microbursts develop rapidly, and their intense wind can exceed a plane's capabilities to recover if they're not avoided. In other words, these invisible wind currents are dangerous killers.

Figure P.2 represents what the Flight 191 pilots likely would have seen, visually and on radar. At the time of the crash, conventional air- and ground-based weather radar could not detect microbursts.

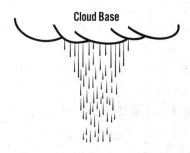

Figure P.2

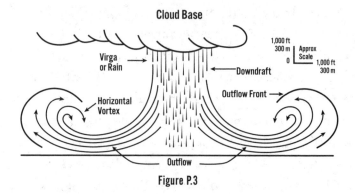

Figure P.3

Figure P.3 more completely represents the wind and rain hazard they would soon encounter. This is the full picture the pilots could *not* see.

As the diagram shows, the dangerous wind field extends outward and beyond the benign column of rain. *It was the invisible wind, not the rain, that brought down Flight 191.*

The pilots couldn't see—and thus couldn't understand—the microburst that lurked undetected in front of them. The radar could show precipitation ahead of the plane, *but it was incapable of showing wind velocities.* And in microbursts, those wind velocities are lethal.

A PATTERN IN THE CHAOS

So, on August 2, 1985—with all the advanced technological systems onboard and surrounding Delta Air Lines L-1011 N726DA, despite state-of-the-art weather briefings and guidance from air traffic control and systems operations control, despite all the simulator and aircraft training these pilots had received, combined with their lifetimes of flying skill and experience—the plane still crashed.

My brain tossed endless questions at me about why this happened. The answers came slowly but surely—not just in this plane crash, but in other catastrophes around the world, past and present: from the RMS *Titanic* and the *Hindenburg* tragedies to the Metrolink train crash to the space shuttle disasters; from the *Costa Concordia* and *Exxon Valdez* maritime mishaps to the Malaysia Airlines Flight 370 disappearance to the B-737 MAX 8 accidents; to business failures and reputational harm at consulting companies such as Arthur Andersen and Enron, to more recent challenges faced by Meta, Tesla, and Amazon, and to the tragedies of mass shootings, police brutality, and the COVID-19 pandemic.

The pattern in the chaos would eventually reveal itself—but only after a series of aviation experiences thrust me headfirst into other industries.

A BETTER BUSINESS MODEL

A ROAD LESS TRAVELED

I've led a quirky life, full of twists and turns. The plane crash became a catalyst in my professional life, propelling me down a road less traveled. Transformed by the event and the realizations I had afterward, I knew I could help.

Within three months of the plane crash, I was in the American Airlines CEO's office requesting a leave of absence. My graduate education in physics had prepared me to work on a project for NASA to design and test a new laser device known as lidar (light detection and ranging) to measure wind shear. NASA also needed test pilots to develop new strategies to avoid and escape dangerous microbursts. I signed up for both.

So I left the airline temporarily to work as a physicist for a company called Coherent Technologies, under contract with NASA and the Federal Aviation Administration, to develop a laser wind shear prediction system— an antidote to the microburst phenomenon that caused the crash.

We presented our results to government officials at NASA's Langley Research Center in Virginia, including the US Air Force and the FAA. While I was there, NASA recruited me into a flight test program to improve pilot wind shear recovery techniques through simulator tests. Over several months in 1987 and 1988, I participated in research developing optimal aircraft avoidance and recovery strategies.

I returned to American Airlines and became its chief safety officer. I began to realize most safety programs focused on audits and accident investigations, while the real risks resided in daily operations, buried beneath unexamined, successful outcomes. Critics of the FAA complained of a "tombstone mentality," where regulatory changes came only at the expense of human lives. As a pilot, I knew that frontline workers encountered risks daily but rarely reported them, especially when their own actions or mistakes were involved.

So I developed a program known as ASAP, or Aviation Safety Action Program. This program transformed the industry by providing incentives for aviation professionals—pilots, mechanics, dispatchers, flight attendants, ground workers, and air traffic controllers—to report and become part of the safety improvement process. The program, a collaboration among airlines, labor associations, and the FAA, has fueled a 95 percent decrease in fatal accidents.[1] As of this book's publication, there are more than 767 ASAPs in the United States.

In 2000, the US surgeon general, David Satcher, MD, invited me to bring my improvement strategies to healthcare. In 2006, I made a move that surprised my friends and colleagues: I elected early retirement from American Airlines, changing careers in my mid-forties to bring my approach to high-consequence industries full-time, from transportation to energy to first responders to law enforcement and beyond.

From 2006 to 2013, I helped pioneer an approach to organizational improvement known as just culture, teaching executives, managers, and employees how to respond fairly and consistently when things go wrong. While teaching individuals was satisfying on a personal level, I was frustrated by the challenges of persuading large organizations to see, understand, and manage risk before disaster strikes. After years of development, I discovered the solution had been hiding in plain sight.

Looking back on my career, I found a pattern in the chaos of catastrophes I had seen and experienced, and a solution to preventing them. In 2013, I started my business, SG Collaborative Solutions, to help high-consequence organizations become highly reliable—a term often used but rarely understood.

In healthcare, my work has led to fewer medication errors and mislabeled specimens, along with lower infection rates, among other outcomes. My clients include scores of the nation's top health systems, such as Mass General Brigham healthcare system, Harvard Medical School, and Tampa General Hospital. I've worked with the American Hospital Association, the Agency for Healthcare Research and Quality, the Institute for Healthcare Improvement, and the American Medical Association. The California Medical Association has supported my cultural model of improvement known as Collaborative Just Culture®. Efforts are underway to make this program a national model for healthcare organizations and professionals.

I've worked extensively with the Federal Aviation Administration, the major airlines, and their trade and labor associations. I've assisted the first responder sectors, including emergency medical response agencies, firefighting and law enforcement organizations, and forensic science laboratories. I've consulted with the Innocence Project and the National Institute of Justice. I've worked with the National Transportation Safety Board, many state departments of health, the professional boards of medicine, pharmacy, and nursing, the Federal Railroad Administration, the Nuclear Regulatory Commission, and the National Highway Traffic Safety Administration.

For most of my career, I've focused on helping high-consequence industries and organizations, where loss of life or damage can happen in the blink of an eye, sometimes on an enormous scale. For them, getting things right most of the time won't suffice. In those environments, success is measured over decades rather than quarters. Yesterday's results won't matter if an accident thrusts your business into the front-page headlines today.

But every business is high-consequence at some level, isn't it? Whether it's to the owners/shareholders, workers, or customers, the success or failure of any business matters.

This book is intended to be a practical guide to reliability for leaders in business large and small. It's also relevant to governmental agencies, labor associations, and groups of people working in teams. It's designed to help you see, understand, and manage socio-technical risk—preventing catastrophes, from plane crashes to pandemics, from medical errors to climate instability, from providing customer service to driving a vehicle.

If you're an owner or manager, you'll discover specific strategies that will foster a better workplace culture and environment, reduce employee burnout, raise retention rates, and improve production and quality. You'll find a comprehensive model to improve your business results with a program combining my work with ASAP and just culture.

Any business can use this book's concepts, principles, and programs to do the following:

- Improve across all organizational attributes
- Prevent failures and adverse events
- Optimize assets and resources
- Enhance cultural alignment—get people pulling in the same direction
- Gain competitive advantages
- Ensure long-term sustainability

The science leading to your success is simple and straightforward, but the applications are not always easy, requiring a more nuanced understanding of how systems, people, and organizations produce results.

But they're within your grasp.

Let's start by comparing a few often-used adages that might be too obvious for our own good.

WORDS TO LIVE BY . . . OR NOT

In business, as in life, we sometimes embrace words to live by—axioms to guide our thoughts and actions. These words help us form mental models to make decisions. For better or worse, we justify our actions with catchy phrases. An example:

The early bird gets the worm.

For business leaders, this might be a rationale for being the first to enter a marketplace with a new product or service. There have been instances where being first—the so-called first-mover advantage—establishes a brand as the original, which can carry significant consumer recognition, resulting in marketplace dominance. Examples include Amazon, the online bookseller that revolutionized online retail sales, distribution, and delivery, and Uber, the pioneering rideshare service.

But what about this maxim, which seems to imply the opposite?

The second mouse gets the cheese.

That implies it might be better to not rush into a marketplace until the early lessons are learned and market forces settle down. History is replete with examples of second-mover companies that entered the market later and outperformed the competition. Sometimes, a second mover benefits from the first mover by appealing to its existing customer base and using marketing strategies that have proof of success. Apple Inc. may be the clearest modern example of this strategy.

There are many other examples of equal, yet opposite-appearing strategies:

He who hesitates is lost.

But how does this square with this adage:

Look before you leap.

Or these sports maxims:

Defense wins championships.

While others say:

The best defense is a good offense.

How often have you heard this:

Winning isn't everything, it's the only thing.[2]

Which is countered with what we teach our children:

It matters not whether you win or lose, but how you play the game.

Or my personal favorite, from Winston Churchill:

"Never give in, never give in, never; never; never; never in nothing, great or small, large or petty—never give in . . ."[3]

and debated by W. C. Fields:

"If at first you don't succeed, try, try again. Then quit. There's no point in being a damn fool about it."[4]

Why point out the often confusing, apparent contradictory nature of these sayings? Do they reflect a strange dichotomy of nature, like the physical properties of light, which act simultaneously like a wave and a particle, depending on the circumstance and type of experiment?

The answer is that socio-technical science requires a better understanding of market forces and environmental conditions than a mere aphorism. We must look beyond the obvious to find what's hiding in plain view. Let's explore this science and how to apply it, starting with a few high-consequence activities you may be familiar with, then move to more everyday applications.

APPLES TO ORANGES

At patient safety conferences across the United States, there's a chart often circulated comparing healthcare to other high-consequence industries and activities. In this chart, the x-axis shows the total number of lives lost per year, while the y-axis displays the number of encounters for each fatality. In tabular form, the chart would look something like this:

Lives Lost/Year	Dangerous	Regulated	Ultra-Safe
>100,000	Healthcare	Driving	
1,000–10,000			
100–1,000			Scheduled Airlines
10–100	Mountain Climbing	Chartered Flights	
1–10	Bungee Jumping	Chemical Manufacturing	Nuclear Power
# of Encounters/ Fatality	1–1,000	1,000–100,000	100,000– 10,000,000

At first glance, comparing death rates appears to show that healthcare is as risky as mountain climbing or bungee jumping. These data, cited without source documentation, are presented at patient safety conferences to inspire healthcare leaders to think differently about improving care. But the healthcare apple isn't necessarily less safe than the oranges around it, for a variety of reasons. While some estimates indicate medical error is the third-leading cause of death in the United States,[5] its risk-reward equation is very different from the other activities in the chart.

Without debating the chart's accuracy, we should ask these questions about each activity:

Are the inherent risks static or dynamic? Mountain climbing, bungee jumping, and healthcare are shown as dangerous, but the nature of the healthcare risk is dramatically different. The risks of bungee jumping and mountain climbing, although significant, center on the dangers of a single threat: hitting the ground or other hard surface. In contrast, healthcare risks are both non-static and dynamic. The causes of unintended healthcare deaths, such as infections, sepsis, falls, misdiagnosis, wrong-site surgeries, and medication errors, are multifaceted, moving targets. Patients and healthcare providers often don't recognize them until harm happens. Unlike mountain climbing or bungee jumping, the socio-technical issues that produce these outcomes usually are not fully seen or understood.

Can the risks be avoided? Except for healthcare, the dominant risks of the activities can be isolated, managed, and in many cases avoided. An airline can cancel flights because of hazardous weather or reroute planes when an air traffic control system fails. Nuclear power and chemical manufacturing plants can suspend or alter production schedules for repairs when something breaks down. Mountain climbers and bungee jumpers can choose not to participate in risky activities if they see and understand the risks.

US healthcare institutions, on the other hand, rarely, if ever, shut their doors because of risk. They do assess patients' conditions before admitting them and often refer them for care depending on a variety of risk factors.

But legal, ethical, and professional considerations compel healthcare providers to treat patients regardless of risk.[6] Unlike the transportation, energy, or service industries, healthcare institutions usually can't avoid the risks of caring for patients, no matter how sick or badly injured the patients are.

How are they regulated? Each activity in the chart is regulated differently. It's no accident that the industries labeled ultra-safe have more stringent oversight.

Are there multiple points of delivery? When an airplane flies or a factory makes a product, that's a single outcome or result, regardless of how many legs of the flight or delivery trucks there are. But healthcare patients have a wide range of possible ailments and conditions, each with its own set of challenges in diagnoses, treatment, and monitoring. Those dynamic, ever-changing challenges mean multiple points of delivery with each patient. And each point has the potential for socio-technical errors and adverse outcomes.

Is the activity human- or technology-centered? Nuclear and chemical power plants are the products of sophisticated engineering system design. They're socio-technical, but the focus of their activity is technical, or system-based. Healthcare, by contrast, evolved separately from the engineering sciences. Healthcare requires human-centered care, on the delivery and receiving ends. As a result, healthcare delivery is much more challenging.

How many lives are saved by the activity? That depends on perspective. Transportation and power and chemical plants evolved with multiple purposes in mind, including saving lives, which they've helped do. But healthcare arose for the *primary* purpose of saving lives otherwise lost because of illness or injury. The number of lives lost through infections and provider errors is in proportion to the number of lives saved. A sure way to lower the unintended death rate would be to limit the number of patients or the kinds of illnesses and injuries treated. But the goal is not to deliver less care; it's to make delivery of care more reliable.

Are the risks worth taking? For mountain climbing, bungee jumping, and driving, the answers to that question are personal. For transportation, chemical manufacturing, and nuclear power generation, there are business considerations, balanced with community and society needs and expectations. For healthcare, the answer is unequivocal: The benefits far outweigh the inherent risks. Becoming more reliable provides more effective and resilient healthcare, improving outcomes and saving lives.

BEYOND QUALITY MANAGEMENT

In the mid-twentieth century, Edwards Deming taught the world a better business strategy: Improving quality reduced expenses, while increasing productivity and market share.[7] Like a Navy SEAL team working to the mantra "slow is smooth; smooth is fast,"[8] he showed automobile manufacturers how to pay attention to systems, processes, and people in a way that balanced productivity and cost. To everyone's surprise, his approach demonstrated that by focusing on quality, optimizing processes could simultaneously cut costs *and* yield higher productivity.

By balancing the competing priorities of customer expectation, product delivery, and cost, the quality management philosophy revolutionized automobile manufacturing and established a path for other industries to follow. Quality methods guided organizations to *document, monitor, and measure,* which produced superior results.

But all industries are not the same as automobile manufacturing, where Deming initially focused his work. Hospitals, airlines, emergency medical services, firefighting, law enforcement, and energy producers, to name a few, are not car companies. These companies often faced disasters that could happen instantly. These high-consequence industries grappled with unique challenges requiring specialized solutions: Operational departments, regulatory compliance, risk management, information technology, performance improvement, and safety departments were needed to help them stay in business and maintain a competitive advantage. But these departments were often seen as silos, each performing specific functions in isolation. So long as everything went according to plan, the organization met operational goals and the business thrived. But as soon as conditions changed and things didn't go as planned—an environmental disaster, an unexpected downturn in the economy, a drop or increase in customer demand, or a supply chain disruption—these silos worked against each other, and the organization lacked resiliency.

Since all organizations engage people, the human resources function arose to address the challenges of managing the workforce. In the late 1990s, the term *just culture* gained popularity as a human resources philosophy, using an algorithm to categorize employee behaviors with the aspiration to improve culture. But attempts to establish a just culture came with their own challenges. How does an organization ensure consistent responses using a complex tool subject to unreliability? Sometimes cultures improved; many times, they did not.

Subsequently, industries turned their attention to the term *high-reliability organization* in hopes of achieving yet another level of improvement. Organizations compared themselves to aircraft carriers and nuclear power plants to achieve desired levels of performance. Naval ships and power plants are the products of sophisticated engineering system design. The focus of their reliability is technical, or system-based defenses-in-depth.

By contrast, healthcare, as we've seen, evolved separate from the engineering sciences and requires human-centered care on the delivery and receiving ends. As a result, healthcare faces a different set of challenges. It turned out that most industries have different challenges, too.

Notably adding to these challenges is that consistent definitions and standards have not been established: What is just culture? What is high reliability? Without answers to these questions, organizations have struggled to achieve and replicate results. One-and-done training, individual certifications without proficiency evaluations and consistency follow-ups, and an array of unaligned or even misaligned activities have not yielded consistent outcomes from one industry to the next.

We need a better business model to guide us. A model based on science that's evidence-based and evidence-producing, one that's easy to understand

and can be employed in a variety of settings, and manages risk in a dynamic, ever-changing world. We need something as fundamental as Maslow's hierarchy of needs—the motivational theory in psychology comprising a five-tier model of human needs, often depicted as hierarchical levels within a pyramid[9]—but with the practical applicability of Deming's quality management approach.

INTRODUCTION TO RELIABILITY

Reliability is, to put it simply, sustained high performance over time. A graph of reliability might look like figure 1.1.

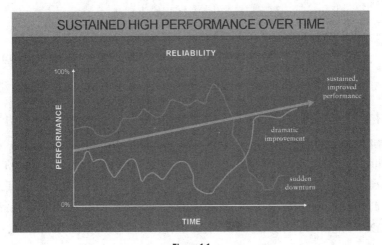

Figure 1.1

Performing on occasion does not equate to reliability. Of the three lines, only the middle line performs consistently. This example does not show high reliability, only consistent improvement over time.

Some activities require consistently high performance. Showing up to work on time, preventing illness or injury, financial investing, and parenting are just a few examples where reliability is important in our lives.

The key point to remember is this:

To be reliable, high performance must be sustainable.

The absence of failure up to a particular time does not equate to the absence of risk; and being accident-free, even for an extended period, does not guarantee future success. Conditions change. Internal and external forces tomorrow may produce results very different from the past.

There are many examples in our everyday lives. Imagine all the people below are usually high performers. But for a variety of reasons we'll soon explore, the unexpected happens:

- A social media company is on the hot seat for lack of privacy protections.
- A straight A student's grades suddenly deteriorate.
- A surgeon operates on the wrong knee of a patient.
- A parent oversleeps, causing a child to be late for school.
- A driver veers out of his lane, causing a collision.
- An adult leaves a swimming pool gate ajar, and a toddler falls into the pool.

It's tempting to focus on *human* performance, isn't it? But we should recognize our activities and the results we produce most often involve tools, technologies, and processes—in other words, *systems*. To understand how we can manage them better and improve our lives, it helps to understand this:

The results we produce are socio-technical.

Don't let that term scare you. It simply means people (*socio*) interacting within systems (*technical*), often within organizations. We have surrounded ourselves with systems—hardware, software, tools, equipment, vehicles, houses, schools, laws, policies, processes, and procedures—to structure our lives. And we share these socio-technical systems with other people who likely see and manage risk differently. The results we achieve are interconnected; our performance has a ripple effect, influencing the lives of those around us.

Our systems may be well conceived, but they can be undermined by human behavior. You can put a speed-limit sign by the side of the road, but how many people obey it? You can install a pool gate that automatically locks when shut, but what happens when a dropped towel gets stuck at the bottom?

Simply putting a device, barrier, rule, policy, or procedure in place may not be enough. Humans are not rule-followers by nature, and we make mistakes.

Partly because of that, the results of most socio-technical systems are less than optimal. Would you consider these completely reliable?

- The smoke alarms in your house
- The power grids supplying electricity
- The medicines and supplements you take
- Spell-check and auto-correct

These systems work—and so do many in our everyday lives—but few are *optimized*. In most cases, we simply live with the results and learn to adjust. In others, we pay for unreliability with our lives.

Take, for example, a stove, a bicycle, or a car. All these are socio-technical machines, and they can fail in many ways—mechanically, through software, or by human behavior: a fire, a collision, or simply being inoperable, or all of the above. Each can cause injury or damage resulting from their operation. The probability of these adverse events happening may be relatively low, but the severity of the consequences can be high.

Because there's utility in operating these machines, we accept the risks and use strategies to prevent or mitigate harm. Wearing a bike helmet reduces the probability of a traumatic brain injury. Children may not understand the risk; it's likely they've never had a serious injury while riding a bike. But parents may have had an accident, or known someone who has, or simply recognized the risk.

A statistical analysis could predict, within a margin of error based on circumstances, the likelihood and severity of a traumatic brain injury for every person who rides a bike. But we don't need to study statistics to reduce the risk. What we need to do is be aware of the risk, wear the right helmet, and, for parents, influence a child's behavior so the child wears a helmet reliably, even when no one's watching. That helps optimize the socio-technical machine.

Reliable systems, people, and organizations share two common traits:

1. **Effective:** Successful at producing a desired result when things go right.
2. **Resilient:** Able to withstand or recover quickly from difficult conditions when things go wrong.

Consider the early days of the automobile industry. The Ford Model T set the standard for manufacturing in its day. Compared to the horse and buggy, automobiles were substantially more *effective* in transporting passengers from point A to point B, when they worked. But, oh my, when things went wrong!

Getting the combustion engine to perform consistently, along with all the other moving parts in the automobile, became a challenge that led many to believe that cars would never replace their equine counterparts. But they did. As the automobile evolved, dramatic improvements were made in effectiveness (the ability to transport passengers smoothly at increasing speeds) but also *resilience* (decreasing breakdowns and other failures). Over decades of evolution, spurred by customer demand and regulatory influence, safety technologies became standard features contributing to the overall reliability of our vehicles.

There are many more examples: airplanes, electrical grids, personal computers and smartphones, and artificial intelligence. Are any of these systems perfectly reliable? No. But through trial and error, many of these products improved resilience: engineers learning from consumer experience and feedback.

To be effective and resilient, systems must respond to their own vulnerabilities (such as software and hardware) and the risks of humans operating within those systems (such as proficiencies, cultural, environmental, and personal influences, and behaviors).

The people part of the equation poses an interesting challenge for us. Why? Because humans have a human bias. When things go right, we'll take the credit. When things go wrong, something inside us wants to assign blame to someone else. The problem comes when we overlook the systemic, environmental, and other performance-shaping factors that contribute to human behaviors. (In a later chapter, we'll examine many of the biases that invade our thinking and discuss ways to recognize and avoid them.)

Throughout history, we have tried to forge the world to meet our needs. The tools that shape our lives in many ways have grown more complex. Modern life is socio-technical: Most everything we produce involves humans interacting with systems. Achieving the results we hope for and expect—in business and everyday life—requires an understanding of this relationship and the science behind it.

A HIDDEN SCIENCE

Reliability is a hidden science, hiding in plain view. It evolved in a crooked line, coming from diverse areas of expertise, segregated by specialties. This hidden science synthesizes engineering, behavioral psychology, neuroscience, ethics, and the legal system. That leaves us with challenges. For instance, engineers know system design but don't always understand human behavior because they don't think like typical humans. Psychologists and neuroscientists understand how people think and act, but don't always know how systems work because they don't think like engineers. And lawyers think differently than all of us.

But if we fit the interconnected pieces of the puzzle together, one at a time, we can use the whole picture to manage risk and get better results. A key first step is this:

Success requires a relentless focus on what you do well and, just as important, what you don't.

The principles and strategies we'll examine go far beyond preventing plane crashes, explosions, and bankruptcies. This science also applies to the corner grocery, the online retailer, and the classroom.

This hidden science can also help you prevent catching a cold or the flu, make better choices in what you eat, and be a better parent. It can make your car safer, your house more efficient, your children do better in school, and the business you run more profitable. The executive, the factory worker, the student, the teacher, the janitor, the doctor, the nurse, the pharmacist, and the patient all can benefit from it.

To get better results, we must recognize the following:

Organizations = combinations of people working within systems

Optimal results require an understanding of the complex ways in which people and systems interact, and how to manage them differently than we've done in the past. That often means avoiding blaming people when a bad result happens, before you make sense of the risk, the system, and the environment in which it happened. And understanding why humans find it hard to follow rules.

Organizational success requires more than advice on leadership and culture. Many books get the order wrong by focusing on the art of leadership, believing that persuasion and influence drive organizational success. While it's true that a few select businesses succeed through force of good ideas and personality, *sustainable* success in business requires more than charismatic leadership: It requires an understanding and application of the hidden science.

MURPHY'S MYTH

You've probably heard of Murphy's Law: "Anything that can go wrong will go wrong."[10] It's used often as an expression of exasperation—a commentary on human fallibility or the inevitability of catastrophe.

But it's a dangerous myth.

We experience risk throughout our lives. Getting out of bed in the morn-ing, going to work, coming home, interacting with people, choosing the food we eat and the amount of sleep or exercise we get are all part of man-aging risk. When we're sick, we go to a hospital. The drive to get there and what happens once we arrive are statistically two of the riskiest encounters we'll face in our lifetimes.[11]

Everyday examples could more than fill this book. Here are a few: not replacing smoke detector batteries, texting while driving, not wearing a bike helmet, eating the wrong foods, and not washing your hands properly.

But while experiencing risk in our lives is inevitable, bad results aren't. Understanding a few basic concepts will make that clearer.

What happens to us isn't random; it's based on probability.

The butterfly effect—the theory that air moved by a butterfly's wings could alter the weather halfway around the world—is an example of prob-ability: the likelihood that something will occur. There are many examples in nature of patterns emerging from probabilities: veins in a leaf, the for-mations of mountains, the winding paths of rivers.[12] All of these represent statistical outcomes arising from probabilities.

It's the same for humans. The events in our lives happen with the same kind of probability—there's a statistical likelihood of any particular out-come. We live within the boundaries of a set of variables, such as our genetics, where we live on the planet, our family and friends, and our envi-ronment. As we experience our way through time, what happens to us is partly by design, partly by choice, and partly by chance. It's a unique path for everyone, even for identical twins. Your path may seem random, but you travel it through probability.

Our world is a risky place. But it's important to understand that although risk is all around us, our world is not strictly random. Yes, there are random processes at work, but these forces interact in mathematical ways.

Let's say you and I are walking down a sidewalk near a busy street and we see a nail lying on the road a few feet from the curb. Although we may have no duty or responsibility to pick up the nail, we consider our options. We could continue walking and hope no car passes by that picks up the nail and causes a flat tire. Or we could pick it up. If we pick it up, have we prevented an accident?[13]

This is the classic question about reliability: How do we prove that we prevented the accident that didn't happen? Let's say we're in a hurry and decide not to stop and pick up the nail. Later that day, the nail punctures the tire of a passing car, causing the car to veer onto the sidewalk and hit a couple pushing a stroller with an infant inside.

In this hypothetical example, have we caused the accident by our act of omission?

Now, you might say we've gone too far. What are the odds of such a combination of events? This is precisely the point of reliability science: Each system breakdown and vulnerability, each human action and omission, contributes in mathematical ways to the results we achieve in our daily lives.

Sometimes we see tragedies result from seemingly insignificant behaviors, previously repeated over time with positive results until the people involved were unable to see and understand the risk, until the accident happened.

Accidents happen to organizations the same way. Relying too much on past success can be dangerous. Sometimes organizations learn the wrong lesson from successful outcomes—not seeing the risk—until catastrophe strikes.

Sure, sometimes we get lucky and avoid mishaps. We could say most potential accidents are statistically unlikely—such as getting struck by lightning, crashing a car, filing for bankruptcy, or flying a plane into a microburst. But getting the odds in our favor, stacking the deck, so to speak, requires science, not luck.

RISK IS PROPORTIONAL AND PERSONAL

Managing everyday risk requires a sense of proportion.

In most cases, the more we're exposed to a risk and nothing bad happens, the more likely we are to keep tolerating it until things go wrong. Then, because of our bad experience, we see the risk in a different light. We develop hindsight, rather than foresight, bias. This tendency to overvalue outcomes, rather than understand risk, leads us astray. In some instances, we overreact to human errors by punishing people when bad things happen, while repeatedly ignoring the same behavior when nothing goes wrong.

Sometimes we worry excessively about things beyond our direct control, such as a plane crash. Or we may have phobias—such as a fear of heights, public speaking, clowns, or spiders—that dominate our consciousness in certain situations. While phobias may be natural responses to fear, they consume too much attention and prevent us from addressing other, more threatening risks in front of us.

We are unavoidably human, which makes managing risk very personal.

Because we are human, and because each of us has experienced our way through life under unique circumstances and probabilities, our ability to manage risk becomes personal. Each of us may see the same risk very differently. The biases we all have can blind us to solutions beyond our personal experience.

We lose our perspective of what the problem is. Outcome biases, phobias, and our unique experiences are just a few human quirks preventing us from managing risk more effectively. Each of us has our limits, including the time, attention, and energy we spend focusing on reliability. The challenge is to balance these resources in the proper proportion, and worry about the right things, rather than the wrong things. Understanding the biases in our personal experiences helps us see risk more clearly.

The good news is the same brain chemistry that makes us fallibly human and adds personal bias in our lives also lets us reason, use judgment, and improve. And there's a logical step to this evolution:

Reliability requires a sequence.

THE SEQUENCE OF RELIABILITY®

Becoming highly reliable requires a scientific understanding of how organizations—socio-technical entities of people working in systems—operate and produce results. The Collaborative High Reliability model and taxonomy starts with applying the socio-technical science in a specific order, known as the Sequence of Reliability.

This sequence matters because it can make you consistently reliable over time and allow you to adapt to any risk while working with a diverse array of people and resources. There are two steps in the Sequence of Reliability. The first step is:

1. **See and understand risk.** Seeing risk means having vision. Understanding risk means knowing why and how it harms us. We must recognize how the risk is perceived by individuals, teams, and the organization at large.

The second step is:

2. **Manage reliability in this order:**
    a. Systems (to become effective and resilient)
    b. Humans (human performance and human behavior)
    c. Organizations (achieve sustainment and become predictive)

For the rest of this book, we'll dive deeply into how this works, providing practical and theoretical value, yielding profound new strategies on organizational and personal improvement. Through a progression of logical building blocks, we'll make complex socio-technical principles easy to understand so that companies and entire industries can reduce risk and achieve better results: financial, operational, and customer-facing. Real-life stories from high-consequence industries will uncover and illuminate this hidden science, making the lessons relevant and easy to apply to any business as well as our personal lives.

We begin with a powerful, familiar metaphor.

SEEING AND UNDERSTANDING RISK

THE ICEBERG MODEL

One of the biggest challenges you face as a business leader is preparing for hidden risks—either because you're consumed with competing priorities that block your view, or because you're not looking in the right direction. Facebook pioneered the social media experience, connecting families and friends like no other platform before it. Protecting consumer privacy was always incidental, until its existence was threatened when the Federal Trade Commission fined the company $5 billion for not protecting users' personal information.[1] In contrast, Apple prioritized its customers' privacy but failed to anticipate supply chain disruptions in China that limited its ability to keep pace with product demand.[2] Similar lessons could be drawn from the decline of businesses such as Kodak, Blockbuster, and BlackBerry.[3]

The trouble we can see in front of us often represents the "tip of the iceberg"—meaning there's even greater danger lurking unseen beneath the surface. This analogy is crucial to managing socio-technical risk. This book focuses on what's below the surface: the everyday risk in our systems and human activities, and the corresponding reliability we're willing to accept.

Whether it's an accounting discrepancy that leads to recognition of widespread fraud, a fender bender that results in an automobile manufacturer's recall, or an aging bridge discovered to have weakened joints, what we can see sometimes represents a fraction of the risk ahead of us—accidents waiting to happen (see figure 2.1).

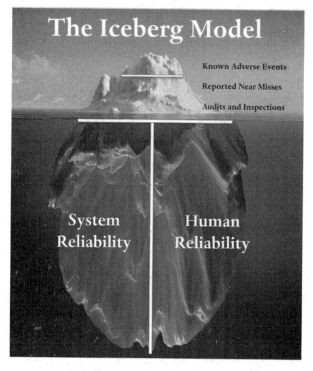

Figure 2.1

Many times, we're overconfident in our ability to see and understand everyday risk. We rely on adverse events, reporting systems, and audits and inspections to warn us of impending danger. Like the *Titanic* before it sank, we celebrate our successes and develop a false sense of security based on past results.

But we often learn the wrong lessons from our successful outcomes. It's human nature to learn from experience. We usually are driven by a desire to achieve a result, and anything that stands in our way represents negative input, an obstacle to success. "Nothing ventured, nothing gained" may guide our thinking. When we achieve the desire result—such as a major sale or a service delivery—we congratulate ourselves on a job well done and reward those involved.

But failure has its consequences. The problem is, we often get great results with vulnerable systems and risky behaviors, until we don't.

Rewarding outcomes, without regard for how the results are achieved, is asking for trouble. So how do we guard against this? We start by taking an honest look at the limits of our optimism. The best leaders in business are not averse to taking risk—a company's success often depends on it—but they do so by making informed decisions, collecting the best data and information available, and recognizing the limits of their sources.

Which recalls Donald Rumsfeld's most famous statement while serving as George W. Bush's secretary of defense:[4]

> As we know, there are known knowns; there are things we know we know. We also know there are known unknowns; that is to say we know there are some things we do not know. But there are also unknown unknowns—the ones we don't know we don't know.[5]

Seeing, understanding, and responding to risk is a non-trivial exercise. What we think we know about a particular risk, whether it's a military or diplomatic strategy, our health, the foods we eat, or the way we run our businesses, may be proven wrong tomorrow. What we believe to be good for us turns out to be bad. We get things wrong.

But we learn. We can shrug our shoulders and believe the world is too complex to understand, or we can evolve our approach. The key to success—in business and our everyday lives—starts with looking ahead.

SEEING AND UNDERSTANDING RISK

The iceberg model guides us to develop two related but distinct skills: seeing and understanding risk. As we've determined, seeing means having the vision to detect what's ahead. Understanding means having the risk intelligence to know how it will affect us. How we respond is based on our tolerance for the risk and the strength of the reward we're trying to achieve.

Let's start with seeing risk. Sometimes we understand the danger ahead but can't see it when it happens because we aren't looking or because it's beyond our field of view.

In business, we might detect changes in revenues that could indicate a temporary lull in customer spending or a harbinger of significant financial shortfalls to come. It may be hard to understand market forces, but without the ability to monitor revenue, we can't attempt understanding. It's like navigating a ship without sonar and radar.

Healthcare professionals face this challenge every day. If providers can't gather the right information, they're left to guess what ails their patients. After listening to a patient's accounting of noticeable symptoms, and depending on the risk, a physician might gather additional, objective data: lab tests, X-rays, or MRIs. Without the ability to see risk, diagnosing can be difficult, if not impossible.

Our human biases, which we'll explore later, often blind us to risk. Executives want to believe it's normal for everyone to be treated equally and with respect, for example, and may not look hard enough when sexual harassment happens in the workplace. In the same way, some past incidents of police brutality and civil rights violations went unreported—but the proliferation of cell phone cameras and officer body cameras has let us see the risk more clearly.

We can define risk as a condition, object, situation, or other threat involving the probability of danger or harm to people and/or property. The harm can be physical, psychological, emotional, financial, or software-related. Risk involves possible adverse outcomes—customer impact, crashes, or patient injury. It could be a chemical spill, a worker injury, or a supply chain interruption, for example. Personal and organizational values, as well as risk intelligence and tolerance, influence how we see, understand, and react to risk.

These definitions apply to individuals, groups, and organizations:

Risk Intelligence: Your ability to perceive the likelihood and severity of an adverse event, most often based on experience, past practice, and previous results. Risk intelligence informs situational awareness.

Humans are biased by direct experience, for better or worse. The experiences that weigh most are the most recent. We tend to believe the results we got yesterday will be repeated today, especially when faced with competing priorities offering strong incentives. A few examples:

- Riding skateboards, bikes, and motorcycles while never wearing a helmet (pleasure vs. safety)
- Getting to work on time while driving over the speed limit and talking on the phone (the necessity of keeping a job vs. safety)
- Going to a family gathering without taking precautions— vaccinations, testing, and/or masking (the pleasure and mental health benefits that come from social interaction vs. health risk)
- Waiting until business rebounds to hire back employees after a layoff (the relationship between cost, revenue, and profit)

In each of these circumstances, our risk intelligence—limited as it may be by our experience—is balanced by our tolerance for risk:

Risk Tolerance: The level of risk you are willing to accept, based on risk intelligence and the strength of the reward associated with the activity.

When the rewards are high, we may be willing to roll the dice and hope for the best. But our tolerance for this risk should be based on facts and reason, not wishful thinking. Smart business leaders have cash reserves, or the ability to borrow, to make up for temporary shortfalls. Foolish leaders expect talent and optimism to overcome whatever market conditions arise.

In business and everyday life, as well as in military operations, this course of action is doomed to fail. It's simply a matter of probabilities. Being lucky is not the best strategy.

Let's look at other everyday challenges of seeing and understanding risk. Making a commitment to seeing and understanding risks is a better approach, but it's not without challenges.

A SCORPION STORY

Sometimes we understand a risk but are unable to see it. A young couple with two small children moved to Arizona from another part of the country, and the family was excited about their new home, which was an older ranch house. A couple of nights after they moved in, the wife said to her husband that the blue-black lights lining the bedroom floorboards looked lovely, that she had never seen that kind of home accent. The husband agreed and marveled at the unique style.

One day, the husband called the previous owner to say how much they enjoyed their new home and asked about the lights.

"Oh, that," the previous homeowner said with a chuckle. "I take it you're not from the desert. Is that right?"

"Well, no. We moved here from the East Coast," the husband said.

"Around here, you must be careful and watch for scorpions, for obvious reasons. But the funny thing is, they glow in the dark when black light hits them.[6] Who would've imagined that? So, I installed the black lights in the floorboards so that we could see those nasty little critters before they could see us. My wife and I slept a little easier at night after that."

ULCERS

Sometimes we see the risk or condition but don't understand it. For most of the twentieth century, physicians believed stomach ulcers were caused by anxiety and a nervous disposition. Whenever patients complained to their doctors, the typical response was an admonishment to relax and lower the stressors in their lives. The medical community could *see* the risk and acknowledged stomach ulcers as a condition. But *understanding* its mechanisms was another matter.

In 1981, to the relief of millions of sufferers worldwide, everything changed. Here's a summary from journalist Pamela Weintraub, who interviewed Barry Marshall, the physician/researcher responsible for an amazing discovery:[7]

For years an obscure doctor hailing from Australia's hardscrabble west coast watched in horror as ulcer patients fell so ill that many had their stomach removed or bled until they died. That physician, an internist named Barry Marshall, was tormented because he knew there was a simple treatment for ulcers, which at that time afflicted 10 percent of all adults.

In 1981 Marshall began working with Robin Warren, the Royal Perth Hospital pathologist who, two years earlier, discovered the gut could be overrun by hardy, corkscrew-shaped bacteria called *Helicobacter pylori*. Biopsying ulcer patients and culturing the organisms in the lab, Marshall traced not just ulcers but also stomach cancer to this gut infection. The cure, he realized, was readily available: antibiotics. But mainstream gastroenterologists were dismissive, holding on to the old idea that ulcers were caused by stress.

Unable to make his case in studies with lab mice (because *H. pylori* affects only primates) and prohibited from experimenting on people, Marshall grew desperate. Finally he ran an experiment on the only human patient he could ethically recruit: himself. He took some *H. pylori* from the gut of an ailing patient, stirred it into a broth, and drank it.

As the days passed, he developed gastritis, the precursor to an ulcer: He started vomiting, his breath began to stink, and he felt sick and exhausted. Back in the lab, he biopsied his own gut, culturing *H. pylori* and proving unequivocally that bacteria were the underlying cause of ulcers.

Today the standard of care for an ulcer is treatment with an antibiotic. And stomach cancer—once one of the most common forms of malignancy—is almost gone from the Western world.

This example illustrates the central challenge present in all of medicine: discerning the cause-and-effect relationship between symptoms and the underlying conditions that cause them. Correlation does not always equal causation. For treatments and cures, what matters first is our ability to see and understand the risk, including the mechanisms by which our bodies are harmed.

INFLUENZA

(Step 1: See and Understand Risk)

Have you ever passed along a cold or flu virus to someone? The odds are we all have. But how would we know? We usually can't see, smell, touch, hear, or taste these germs. If we could, our actions to avoid them would be very different. Our inability to see them *removes the feedback loop that is essential to learning from our experiences*. When we drive a car and start to drift out of our lane, we receive instant visual and sometimes tactile feedback.[8] Not so with viruses. Not seeing them poses a problem.

Medical scientists say that many of our efforts to combat infections—from antibacterial soap to antibiotics—not only aren't effective but also have significantly reduced our defenses against certain types of bacterial infections.[9] So our inability to fully understand a particular risk (the second component to managing one) can lead to less-than-hoped-for results and negatively affect our ability to manage risks in other areas.

The primary system we've put in place to combat influenza shows how we manage the risk. In addition to hand hygiene and other personal measures, vaccinations provide our most effective widespread system of defense. Over the past century, vaccinations have transformed healthcare across the globe, inoculating us against the ravages of disease and saving millions of lives. They are a form of the "herd effect"—what happens when a large percentage of a population has become immune to an infection and provides a measure of protection for people who are not immune. Each year, vaccines are prepared in advance to provide a large-scale defense against influenza.

Who decides what strains of flu go into the vaccine each year, and how do they choose? All year, 142 national influenza centers in 113 countries collect data on the flu viruses affecting the world's population. They monitor which strains are making people sick, how efficiently those strains are spreading, and how well previous vaccines have worked to combat their targeted viruses.[10]

These smaller centers then pass the results to one of five World Health Organization Collaborating Centers for Reference and Research on Influenza in the United States, United Kingdom, Australia, Japan, and China, including the Centers for Disease Control and Prevention in Atlanta.

Scientists at the five main centers analyze the data together to identify new flu strains and determine which strains are most likely to spread and cause illness in the upcoming flu season. Consultants from each center then meet each year in February to determine the recommended composition of the vaccine for the Northern Hemisphere and in September for the Southern Hemisphere.

The data they use are reported through several channels. Clinical laboratories and hospitals monitor where and when flu cases occur, what strains are detected, and what kinds of patients are affected. Patients who have flu-like symptoms with no other obvious cause but who do not have confirmed cases also are recorded. Any changes in the strains of flu and the geographic reach of each strain are also tracked.

Another factor that can determine which strains will be included in the current flu shot is the ability to produce a working vaccine against each strain. Every vaccine must be tested and approved by the Food and Drug Administration before it is used. If production is particularly slow for any reason, that strain will not be included on the World Health Organization's list.

So, what are the results of this systemic approach? The Centers for Disease Control and Prevention conducts studies each year to determine how well the vaccine protects against influenza illness. While vaccine effectiveness can vary, recent studies show that vaccination reduces the risk of flu illness by 40 to 60 percent during seasons when most circulating flu viruses are well matched to the vaccine.[11] In years when the flu viruses are not well matched, the protections drop substantially. But get your flu shot. The herd immunity effect is real, and the shot may lessen the severity and duration of your symptoms. Some protection is better than none.

The conclusion? The key challenge in making the flu shot more reliable is in becoming better at predicting the dominant strain each year, its location, and prevalence. In other words, seeing and understanding it.

(Step 2: Manage Reliability)

In a perfect world, every flu and cold virus could be recognized, isolated, and reported to a centralized data repository.[12] And medical research could make more effective influenza vaccines[13] readily available, based on our ability to pinpoint and predict the geographic locations where these strains are most likely to surface.

Let's also suppose that better personal barriers become available for individual use, such as masks that kill flu viruses on contact.[14] And while we're imagining a better world, let's predict that someday we'll be able to detect certain viruses with the aid of optical devices, like our ability to see and understand microbursts in aviation. That would influence our behavioral choices as another line of defense against acquiring and spreading these viruses. Shaking hands and touching certain doorknobs might become recognizable hazards. And in the unlikely event that someone contracts a flu or cold virus, medical research would lead to ways we could kill or neutralize the virus as a form of recovery.

First seeing and understanding risk, then managing system performance, would give us a greater chance of substantially reducing the occurrence and spread of these viruses, as we've done with certain other communicable diseases such as rubella in the Americas and rabies in certain countries.[15]

But that's only part of the process. To get optimal results, we also would have to manage human performance (people getting their shots) and organizational performance (hospitals, businesses, and schools ensuring herd immunity).

But sometimes the more reliable our system is—both effective and resilient—the less reliable our human behaviors are. Of course, that can be a good thing if we can come close to eliminating targeted diseases. Elimination means reducing new cases to near zero but needing ongoing measures to prevent diseases from reestablishing, according to the World Health Organization.[16] Examples include mumps, measles, whooping cough, and smallpox. But there has been a resurgence in recent years because of people choosing not to get vaccinations.

Elimination may not be enough. Unless we can eradicate these diseases—permanently cut new cases to zero, with no further efforts necessary, according to WHO—we'll need to keep our focus on human and organizational reliability to reach our reduction goals.

While that may sound ambitious, a future of dramatically reduced influenza and colds is within our grasp, if we apply the Sequence of Reliability.

A PREDICTABLE PANDEMIC: COVID-19

On February 28, 2020, the WHO-China Joint Mission on Coronavirus Disease 2019 (COVID-19) sounded this alarm for the global community:

> The COVID-19 virus is a new pathogen that is highly contagious, can spread quickly, and must be considered capable of causing enormous health, economic and societal impacts in any setting. It is not SARS and it is not influenza. Building scenarios and strategies only on the basis of well-known pathogens risks failing to exploit all possible measures to slow transmission of the COVID-19 virus, reduce disease and save lives.

Unfortunately, it would take the United States months and millions of lives to recognize and learn from the experiences described in the report. Within two months of this report's publication, COVID-19 overtook heart disease as the number one cause of death in America, killing more people than cancer, accidents, strokes, diabetes, influenza, pneumonia, kidney and liver diseases, suicide, Alzheimer's, Parkinson's, and all other diseases combined.[17] At the time of this book's writing, the full scope and impact of the pandemic's devastation remains unknown. What is certain, however, is the exponential growth of COVID-19 is but one of many existential threats to humans. Understanding and applying the Sequence of Reliability can help us manage COVID-19 through better mitigation and suppression and help us avoid future catastrophes as we learn to be predictively reliable.

Why did this disease spread so rapidly? The short answer is that we failed to see and understand it, allowing the virus to spread undetected from Wuhan, China. Like the pilots on Flight 191, leaders around the world failed to recognize and respond to the lethal SARS-CoV-2 virus as it gained momentum. While infectious disease experts and epidemiologists offered warnings of the viral storm ahead, past methods of containment relied on symptomatic expression. In other words, we *mistakenly believed you were contagious only if you had a fever.*

The Centers for Disease Control (CDC) posted this on its website in March of 2020:

> People are thought to be most contagious when they are most symptomatic (the sickest). Identifying those who may be infected is crucial. Testing should be done and the person isolated as soon as someone begins to show signs of symptoms.
>
> Some spread might be possible before people show symptoms; there have been reports of this occurring with this new coronavirus, but this is not thought to be the main way the virus spreads.

Why did the medical community make this fatal mistake? Because experience taught us the wrong lesson. During the 2003 SARS outbreak, international gateway airports set up screening barriers to prevent passengers from boarding planes when they exhibited symptoms such as fever.

Similarly, with COVID-19, because we missed this critical first step, everything we did afterward in America and elsewhere—from social distancing to stay-at-home orders; from provisioning of personal protective equipment to testing—failed to stop the virus from propagating. In fact, our inability to see and understand the nature of this strain of coronavirus contributed to catastrophic results. Nothing else the world would do afterward could replace the lives lost or compensate for the global economic and psychological damage left in the wake of this pandemic.

Was this pandemic foreseeable? In Nassim Taleb's *The Black Swan: The Impact of the Highly Improbable*,[18] he cautions readers not to focus on the "normal," but to look for outliers located at the extremes. (It's likely that Taleb would consider the COVID-19 pandemic to be a Black Swan event.) He says, "the normal is often irrelevant."

But our conclusion differs: There's coding in the DNA of adverse outcomes, and it's embedded in the everyday positive results we achieve. Seeing below the surface, deepening our vision beyond past events, actively looking for Black Swans in everyday success, provides a clearer picture of risk and how we can manage it. We shouldn't wait for a catastrophic event to be prepared for disaster. The signs of Black Swans are lurking below the surface, hidden in the everyday outcomes we produce.

ANTIMICROBIAL RESISTANCE[19]

(Step 1: See and Understand Risk)

Antibiotics and antibacterials have become common tools for fighting the viruses and bacteria that put our health at risk. But how effective are they? Ask yourself if you've ever experienced the following:

- Received a prescription for antibiotics, but it turned out you had a viral infection, such as a cold or the flu, rather than a bacterial infection.[20]
- Been told by your doctor that you must take all of a prescribed antibiotic for a bacterial infection to kill all the bacteria, and not to stop when you start feeling better.
- Bought antibacterial soap, believing it must be better than ordinary soap because it sounded more scientific.

Antibiotics are often called "wonder drugs" of the twentieth century,[21] but their widespread use has come under increasing scrutiny.[22] It's now believed that misuse and overuse of antibiotics is contributing to a class of superbugs that could "kill more people than cancer," a United Kingdom government report warns.[23]

It's commonly understood that antibiotics are ineffective against viruses. But a recent study by the National Institutes of Health says one class of antibiotics applied preventively to certain mucous membranes increased resistance to a range of viral infections, including herpes simplex, influenza A, and Zika.[24]

Similarly, antibacterial soaps are disappearing from grocery store shelves after the Food and Drug Administration banned nineteen "antibacterial" additives commonly found in over-the-counter soaps,[25] noting that antibacterial products are "no more effective than soap and water, and could be dangerous."[26]

What are we to take from these apparent contradictory findings? Our world is a risky place. Managing the threats of germs[27]—bacteria, viruses, and other types of infections—requires seeing and understanding the risks. While physicians will continue to prescribe antibiotics (appropriately or not), and we will continue to buy cleaning products marketed to protect us, the results we get depend directly on getting the science right first. We should continue to invest in scientific research to illuminate the biological and chemical mechanisms below the surface. Then we can design and manage systems of delivery that account for our human and technological limits and are effective whether things go right or wrong—systems that are both effective and resilient.

(Step 2: Manage Reliability)

The term *antimicrobial stewardship*[28] refers to how we judiciously and responsibly use our antimicrobial resources. It sounds simple, right? But let's break this down a bit further.

The risk of infection caused by germs is difficult to manage unless we detect and understand these invaders. As we discussed with influenza and the common cold, imagine if we could devote sufficient worldwide resources to the challenge of antimicrobial resistance, and isolate microbial threats—bacterial and viral—with the optimal antimicrobial solution. (That would be possible only after multiple stages of research because of the complexity of each microbial threat.)

As this success happens with each microbial, our attention would turn to the first part of step 2 in our Sequence of Reliability: enhancing our "systems of delivery" performance. What do we mean by that?

Once we've researched and isolated the optimal antimicrobial, we must then develop it and make it available in sufficient quantities, and at affordable cost, for widespread distribution. And since our systems of healthcare delivery are socio-technical, the next two parts of step 2 (improving human and organizational performance) become crucial. That means that people and organizations are engaged in the decisions and applications of this research: manufacturers, healthcare providers who prescribe the medications, caregivers who administer and monitor them, patients who get them, and government regulators, private employers, and professional associations who oversee how they're delivered.

Sounds complex, doesn't it? It is. But the pattern can be simplified, understood, and made more effective through the Sequence of Reliability. The sequence matters: One measured step before the next will lead to better solutions.

THE FOODS WE EAT

(Step 1: See and Understand Risk)

Each year in America, more than 97 million of us spend more than $60 billion on diet products, in hopes of losing weight and improving our health.[29] But is a healthy weight just a matter of balancing the calories consumed with the calories burned? Or is weight loss, and the larger health effects of our diet, more complicated than a simple formula?

There is no shortage of nutritional advice in popular culture. It's hard to avoid magazines shouting about the latest diet when we're in the grocery store checkout line. Like never before, the diet choices can seem overwhelming: DASH,[30] Paleo, Atkins, low-fat, low-carbohydrate, Mediterranean, and countless others. But do more choices equal greater success? Consider this statement from the *State of Obesity* report:

> Obesity is one of the biggest health concerns in communities across the country, with about 70 percent of county officials ranking it as a leading problem where they live. Factors related to obesity are also rated as communities' priority health issues, including nutrition and physical activity at 58 percent, heart disease and hypertension at 57 percent and diabetes at 44 percent.
>
> There has been progress to address the epidemic. After decades of increasing, the national obesity rate among 2- to 19-year-olds has begun to level off and the rise of obesity among adults has slowed over time. Yet obesity remains a bigger threat to our health and country now than it was a generation ago. If trends continue, children today could be the first generation to live shorter, less healthy lives than their parents.[31]

One result of obesity is the staggering contribution to our rising healthcare costs, including cardiovascular disease, diabetes, and cancer.

Our species evolved by eating for survival. The availability of food dominated our diets, and the time and resources we spent to acquire it consumed vast amounts of energy. As food acquisition, production, and distribution grew more efficient, our available choices increased, the labor required to acquire food decreased, and we became obese. That may be an oversimplification, but America's growing dietary trends make it hard to refute this conclusion: Our socio-economic advances have contributed to a national rise in obesity.

Our goal is to learn how to improve our everyday lives by applying fundamental principles of reliability. That means taking the first step in the Sequence of Reliability: see and understand risk. To help us make good dietary choices,[32] we must grasp the science behind nutrition and optimal health.[33] While this can be difficult, the best strategy is to confer with your doctor to help sort out the contradictory dietary claims and match diets and medications with your personal risk profile.

This might sound like a statement supporting nutritional research and consultation with your doctor, which it is. Optimal health—including diets, medications, and exercise—requires a *sequence*.

(Step 2: Manage Reliability)

Dieting has long been considered a function of willpower. We believe that if we exercise and eat the right foods, in the right amount, our weight (and therefore our health) will be optimized. But that's easier said than done if we don't know the right foods to eat. Focusing on willpower is out of sequence.

While there's no denying that our behavioral choices can play a crucial role in managing our weight, diets provide a *system* in which to make those choices. If we choose the wrong diet, we probably won't get the results we're hoping for.

What's the value in thinking of diets this way? It's recognizing that without an effective system, or in this case, an effective dietary plan that works for our individual metabolism, no amount of willpower will lead us to sustainable weight loss and maintenance. One consequence of not having an effective dietary system is the "yo-yo effect,"[34] where we follow a pattern of losing, then regaining, our undesired pounds. Is yo-yo dieting merely a lack of willpower? Or perhaps also a less-than-optimal dietary strategy?

There are two important points here: For weight loss to be effective, we must first select a diet that is (a) effective in helping us shed pounds when we adhere to it, and (b) user-friendly enough to facilitate sticking to it. Understanding the science of nutrition must come first, followed by the correct socio-technical sequence of selecting the right *system* (diet), then managing *human performance* (willpower) and *organizational performance* (a business, school, or other facility promoting healthful eating).

Again, this is easier said than done. But the sequence matters more than our willpower.

DRIVING APPS AND AUTONOMOUS VEHICLES

(Step 1: See and Understand Risk)

We've all been stuck in traffic. There could be any number of reasons:

- We chose the busier route because we enjoy spending time away from work and other people.
- An immediate accident, road condition, or weather ahead.
- We took a wrong turn because of human error.
- We chose the route because of experience, a map, or someone's direction, but it turned out to be less than optimal on this day and time. The delay could be caused by an accident, road closure, or other condition that wasn't known beforehand.

Three of those results are caused by human performance, and one is unavoidable. If we are trying to optimize our strategy and spend a minimal amount of time in traffic, selecting the right *system* by which to navigate is important. Experience may be a great teacher in some circumstances, but a better approach is to use technology to improve our results. Thus, the increase in popularity of software applications.

What do these traffic apps do better than humans? *See and understand* traffic. They monitor and predict traffic flow and try to optimize routes using mathematical algorithms based on input from GPS, cell-tower sensors, and users. They're not perfect, but for a variety of reasons, these systems are more reliable in ways that humans can't be. Some apps even advise us when to expect a pothole, red light cameras, or police officers. By integrating social media and crowdsourcing features, these apps[35] also help us collaborate with large groups of people beyond our immediate vicinity. Amazing, isn't it? But it's based on engineering science that makes the risks clear to us.

(Step 2: Manage Reliability)

Are these apps fully capable of processing information in the same way as people? No. But increasingly, apps are evolving toward autonomous capabilities, which will have substantial impact on our lives. So how does the Sequence of Reliability work when applied to the evolution toward autonomous vehicles? Let's look.

There's no doubt that artificial intelligence is beginning to show exponential growth in our lives.[36] We can expect continued development for the years to come.[37] The challenge, however, will be how to best transition the applications of AI into our lives. There will be human consequences, including job losses, lawsuits, and the uncomfortable feeling of giving up control of the steering wheel.

Following the Sequence guides us to see and understand the AI risks first. There will be many psychological, physical, and emotional effects as humans adapt to an increasingly automated world. We can predict the various challenges ahead as automation increases inside our cars. Drivers will face confusion between the autopilot and their own control over the car. "What's it doing now?" will become a common question. Commercial aviation faced this challenge in the late twentieth century as planes grew increasingly automated. But there are two key differences: (1) Most US drivers are not professionally "trained to proficiency,"[38] and (2) autonomous vehicle software has not yet been standardized.

Both differences point to an early, if debatable, prediction: Once the technology matures to acceptable reliability, a greater number of lives will be saved when we remove the human component from the driving system.

When we manage everyday risk, it's easy to get the steps wrong by focusing prematurely on human behaviors, or even systems, before we see and understand the dangers. We may focus on handwashing and getting our flu shot, but unless the Centers for Disease Control and Prevention matches the shot to the virus, our herd immunity will be less than we hope for. We may diet repeatedly, but we won't achieve our optimal weight and health without understanding the way our bodies metabolize food. We may want police to issue tickets for breaking rules and causing crashes, but we won't prevent most accidents that way.

It's natural to focus on people and their actions, often because of our biases. But that's not likely to produce the desired results. The sequence matters, and following it brings us closer to the outcomes we want.

Especially when our lives depend on it.

BRAIN INJURIES

By the turn of the twenty-first century, traumatic brain injury[39] had become a growing concern among the medical community, as described in the prophetic warning published in 2001 below:

> Traumatic brain injury (TBI) is one of the most prevalent causes of morbidity and mortality all over the world. More than 350,000 individuals are admitted each year as a result of TBI in the USA alone (Kraus et al., 1996). This disease affects mainly young adults in their productive stage of life, producing long lasting disabilities in 25% of cases. This represents an enormous social and economical cost estimated to be around 38 billion dollars per year in the USA (Max et al., 1990). However, at the present there is no available treatment to reduce the extent of cerebral damage following brain injury, other than supportive intensive care.[40]

Since this warning, the TBI concern has expanded to include the following:

- Professional contact sports, including boxing, football, mixed martial arts, wrestling, and soccer

- Youth and adult recreational activities including skiing, horseback riding, bike riding, trampoline jumping, gymnastics, and cheerleading
- The very young and the elderly—in the home and in day- and long-term care facilities
- Domestic abuse
- Military operations
- Household accidents
- Car and motorcycle crashes

For many years, our threshold for concern with head injuries was the medical term *concussion*.[41] But let's consider this as just the tip of our iceberg model. To understand this risk fully, we must dive deeper below the surface. And there's a specific type of brain injury known as chronic traumatic encephalopathy[42] (CTE), defined as:

a neurodegenerative disease that is associated with changes and deficits in cognition, behavior, mood, and motor skills. It is believed to be caused in part by exposure to repetitive head impacts, including concussions as well as subconcussive trauma (i.e., head impacts that do not cause symptoms of concussion).

Evolving medical research indicates that injury and diminished brain function can occur long before concussion symptoms are present. In fact, an article in the *Washington Post* reported:

A new study has found further evidence linking hits to the head rather than concussions to the onset of chronic traumatic encephalopathy, the neurodegenerative disease traced back to the kind of head trauma experienced by football players, other athletes, and combat veterans.

"The concussion is really irrelevant for triggering CTE," Dr. Lee Goldstein, an associate professor at Boston University School of

Medicine and College of Engineering, and a corresponding author of the study, told the *Post*. "It's really the hit that counts."[43]

As we examine the examples listed previously, our vision comes into focus: Each of these activities is a socio-technical endeavor, involving people living—that is, working and playing—inside systems. Sure, we can modify the rules about contact sports and add layers of protection in the equipment we use, but without fully seeing and understanding the risks involved, nothing we do to manage the risk will be optimal. Tragic deaths and debilitating mental conditions will continue to result from these activities. Should we stop them? (In the case of domestic abuse, the unequivocal answer is yes.) Should we pause our daily lives and stop most of our daily activities? We won't and couldn't do this in many cases. But can we improve?

Yes. We can, we should, and in many examples, we will. Applying the Sequence of Reliability to the risk of TBI and CTE will achieve better, even optimal results.

A SERVICE ANIMAL STORY

Lisa was a young, athletic professional woman in her midtwenties when she met her future husband, Dave.[44] He was everything she could hope for in a potential mate. Like her, he was intelligent, funny, compassionate, and athletic. In fact, he had just signed a contract with a National Football League team and was on his way to a successful NFL career.

In his third season, he became a starting defensive back for the team and was just beginning to establish himself as an everyday player. Midway through the season, he began having bouts of vertigo, which soon affected his play on the field. The team had grown cautious in its approach to managing concussions. The league's protocols and guidelines were becoming increasingly clear and prescriptive whenever a player reported feeling dizzy or otherwise showed visible signs of a concussion during a game. Yet Dave had shown no signs of a concussion during any NFL games. He had reported being concussed in high school and a couple of times in college, but what high school, college, or NFL player hadn't? When he thought about it, he may have even had a concussion playing peewee football early in his childhood. But he couldn't remember. Soon, there were other things he couldn't remember, even in his daily life.

Lisa was more than concerned. She worked for a large hospital system in a nonclinical capacity, but she had access to several top doctors and nurses who advised that Dave be evaluated by a neurologist, which she did. The results of the tests were not good: Dave was diagnosed with severe chronic traumatic encephalopathy and was told this disease would affect him the rest of his life. Shocked and saddened by these results, they sought second and third medical opinions. The results were unchanged. So, it was an easy decision when Dave announced his retirement at the end of the season. The news coverage was minimal, although one or two reporters pressed Dave and Lisa for details. They said it was a personal decision, and they would remain loyal fans of the NFL and appreciated the team's support for their decision.

But their life together changed dramatically. Dave had always been independent and active, but now they were told he was at risk of seizures, which soon came. He couldn't be left alone, so they hired a "sitter" to be with him when Lisa couldn't be. The seizures usually required a rush to the emergency room. The doctors were doing the best they could in treating him, and they were exploring a range of medications and therapies to manage his disease.

Then one day at work, someone told Lisa about a program providing service animals who helped with CTE patients. Lisa's first thought was, *Service animal? He's not blind. How on earth could a dog or other animal help?* But she thanked her friend and decided it couldn't hurt to make an inquiry. What she found was a wonderful new approach to improving the lives of people suffering from CTE. This quote from a *National Geographic* news report explains:

Over the last decade a new kind of service animal has emerged. Seizure alert dogs warn people with epilepsy of an oncoming attack minutes—sometimes hours—before it occurs. This allows the person time to take seizure blocking medication, get to a safe place, or call for assistance.[45]

The article continues:

How dogs detect an oncoming seizure in a human is a mystery. Some trainers and researchers think they detect subtle changes in human behavior or scent before an episode occurs.

Although the mechanism by which this remarkable feat happens may remain unknown, it's clear that certain dogs demonstrate the ability to detect precursor symptoms of a seizure that remain undetectable by humans. In other words, these dogs help us *see,* if not fully understand, the risk of an oncoming seizure. It's the first part of the first step in the Sequence of Reliability, allowing us to embrace the remaining steps with a better chance of achieving positive results.

And Dave and Lisa? Their lives have improved dramatically. Although Dave understands he'll live with CTE for the rest of his life, the quality of their lives has reached a new, improved normal. They are active, enjoy recreational pursuits, and are focused on seeing, understanding, and managing other everyday risks in their lives with improved success.

SYSTEM RELIABILITY

WHAT SYSTEM RELIABILITY MEANS

Systems fail. Whether it's the ice cream machine at McDonald's[1] continually frustrating customers; or the Texas power grid failure that left 4.5 million homes and businesses without power and killed at least 246 people;[2] or the Minnesota I-35W bridge collapse that killed thirteen people and injured 145;[3] systems break down. In many endeavors, this is a matter of life and death. In business, this can mean the difference between profitability and bankruptcy. For all leaders, it's important to understand how systems fail—as well as how they work—and to manage them accordingly.

Once we see and understand risk, the next step is building system reliability. Systems come in a variety of forms: large (macro) and small (micro). There are infinite varieties of macro systems:

- Our solar system: the sun, planets, moon, and other rotating bodies. Within this are other systems, such as Earth's ecosystem.
- Governments: geopolitical systems across our planet.
- Highway infrastructure: roads, bridges, traffic laws, stoplights, signs, etc. Each of these is a subsystem.
- Education: buildings, desks, devices, books, policies, curricula, students, teachers, etc.
- A Wi-Fi network: groups of components providing wireless access to the internet.

- Organizational systems: hardware, equipment, software, rules, policies, and procedures such as time and attendance requirements.

Systems can stand alone with little or no human involvement, such as mechanical parts or software, or they can be socio-technical, involving interactions with people. Socio-technical systems are the *support structures* and *controls* we put around ourselves to get a result.

On a personal level, systems can involve strategies and routines:

- Using alarm clocks to wake up at a predetermined time
- Oral care and dental hygiene, including our choice of dentist and toothbrush, and our schedule for brushing our teeth, using mouthwash, and flossing
- Making grocery lists
- Studying before an exam
- Following an exercise regimen
- Dieting and cooking recipes
- Travel itineraries
- Software for paying bills and taxes

We put these support structures and controls around us to achieve specific results. In organizations—including businesses, the military, and other groups—the support structures and controls are applied broadly. But whether we're using personal or organizational systems, our aim is to both *support* the activities involved and *control,* or limit, human performance.

Our highway system is a good example. Roads and bridges provide the *support structures* that let us drive from point A to point B. The speed limit signs, traffic lights, and law enforcement officers provide the *controls* for limiting our behaviors.

The gap between our expected results and actual performance is system failure. This gap is an opportunity for resilience—the ability to recover from failure. For example, waking up on time for work may be our goal. An alarm clock can be an effective system for achieving that. But have you ever overslept using an alarm clock? Was it because of alarm clock malfunction, such as a battery or electrical failure? Or was it the result of human behavior, such as setting the clock incorrectly or hitting the snooze button and going back to sleep? Regardless of the reasons, the results we get with systems are often less than 100 percent.

When they do fail, system resilience becomes important. Knowing systems will never be perfect, we can predict systems to fail and manage them accordingly.

SYSTEM FACTORS

How can we predict and manage system performance? The answer begins with understanding what shapes system performance—the influences that determine the results systems produce.

Figure 3.1 does not represent all the potential influences on system performance. But grouping these common factors as a honeycomb shows they are interconnected.

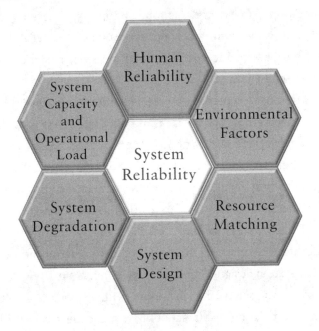

Figure 3.1

The proportions—or relative strength of these influences—will vary widely, depending on circumstance. But we can see how these factors contribute to the results we get from our systems.

System Design: The best systems start with system design, often called design specifications. Every system is designed to do something. Consider a telephone. It's designed to transmit and receive voice communications. The system can be a set of wires or cables stretched between points, a network of cell towers across a geographic area, or satellites orbiting through space. The function, utility, and reliability of the telephone system will depend directly on our system design.

All systems have features or functions that the system is *optimized* to perform, and others that the system may perform, but perhaps less reliably. For example, mobile phones are designed to provide communication "on the go," over a wide area, and may be designed to work best in specific areas where network towers are available. Mobile phones began as marvels of convenience, and we accepted an occasional dropped call as the price we were willing to pay. Over time, as mobile phone systems and technology have improved, we've come to expect convenience *and* reliability. Phone companies have evolved to compete for our service based on reliability, among other selling points.

On the other hand, a corded phone in an office or phone booth (are you old enough to remember those?) lacks mobility, but it may provide greater reliability and call clarity than our mobile phones. All systems have design trade-offs, where reliability must be balanced with other constraints and objectives, including availability of resources, functionality, and cost.

System design plays a key role in relation to the other factors shaping system performance. *System design sets the limits on our socio-technical reliability.* Another way of saying this is we will get no better results than the limits of our system design. Think about aviation. No matter how well we train our pilots, the safety of flight begins with airplane reliability, which starts with system design. Pilots' actions have great effect as well, of course, but no pilot can fly a plane that can't fly.

It's the same in every other socio-technical endeavor, from healthcare to energy, from parenting to school systems, from sporting events to household appliances, from community projects to government institutions. The results we get depend on system design. And seeing and understanding risk is crucial to how well we design our systems.

System Degradation: Systems deteriorate over time. Hardware wears out, software becomes outdated, and policies, processes, and procedures may not remain effective in managing evolving risks. Recognizing system degradation allows us to develop preventive maintenance programs, apply software updates, and revise our policies, processes, and procedures to match the needs of the changing operating environment. Examples are all around us:

- Maintenance schedules for our cars and homes
- Updates to our phones and computers
- Health maintenance plans, including exercise, diets, and scheduled appointments
- Court decisions that lead to improved justice systems
- New workplace anti-harassment policies to create better working environments

Seeing and understanding system degradation provides better management of system performance.

Resource Matching: System performance can suffer from mismatched resource allocation. Sometimes the resources needed to run a system are misplaced. The challenge is applying our resources in the right areas:

- A gas station with plenty of diesel fuel, but not enough unleaded regular and premium
- A school athletic department with ample equipment and facilities for one sport but not enough for another

- A 64-bit computer running software optimized for a 32-bit system
- Neighborhood streets accommodating cars and trucks, but without bicycle lanes to support a growing trend in commuting
- A community hospital with a state-of-the-industry helipad for air medical transport, but not enough ground-based ambulances to meet the need of a growing urban population

System Capacity and Operational Load: These two factors influencing system performance must be considered together. Both are related to resource matching. We typically design systems for a specific capacity, or load, and when that capacity is exceeded, system performance suffers:

- Manufacturers rate automobile tires (and vehicles) for specific temperature-dependent inflation pressures, load bearing capacity, and mileage for wear and tear. Tire and vehicle performance depend on those.
- Computers are designed with limited disk space. Performance degrades as use approaches capacity.
- Speed limits for cars, trucks, planes, boats, and trains are determined under good weather conditions. When weather and other influences deteriorate, lower speeds may be safer.
- Schools and classrooms are designed for specific student-teacher ratios, based on educational needs and building capacities. When these limits are exceeded, educational performance can suffer.[4]
- Airplane performance is significantly affected by several variables, including weight and location of the passengers and cargo, temperature, altitude, and atmospheric conditions, all of which are specified in the aircraft's certified design limitations.

External and Environmental Factors: These factors, too, can have powerful effects on system performance. Some examples:

- Bad weather affects the military, businesses, schools, Congress, and transportation systems—including roads, airline schedules, and rocket launches and recoveries.
- Extreme temperatures, water intrusion, and physical jolts affect computer performance.
- Malware affects computer software.
- Natural and human-caused disasters can devastate communities.
- Changing market forces affect businesses, stock prices, and customer demand for products and services.

Human Performance: Human performance affects all socio-technical systems. Even systems designed to operate autonomously are designed by humans, or by software originating with human input. In some cases, human performance overrides system design limits. In other instances, human performance simply yields less than optimal results:

- A bus driver exceeds the speed limit, which leads to a crash.
- A healthcare professional misses a recipient verification call and sends a fax with confidential patient information to the wrong recipient.
- A zoo worker skips a step during a maintenance inspection and fails to notice a large hole in the fence around a wild animal exhibit.
- A restaurant chef mistakenly undercooks a poultry dish, leading to customer food poisoning.
- An official timekeeper at a football game forgets to reset the game clock after a penalty, time runs out, and the game ends prematurely.
- A software developer fails to document crucial steps in a program, leading to system failure and subsequent rework.
- A parent forgets to set the clock forward one hour for daylight saving time, and the kids are late for school.

All of these examples produce less-than-optimal results. That leads us to ask: Can people improve system performance, or at least compensate for system vulnerabilities? The answer, of course, is yes.

But remember that system design limits socio-technical performance. Without a system to support and limit human performance, even reliable human behaviors will not get us the results we desire. That's why championship sports teams working within a well-designed system typically outperform a team of all-stars. In most cases, human performance alone won't compensate for a lack of a well-designed system.

Recognizing this is important to our success.

A CHECKLIST STORY

By 1995, John had been a cardiothoracic surgeon for more than two decades. His path to medicine was driven by an uncommon curiosity. Before practicing medicine, he'd worked in his dad's generator repair shop, studied the classics at Brown University, earned an electrical engineering degree, and took up flying as a hobby. Attention to detail, methodical procedures, and engineered systems fed his curiosity. He wondered why flying is so different from medicine, when the crucial interactions between people and technology are so vital to success in both.

One night after doing surgery to insert an aortic valve in a patient, John lay awake in bed, worried. The surgery had gone as he expected, but the process of taking the patient off the bypass machine had not. The patient's blood pressure and other vital signs decayed rapidly, indicating a premature removal. He ordered the patient back on the bypass machine, and the surgical team repeated the steps required to safely transition back off bypass. The transition then happened as expected.

As he reconstructed the steps leading to the interruption, John knew something was wrong. All the surgical team members—himself, the perfusionist who ran the machine, the anesthesiologist, the circulating and scrub nurses and technicians—were experienced surgical professionals. But together, the team didn't perform as it should have. He didn't know exactly *what* had gone wrong, but he knew *something* had gone wrong, and he felt responsible.

The next day, John brought to the hospital a straightforward, aviation-style surgical checklist with eight steps to be performed in sequence when taking a patient off bypass. He asked the hospital's surgical team members if they would be willing to participate in a ninety-day test using his surgical checklist. His goal was to demonstrate improved reliability using a simple aviation tool, one that all pilots use every day.

An anesthesiologist and a nurse thought he was on the right track and were willing to participate. But the rest of the team involved in the surgery didn't see the problem. Everything had turned out fine. A test John had ordered after the operation showed no anomalies. So, John asked other surgeons at the hospital to participate. But in their experience, the checklist was unnecessary, time-consuming, and a possible distraction. Their attitude seemed to be, *Sure, heart surgery, like all surgeries, is risky. But the medical risks are known beforehand, and everyone agrees the risks are worth taking.*

But in John's mind, shaped by years of engineering system optimization and personal experience, status quo wasn't good enough. He thought they could do much more. He wanted to become more reliable in the delivery of medical care. His colleagues, he thought, simply didn't see and understand the risks the same way he did.

A rigorous, step-by-step approach isn't confining; it's liberating—it opens us to possibilities we couldn't see otherwise. And applying the Sequence of Reliability can help us understand everyday risks.

AN EVERYDAY EXAMPLE

Imagine we're a group of citizens who want to build a school system in an underserved community to educate children in grades K–12.

We start with *system design*: establish our educational objectives, then seek funding for them. We set curricula for each grade and standards to measure progress.

We recognize components of our system will degrade, requiring monitoring, maintenance, refurbishment, and eventually replacement. Buildings deteriorate and require maintenance. Supplies and technologies wear out and become outdated. There will be staff turnover, and teachers must be retrained periodically.

Resource matching requires us to continually assess how we're allocating our limited resources. If we're not careful, we'll find mismatches among our time, money, and effort and where they're needed. Successful budgeting requires planning for changing needs, including unforeseen expenses. An abundance of teachers trained to teach primary school students wouldn't fill our need for secondary education, and vice versa. Or an ample number of science instructors might not meet our requirements for arts education.

Ideally, we would balance our school system *capacity and operational load.* Let's say our school is designed for class sizes of fifteen to twenty students per class, and we are limited to a specific number of classrooms. Imagine that an external event such as a flood or tornado destroyed a school in a neighboring town and our school board agrees to accept its students. The ᴜperational load would overwhelm our system capacity. We may have to look to overflow strategies such as temporary classrooms or renting off-campus space.

At every level—administrators, teachers, students, environmental workers, and security staff—*human performance* will affect our school system's performance, for better or worse.

We must consider all those factors as we make our school system more reliable, but we must master one of them first.

SYSTEM DESIGN

The factors influencing system performance are interconnected, but one is more important than the others: system design. System design is crucial to both *effectiveness* and *resilience*, allowing us to manage all the other factors more reliably.

Engineers use these three strategies in sequence to manage system performance:

1. Barriers
2. Redundancies
3. Recoveries

Don't be intimidated by these terms—in engineering, they don't have the negative meanings we usually associate with them. We often think of barriers as obstacles to success. But in reliability science, barriers to failure lead to success. Efficiency experts think of redundancies as wasteful and unnecessary; being made redundant may mean losing your job. In reliability, redundancy is an essential defense against failure. Some people might attach social stigma to recovery, such as in drug, alcohol, or mental health rehabilitation, but recovery strategies are essential to reliability.

These strategies are easy to see, understand, and apply.

BARRIERS

Barriers = obstacles put in place to prevent failures

Barriers do this by reducing threats and hazards (external and internal) or by limiting human performance. Barriers take many shapes and sizes. Here are a few of the barriers we see every day:

- **Physical:** A fence, designed to keep people or animals out or in.
- **Electrical:** A ground fault interrupter on outlets and devices, designed to break a circuit when there's a short. They're required near water to prevent electrocution.
- **Software:** A username and password or anti-virus protection.
- **Biological:** An antibiotic to treat a bacterial infection.
- **Permanent:** An around-the-clock speed limit on a roadway.

- **Temporary:** A speed limit in a school zone, in effect on certain days and hours.
- **Psychological:** Surveillance cameras and warning signs that appear to be physical but may also impose a psychological barrier.
- **Laws, regulations, policies, or procedures:** Providing guidance for human performance.
- **Multiple barriers:** A car's fuel filler opening. This serves several functions. The first barrier is the door, which prevents unauthorized access. The gas cap keeps fuel and fumes in the tank. A tether keeps you from losing the cap. There's one more. Inside the filler neck is a small restrictor that limits the size of the nozzle you can insert. It's designed to prevent you from putting the wrong type of gas in the tank.

Some barriers are elegantly simple in their design. Figure 3.2 shows two barriers with similar but different purposes. One has a more *resilient* design than the other.

Both are covers, providing a barrier against entry and exit. Have you ever seen a street hole cover any shape other than circular? If it were a different shape, it could be turned at such an angle that it could fall down the hole. A round street hole cover is designed to be *resilient*—protecting people underneath. No matter which way you turn a round street hole cover, it won't pass through the hole if the structure is intact.

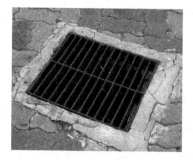 

Figure 3.2

Other barriers seem simple, but require complexity. Look at this series of color-coded medical device connectors in figure 3.3.

Figure 3.3

Though rendered here in black and white, the fittings, from left to right, are plates for: two oxygen ports (green), medical air (yellow), nitrous oxide (blue), a red dial, and medical vacuum (white).

Are the color codes enough of a barrier to prevent someone from inadvertently hooking up the wrong fitting? What if someone were color-blind? Each fitting is physically different than the others so that it's impossible to hook up the wrong one.

There's a lesson here. Sometimes we can design system barriers that lower the risk dramatically without having to change human behavior.

One example of this is the gas pump. Engineers design gas pumps to be effective at pumping gas, and resilient when things go wrong. That can happen when you pull away from the gas pump with the hose still attached: The hose is designed to break into two pieces.[5] One remains with the car and the other with the pump. Check valves on both sides of the breaking point prevent fuel from leaking out of either half. The check valves are barriers, significantly reducing the risk of a spark leading to an explosion.

Other barriers can't eliminate the risk of human error. Spell-check isn't 100 percent reliable partly because we often ignore spell-check warnings (it's called alert fatigue). Speed limit signs are barriers, but how many people exceed the limit when the police aren't around? And medical gloves are designed as a barrier against germs and other hazards, but healthcare providers sometimes cut off the fingertips for sensitive tasks such as inserting intravenous needles.

No barrier is 100 percent effective all the time. We can't assume a barrier is reliable simply because we put it in place.

In fact, barriers fail in multiple ways. They can be ignored, worked around, or fail on their own. When examining a barrier, it helps to imagine all the ways in which it would not work as designed. While we may not always know *when* a barrier will fail, with a little imagination it's possible to predict *how* and *where* it will fail.

That's not enough to become reliable, though. We need a just-in-case plan.

REDUNDANCIES

Redundancies = parallel working components and/or backups

Redundancies contain multiple system elements and use checks and balances to achieve reliability. When things are going right during normal operations, parallel components, such as dual wheels on a truck, provide extra reliability. When things go wrong, we rely on backups, such as a spare tire. Both are redundancies. Redundancies come in many varieties. A few examples:

- **Physical:** A door with two locks.
- **Electrical:** Alternate power supplies, such as generators or multiple-source outlets. The red markings on certain outlets indicate the side of each outlet that will continue to supply electricity from a generator or battery in case of a main power failure.
- **Software:** Backups and auto-save features.
- **Biological:** Different medications designed to treat the same condition.
- **Multiple people and processes:** Double-checks and "second opinions."

Aviation provides a good example of the importance of redundancies. See figure 3.4.

Figure 3.4

How many redundancies do you see in this aircraft photo? It's obvious there are two engines. One can allow the aircraft to fly, but two, you would have to agree, is much better. You'll also see two tires on each wheel assembly, two landing lights, two front windows, two side windows, and two sets of windshield wipers on each window powered by separate electrical systems.

Inside the plane, there are, of course, at least two pilots and multiple flight attendants.

What you may not know is each aircraft has at least three independent hydraulic systems to move the flight controls. There also are at least three, and sometimes four, independent electrical systems. And there are multiple systems to control cabin pressure.

There's one final redundancy: Beside each pilot's seat are *two* coffee cup holders, both essential to reliability.

You can start to see why aviation has become one of the most reliable industries in the world. That's because aviation engineers understand system design and system reliability.

But redundancies work best when they're truly independent. An aircraft has two or more separate fuel tanks, typically located in each side of the wing. But if the fuel in both cells comes from the same source and is contaminated, the fact that the cells are redundant doesn't help. Contaminated fuel in either cell could cause engine failure.

What if the airplane is taxiing and runs over a board with several nails in it? Both tires on the assembly could blow at the same time.

Are the pilots truly independent? In general, yes. But sometimes what we think is independent might not be so. There are many ways in which a pilot might become incapacitated. On long-range flights, for instance, the pilots are supposed to eat different meals to lower the likelihood of food contamination affecting both.

Similarly, healthcare professionals must be independent when functioning as redundancies. Certain medications require two or more nurses to check the accuracy of them.

The challenge is ensuring the nurses aren't too trusting of each other. To be reliable, both nurses must perform their functions independently and not assume the other one has acted properly.

Sometimes the more we trust others when we work together over time, the more we lose our ability to be truly independent. This can occur in any setting where teams of individuals are working together, depending on each other. And sometimes, we would suspect that people with the greatest skill may be the least likely to make a mistake.

Designing multiple components usually results in a greater chance of success. Redundancies can increase those chances, although they have vulnerabilities. But what happens when both barriers and redundancies fail?

RECOVERIES

Recoveries = ways to correct when things go wrong

Recoveries are additional layers of protection after barriers and redundancies fail. In many cases, it may be possible to reverse harm using recoveries. Like barriers and redundancies, recoveries come in many different forms:

- **Physical:** A parachute or a spare tire.

- **Software:** The system-restore function on a computer.
- **Biological:** Reversing agents and antidotes applied after a medication has been improperly administered.
- **People, equipment, and processes:** A lifeguard or a roadside assistance program.

Recoveries can treat psychological conditions, using psychiatrists, psychologists, and counselors. Recoveries can involve multiple people, such as in-group therapy. Recoveries often require fewer resources and initial investment than barriers or redundancies. The downside to recoveries is that something bad may have already happened. Of course, the upside is that recoveries may be able to reverse the harm.

The harm may be small—you're locked out of your car because the battery or Bluetooth in your car's key fails. The recovery device—an old-fashioned key attached—lets you in (see figure 3.5).

Figure 3.5

Or the harm may be big, such as the US economic downturn in 2008. Congress passed the Economic Stimulus Act that year, boosting the economy and avoiding a recession.[6]

Humans have been building in redundancies for centuries. More than one thousand years ago, the Chinese had the foresight to put firecrackers inside the walls of homes they were building. If a house caught fire, the firecrackers would explode and wake up the occupants. An ingenious form of recovery.

As we've seen, barriers and redundancies—designed and often implemented by humans—aren't foolproof. That's why we need recoveries, which sometimes are the best we can do when bad things happen.

Recoveries are essential to reliability. Like the other strategies, there's a key to effective recoveries: Apply them early and often enough to minimize harm after barriers and redundancies have failed.

The system design strategies of barriers, redundancies, and recoveries form lines of defense against failure. But we must recognize that each design element will have vulnerabilities and fail points—some we can accept and some we can't. Our challenge is to understand these failure points, along with their probabilities, and match the *combined* system strategies with the risks we're managing. An email with a grammatical error may cause nothing more than embarrassment. But with a life-threatening medical condition, a less-than-reliable system can be deadly.

A HOSPITAL STORY

One day a nurse was walking past a central monitoring station in a hospital cardiac unit. She heard an alarm and went immediately to the patient's room. She wasn't sure which alarm was sounding, so she tried to isolate the possible sources.

The first piece of equipment she came to was the cardiac monitor alarm. She turned it off. The alarm kept ringing, so she turned off the next piece of equipment, and so on, until she discovered the device that was sounding. After shutting it off, she determined it was a false alarm, and went back to the central monitoring station.

But she forgot to turn the cardiac monitor alarm back on. Not long afterward, the patient went into cardiac arrest and the alarm didn't sound. The patient died.

Healthcare regulators and other government officials investigated, all focused on the nurse's behavior. Eventually, a local newspaper heard about it and sent a reporter to interview the patient safety officer. Near the end of the interview, the reporter asked, "What have you done with the nurse who caused this patient's death? Have you fired her?"

The patient safety officer replied, "We don't think that's the best solution. We think this was both human and system failure, and we want to understand both better so we can minimize the risk of it happening again."

The patient safety officer later approached the manufacturer of the cardiac monitor alarm and asked a simple question: "Can you reprogram this device so that if someone turns it off, either by mistake or deliberately, and the unit is working properly, it can turn itself back on after a short time? Can you put it on a timer and have it reboot itself?"

The reply: "Of course, that's easy to do. We didn't know you wanted us to do that."

The patient safety officer then said, "Well, we want you to do it now."

By using recovery—a simple design strategy—the hospital reduced the likelihood of that kind of death happening again.

Systems and humans will never be 100 percent reliable. But if we understand and apply these strategies, we can improve our reliability. We may not always predict *when* people will make mistakes, but with a bit of effort we can predict *how* and *where* they will fail and apply a combination of system strategies to help protect us.

Our lives may depend on it.

HUMAN RELIABILITY

THE FALLIBLE HUMAN

We're all human. What makes us unique as individuals is the product of our biology, environment, and experiences. But we all have one thing in common: We all make mistakes. There are no exceptions.

Although human failures are inevitable, like systems, we can manage them. But first we must see and understand *how* people perform, what motivates them, and the influences on their behaviors. For leaders, this starts by applying what you've learned so far about risk and systems.

A DRUNK DRIVER

Let's examine an example in our everyday lives.[1] A soccer coach is taking kids to a game when a drunk driver collides with the minivan.

The drunk driver had been previously arrested and convicted for driving under the influence, but a judge overturned the conviction due to problems with the breathalyzer calibration that was performed by a non-accredited laboratory.

In retrospect, it's apparent that the state's decision to have the breathalyzer calibrated by a non-accredited provider could yield issues with reliability, which in this case allowed a driver to avoid conviction, leading to the drunk driving tragedy. But were the downstream consequences of the state's decision seen and understood in advance?

This example raises two important questions:

1. What values were at play in the judge's decision?
2. Was the risk acceptable in a society governed by laws and due process?

We'll examine these questions later in detail when we explore the purpose and limitations of our justice systems.

But for now, you're likely wanting to know what happened to the kids and the soccer coach hit by the drunk driver, right? I'll turn the question back to you: Does the actual outcome of the collision—whether it involves no injuries, minor injuries, or tragic loss of life—matter when it comes to how we see, understand, and manage the risk?

Think about it as you continue reading.

A MEDICAL MISTAKE

In 2006, as my father approached eighty years old, he was diagnosed with cardiovascular disease. He also had a relatively rare blood cancer known as polycythemia, where his body produced too many red blood cells. For him, the symptoms were itchy red spots across his abdomen. His primary care physician diagnosed the condition, and the treatment was straightforward: Every three months, he had a phlebotomy, a simple procedure where clinicians drew a pint or two of blood, effectively reducing his red blood cell count. His symptoms all but disappeared, and the disease was manageable.

But his coronary artery disease persisted, resulting in shortness of breath, mild episodes of angina, and a growing frustration with not being able to do the things he was used to doing—walking the dog, going to baseball games, and visiting friends. His cardiologist recommended the insertion of three stents to restore blood flow to his clogged arteries. My dad liked his genial and communicative cardiologist and trusted his extensive knowledge and skill. And it didn't hurt that they pulled for the same baseball team. So when the cardiologist recommended the heart catheterization, Dad immediately gave his informed consent.

Two weeks later, I went to the hospital with my father. As we sat down with the cardiac nurse in the pre-op area, I pulled out a plastic grocery sack with Dad's medications. I knew that neither of us would remember all the names and doses, so I wasn't taking any chances in getting them wrong. The nurse diligently wrote down each medication and dose, asking when each one had last been taken. When she saw he had polycythemia, she asked, "When was his last blood draw?" Dad said, "It was two months ago, just before the start of Opening Day. I remember it because I drove directly to the ballpark afterward. We lost." The nurse wrote down the date and asked when Dad was scheduled for another phlebotomy. "Next month," he said. "Right around the All-Star break."

The stent insertion took almost three hours. When the cardiologist finally emerged, he said the procedure went "picture perfect." He showed me the before-and-after catheterization images on a computer monitor. Even with no clinical training or experience, I could clearly see improvement in blood flow. "Everything will be just fine. Your dad will notice a big difference in his life once he's up and getting around," the doctor said. "He should be able to make the next game when the team comes back in town the day after tomorrow."

An hour later, as my father lay in his bed in cardiac recovery, his face told a different story. When I asked him how he was feeling, he said, "I've felt better." I went to the nurse's station and said, "I think something's wrong." We returned to his bedside, and my father said he felt pressure across his chest. The nurse, watching the cardiac monitor, took his blood pressure, which was low. "Is that normal?" I asked. She said, "Well, yes and no. It's not uncommon to see a drop in blood pressure following stent insertions. I'll keep an eye on it." She told my father, "Everything's fine. Try to rest."

But when she left, I could see Dad was feeling more than discomfort. I followed the nurse into the hallway and asked her again, "Are you sure this is normal?" She said, "Well, just to be on the safe side, I'll administer a nitro pill under his tongue. If anything's wrong, that should make him feel better." She returned a moment later with the nitroglycerin.

After a few minutes, the pressure grew worse. "What's wrong, Dad?"

"I don't know, but I've never felt this before."

I was out the door and down the hall. "Something's not right," I told the nurse again. She stopped what she was doing and looked up.

"What do you mean?" she said.

"The pill doesn't seem to be working. He says the pain is worse."

"OK," she said. "I'll administer another nitro pill. Give me a few minutes."

"Please hurry," I said as I ran back to my father. His face was drained of color. His hands felt clammy. I could see him gritting his teeth as he spoke. "It feels like an elephant is stepping on my chest."

The nurse came in and quickly handed my father another pill without greeting him. She stood before the cardiac monitor and wrote something down. Then she was gone. I felt helpless. This was the same feeling I had twenty years earlier watching Flight 191 on its final approach—I could sense what was happening but was powerless to do anything to stop it. My father was in distress, but all I could do was watch and will the plane to reach the runway. So I ran down the hall.

"Something's terribly wrong. The pills aren't working. He's not even able to speak, he's in so much pain."

"OK, I'll call the doctor and administer morphine. That should work."

She rushed to the medication dispensing unit. She appeared to be having difficulty unlocking the machine. I could hear her calling the pharmacy on the radio draped over her shoulder. "My code isn't working," she said through the radio. "Can you unlock the device?"

I raced back to my father's room and grabbed his hand. "It's going to be OK; she's getting a stronger drug." He smiled, but I could feel the cold in his hand and watched as his face grew the color of ash. Then a physician walked in. "Something's wrong," he shouted, confirming the obvious. "Get this patient back down to the cath lab immediately."

Three hours and forty-five minutes later, the cardiologist once again emerged from the surgical suite. But this time he was drenched in sweat. "There's been a complication," he said. "Your father must've had an allergic reaction to the blood thinner we were using. All three stents were occluded, blocking the blood flow. I reinserted new stents inside the existing ones, and the blood flow has been restored. It appears your father may have had a cardiac infarction, or heart attack, during the time the blood flow to his heart was restricted. I won't know the extent until we conduct further testing. We'll measure enzymes and I'll order an echocardiogram to analyze the extent of the damage to his heart. But don't worry, I've switched his blood thinner and we'll monitor him overnight. I don't expect any further complications."

Once again, I was caught between the world of my experience and the reality before me. I didn't think Dad had ever had an allergic reaction. But who was I to question this physician? All his years of clinical practice and medical expertise must surely be trusted, right? Without thinking, I blurted out: "But, Doctor, what about his polycythemia?"

His face grew taught, and he suddenly jumped back, as if I had punched him in the chest. "I don't know what you're insinuating, but I wouldn't have done anything different." He turned abruptly and walked away without saying another word. I looked around at two nurses standing beside me. Their faces were blank and silent. Then they, too, walked away.

I spent the night on the recliner next to my father's hospital bed. I tossed and turned, but it wasn't the chair that made me uncomfortable. What happened? What could have been done to prevent this?

Before the sun rose that day, I would know the answer to the first question. The answers to my second question would come later.

At 5:00 a.m., the cardiologist walked in. "I want to apologize," he said. "I've been up all night thinking about your dad. It wasn't the blood thinner that caused this unfortunate event. It was the polycythemia, just as you suggested. It's likely the excess red blood cells coagulated around the stents, restricting the blood flow, which led to his heart attack.

"I went back and reviewed his chart, and the nurse had clearly noted this condition, and that he would be due a phlebotomy soon. I should have noticed this ahead of surgery and ordered the phlebotomy before surgery. But I didn't read the chart. I knew your father. I was focused on getting the procedure done so he could get back to enjoying his life. I don't know what to say. This has never happened to me before, and I promise you it won't happen again."

For a few moments, my mind became a wrestling match between emotion and rational thoughts—my personal feeling of anger at the doctor was at odds with what I had learned from my professional experiences in aviation. My original thought of *What could have been done to prevent this?* was being pinned to the mat by the question, *How could a medical professional make this mistake?*

"Thank you, Doctor, for being honest and telling me what happened. I understand how you must feel, too. But with all due respect, this didn't just happen to you, it happened to my father. I have no doubt this experience will remain with all three of us."

As he walked away, I realized my question of *What could have been done to prevent this?* was complicated. The solution ran deeper than punishing the doctor. A lawsuit or licensing action would likely only make the situation worse, chilling the culture of reporting for other physicians in the same practice or hospital. The answer was hiding in plain view but would pose challenges in a healthcare community unfamiliar with socio-technical science.

WHAT HUMAN RELIABILITY MEANS

Most days, the socio-technical combinations of system and human performance produce positive results. Ironically, these same combinations also cause disasters. When that happens, we often focus on human behavior. Who did this? Who's responsible?

One reason is that we lean toward the familiar. Sometimes we mistakenly believe we understand human behaviors because we're human, too. But in complex organizational accidents, context matters. Mentally walking in someone else's shoes is not the same as being there when the disaster happens. Another reason is that we often don't fully understand systems, believing them to always work as designed. As we've seen, it's a dangerous game to think systems are 100 percent reliable.

Armed with a scientific understanding of the limits, vulnerabilities, and failure points of systems, we now must wrestle with the quirky component of the socio-technical equation: us.

At any given moment, every human will be less than perfect. The gap between human performance and 100 percent reliability represents "human failure."

Understanding this gap presents opportunities for improvement, or resilience. It's our way of bouncing back to higher performance when things go wrong. Knowing that people won't always live up to our expectations, we can predict that they will fail—and manage human performance differently to improve.

To understand human reliability, we start with an observation about human performance within systems:

Often, the more reliable our system, the less reliable the human.

This can happen when people drift into complacency or become less proficient because they rely on automation. There are many everyday examples:

- Our recollection of phone numbers and email addresses when the information is stored in our digital devices.
- Our ability to spell and use correct grammar without spell-check and auto-correct software.
- Our manual proficiency at flying aircraft or driving vehicles after using advanced automation for prolonged periods.
- Our cooking skills after eating out for extended periods.
- Our in-person social skills after communicating on digital devices for long stretches.

A pattern becomes clear: Any activity that requires manual or cognitive dexterity can degrade over time with lack of use. This is especially true for proficiency-based tasks. Some activities require not just knowing how to do something, but also recent practice and a cycle of improvement. While it might be true that we never forget how to ride a bicycle, other tasks such as flying an airplane or performing surgery depend on more than just muscle memory. High-consequence industries recognize this and expect human performance to degrade the further removed a person is from performing the activity. Once that's recognized, practice can help. Practice doesn't always make perfect, but it does improve proficiency. For example, big-city fire departments routinely train for high-rise fires, even though they may go years without fighting one.

We can make our organizations more reliable by balancing system and human performance. Computers and automation perform some tasks better than humans, such as mathematical computations.[2] With other tasks, humans (for the time being) excel over automation, such as natural language processing and value-based judgments. An autonomous vehicle may provide safer transport, but (for now) can't be a Good Samaritan and help people stranded on the roadside.

Remember, our goal in being reliable is to be *effective* and *resilient*. This often means focusing on human proficiency—even when it's not needed during normal operations—so we can recover when things go wrong and require human intervention.

On one extreme, we get better results when we can engineer human performance out of the equation, such as the automatic shutoff valve at the gas pump. But in some situations where the mechanical or software reliability is crucial, we must rely on human performance to help maintain system resilience.

Aviation again provides an example of learning to adapt to automation. As engineers added increasingly sophisticated autopilots and software to commercial aircraft, "human error" accidents declined. But several accidents happened when the automation confused pilots—who didn't know whether humans or the systems were controlling the plane.[3] As a result, airlines placed greater emphasis on pilots maintaining their manual flying proficiencies, while training them to use the appropriate level of automation for particular tasks.

For example, on extreme low-visibility approaches in foggy weather, pilots depend on autopilots to steer the aircraft to a safe landing. At the same time, the pilots are poised at the controls, monitoring and calling out conditions at specified points along the flight path, ready to take over with manual control should things go wrong. This has proved to be a highly reliable process, although the current level of success came only after a history of trial and error.[4]

In balancing human and system behavior, we must remember that people fail not just because we're an imperfect, unpredictable species. Many interconnected factors influence human performance.

And we can manage them.

THE SEQUENCE OF HUMAN FACTORS

How do we predict and manage human reliability? By understanding what shapes it: the influences, external and internal, that determine the results humans produce (see figure 4.1).

Figure 4.1

As in our discussion on system reliability, this illustration does not represent all the potential influences on human performance. But grouping these common factors as a honeycomb shows they are interconnected.

The proportions—or relative strength of these influences—will vary widely, depending on circumstance. But we can see how these factors contribute to the results we get from people.

But there's an important sequence in how we should review and manage human reliability. We must begin with these human factors *before* we can understand and manage behaviors. Why a sequence? Because our behaviors are driven by these performance-shaping factors, and to manage them we must fully understand these factors first.

This is where early applications of just culture missed the mark by focusing on duties, breaches, and behaviors, as we'll examine later. Addressing behaviors without their underlying contributors most often leads us to less-than-desired results, including perceptions of injustice. When managing people, optimal outcomes require a sequence.

Performance—Knowledge, Skills, Abilities, and Proficiency (KSAPs):[5] These are the qualifications that make us more likely to perform reliably. Throughout our lives, our capacity to perform is growing, diminishing, or plateauing. These factors provide a way of managing that capacity. Some examples where human performance depends on knowledge, skills, and abilities include the following:

- A pro football team with a poor passing game trades for a veteran wide receiver with speed.
- A hospital near a new retirement community recruits doctors, nurses, and technicians trained in geriatric care.
- A developer building a desert community hires an architect with the vision and engineering skills to design adobe-style homes.
- A school district with a rapidly growing immigrant population hires more certified English as a second language teachers.

Human reliability in any field—business, sports, education, and parenting—starts with knowledge, skills, and abilities. We don't expect perfection, but we do have expectations of basic qualifications. Acquiring and maintaining knowledge, skills, abilities, and proficiency is a lifelong process influencing human reliability.

System Factors: The elements of the system in which people operate—the support structures and controls we place around them—influence their performance. For example:

- Training
- Policies, processes, and procedures
- Environment
- Equipment
- Distractions, stress, fatigue, and burnout

Personal Factors: The things that affect us individually, that are unique to ourselves, influence how we think and act—for better or worse. Personal factors may include:

- Health
- Personal conflicts
- Our past experiences
- Distractions, stress, fatigue, and burnout

You'll notice that distractions, stress, fatigue, and burnout appear on both lists. These can originate in the system, sometimes because of operational necessity. But people often bring these influences into the organization. When examining how bad outcomes happen, we must look closely at the system and the personal contributors and how they're intertwined.

Culture: No model of human performance is complete without examining culture. As management consultant Peter Drucker supposedly said: "Culture eats strategy for breakfast."[6] We might rephrase that as "Organizational culture eats system design and personal factors for lunch."

Culture can be a powerful, complex set of influences on human performance and behaviors. Culture has inspired an entire genre of literature, describing the various ethnic, social, political, and organizational effects on our lives. There are books on learning culture, reporting culture, just culture, and culture of excellence, to name just a few.

Many of these books isolate cultures as representing a single value, such as safety. But they don't recognize the complexities of multiple competing values, such as cost and customer satisfaction. Culture is a dynamic, evolving influence. You could say it's like the weather, but that's an oversimplification. Weather forecasting has improved dramatically in the digital age, and rarely does weather catch us by surprise, at least on a large scale. Culture, on the other hand, is more difficult to define, much less forecast with certainty. Yet it is one of the most persistent influences on human reliability.

For example, cultural inequalities and discrimination—toward race, gender, sexual orientation, and religious beliefs—have influenced human behavior throughout history. In the workplace, this can result in harassment. On school playgrounds and social media, it takes the form of bullying. In both examples, a negative culture chills personal and organizational reliability.

Conversely, positive cultures can produce superior results. Inclusive, team-oriented behaviors directly affect human performance: Examples in sports, business, and scholastic achievement are many. In any field of human performance, positive cultures play an important role in successful results.

Cultures arise from societal groups, including geographic, racial, ethnic, religious, educational, governmental, recreational, professional, and organizational communities. Cultures can appear homogenous or diverse, aligned or chaotic, traditional or modern. Cultures evolve like organisms and can morph from one day to the next. In the digital media age, the number of cultural influences on our lives has increased, and the speed by which these influences propagate has increased dramatically. Cultural phenomena can grow virally and disappear from public consciousness as quickly as they appear.

Cultures interact, and sometimes collide. (We've all heard the expression *culture clash*, which can be a very real phenomenon, even within the same household, especially during the teenage years.)

Culture—whether through leadership or peer pressure—can improve or degrade human performance. Think of a star basketball player who inspires her teammates to be better by staying on the court after a tough loss to practice free throws; or a group of high schoolers who bullies others because of peer pressure.

In America, culture is the reason we shake hands when greeting other people—increasing the spread of germs and the risk of infection. Culture also accounts for the way we buckle up before driving our cars, then hit the gas and drive over the speed limit while talking on our cell phones. Culture influences whether we choose paper, plastic, or recycled bags at the grocery store. Culture determines whether we follow policies, rules, and procedures when we're working, especially when others are watching.[7]

Culture influences the way we see the world through our own experiences and filters how we interpret the experiences of others. Our path through life is guided by our biology, environment, and experiences, and culture is interrelated to all three. Recognizing this connection is important to understanding culture's role in influencing human performance.

Culture—in the workplace, home, or school—directly affects our behaviors and indirectly affects the other influences.

Perceptions of Risk and Competing Priorities: How we perceive risk depends on at least two consequences: real harm and artificial danger.

Think about driving a car. Most of us routinely drive slightly over the speed limit, because we think the likelihood of a crash is low. In the back of our minds, we know speeding adds risk, but if we haven't recently had a car crash, the possibility of an accident is distant and uncertain. This is a weak influence on our behaviors.

On the other hand, if the weather is bad and the roads are hazardous, we recognize the risk increases, so we slow down, self-limiting our behavior. This influence is stronger when we perceive the risk of harm to be increasing.

Immediate and certain consequences are strong; distant and remote consequences are weak.

Watch what happens the next time you see a police officer parked on the side of the road. We slow down. Every time. We may even slow down when we're not speeding, because we're used to driving over the speed limit. Of course, as soon as we drive around the corner, we speed up. We may even flash our lights at the cars coming the opposite way to warn drivers of the *artificial danger*—the likelihood of getting a ticket. It's an immediate and likely consequence. In these situations, it's not the risk of an accident (remote) that drives our behavioral choices; it's the risk of a ticket (immediate). Artificial danger is powerful, but only for a moment, until we get around the corner.

Which brings us to the tension between perceptions of risk and competing priorities. Why do we normally speed when driving? Because we're driven by competing priorities. We might be running late, or we find it enjoyable, or we rationalize that almost everyone else is speeding, too. We're caught between the remote and uncertain consequence of having an accident or getting a ticket, and the immediate benefit of getting somewhere faster.

In every area of our lives, we face multiple values and priorities, which we must balance to become highly reliable. That's crucial to understanding human performance. Perceptions of risk and competing priorities go together. They dominate our behavioral choices and often determine human reliability.

All these interconnected forces are constantly changing, in their influence and their proportions. At any given time, one or more can outweigh the others. For example, our basic needs of food, shelter, and clothing might overwhelm the other influences. Similarly, our competing priorities can outweigh the combined influences of culture, systems, and perceptions of risk.

Now we turn our attention to managing human behavior—armed with the knowledge and skills to make us more reliable.

HIDDEN PATTERNS

There are two broad categories of human behaviors:

1. Choices
2. Human Errors

Understanding the distinctions is important to managing human performance.

In 1999, the Institute of Medicine published a report, *To Err Is Human.*[8] It became a rallying cry throughout healthcare because of its purpose— to prevent patient harm by focusing on human error. Unfortunately, this approach contributed to a misunderstanding of the socio-technical science of reliability. Although it's counterintuitive, human error—in mathematical terms—is not the dominant behavioral risk in healthcare, nor in our everyday lives. What is the dominant risk?

Can you count the times you've made a human error while driving, such as accidentally running a red light? Most of us can do it on one or two hands.

But how many times have you chosen to not follow a rule when behind the wheel, such as talking or texting on a cell phone? None of us could accurately estimate the number of these choices we've made in our lives. But that number—and the increased risk—far exceeds our human errors and the risks they pose.

It's hard to be convinced that our *choices*, not our *errors*, add up to the greatest risk in our lives. After all, we almost always blame human error as the "probable cause" when someone fails. What we're overlooking is the *combination* of choices and errors—and why we make the choices we do.

Adverse outcomes, or accidents, are most often combinations of human performance-shaping factors, system factors, and lack of resilience, followed by behavioral choices resulting in human errors that lead to an adverse result.

Figure 4.2—while not putting numerical values or estimates on each of the ways in which a bad event could happen—shows how contributors are connected.

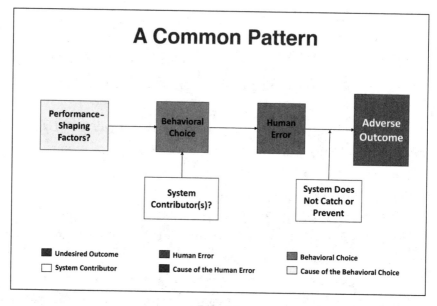

Figure 4.2

Using our example of running a red light, let's look at some ways that might happen:

System Performance

- Brake failure
- Unintended car acceleration
- Traffic-light failure

Human Performance

- Being chased by someone intent on harming us (choice)
- Taking someone to the emergency room (choice)

- Racing a yellow light through the intersection (choice)
- Coming to a rolling stop (choice)
- Becoming incapacitated: falling asleep or having a stroke, heart attack, or other medical condition, including death (human error)
- Hitting the accelerator instead of the brake by mistake (human error)
- Not seeing the red light because of a distraction (human error, often preceded by a choice)

In your experience, which of these ways are most likely? Most people would agree that racing a yellow light, making a rolling stop, and missing the light because of a distraction are most common. All of them involve choices. While we may not choose to run the light, we often choose the behavior that causes the distraction. It could be checking our cell phones, turning our heads to talk to the kids in the back seat, or reaching down to pick up something off the floor.

Choices often precede our human errors. In most instances of human error, choices are the *probabilistic* contributors. That means the choices we make don't always result in human error, but they increase the likelihood, or probability, of human error.

To understand our choices and errors—and the way humans think—we must study another hidden pattern.

TWO MODES OF THINKING

Daniel Kahneman, co-winner of the 2002 Nobel Memorial Prize in Economic Sciences, wrote *Thinking, Fast and Slow*, in which he concludes humans think in two basic modes: fast and slow.[9]

He calls the first mode System 1. Our brain is on autopilot, where our facial muscles are relaxed and we feel comfortable and confident. Kahneman suggests we spend most of our time thinking in System 1.

In this mode, he says, we're thinking fast, moving around, and making decisions. In fact, we're managing risk. Think about a task you're good at—

running a meeting, making a sale, painting your living room, or mowing the lawn. Those activities require fast, pragmatic decisions. You probably feel confident, operating on training, experience, and instinct. This is the mode in which we've evolved to think over generations of human experience. We've been running from the saber-toothed tiger and making fast decisions for millions of years.

But the System 1 brain is susceptible to human error. Snap decisions are often right, but sometimes they're wrong. Depending on circumstance and the system around us, these results can be benign or deadly.

Have you ever driven to work and realized once you arrived that you don't remember a thing about the drive? That's System 1 thinking. We're performing lots of different mental activities simultaneously. Or at least we think we're doing them simultaneously when we're processing them in a series.[10]

Kahneman calls our other mode of thinking System 2. This is our deliberate mode, where we must stop and think slowly. Doing your income taxes by hand or calculating the amount of water needed to fill a swimming pool requires using our brains differently than we do in System 1.

Our facial muscles tend to reflect our mode of thinking, Kahneman says. With System 1, our faces tend to relax, and we often smile. With System 2, we may scrunch up our faces when we're concentrating. This is especially true when we struggle to learn a new task, like a child sticking out her tongue while learning to read or write.

The System 2 mode of thinking can also be misleading. In his book *Blink*, journalist Malcolm Gladwell says our initial, instantaneous (blink) reactions often turn out to be more accurate than our deliberate analyses.[11] Have you ever taken a multiple-choice test and your first, instinctive choice turned out to be correct? And the more you analyzed the question, the more you became unsure of your response? As Gladwell points out, one theory of test-taking suggests that we should let our first impression be our guide. This would be our System 1 brain.

But a System 2 brain is more methodical, logical in some ways, and it requires a greater effort of thought. That's why Kahneman says we spend less time during the normal day thinking with our System 2 brains. And as we grow more proficient in a skill-based task, we spend even less time thinking deliberately and slowly.

We engage different modes of thinking throughout the day. We might daydream or get distracted while driving to work. When we get to the office, we may still be on autopilot with our System 1 brains and remain there for much of the workday. At other times, we shift to our System 2 brains when critical thinking skills are required, such as writing a report on a new product.

Understanding these two modes of thinking, and our natural tendencies to fall into one mode over the other, will help us become more reliable.

HUMAN ERRORS

Not all human errors[12] are created equal, but they share a common definition of being inadvertent:

Human error = actions or thoughts taken without intent,
or by accident

Human errors come in a variety of forms, each with its own characteristics.

Slip: A slip can be a physical or cognitive action we wouldn't intend to do but can easily happen.[13] The classic example is an accidental fall, like someone in a comedy routine slipping on a banana peel. Many everyday actions can be considered slips:

- A baseball player dropping a fly ball
- A driver bumping into another car while parallel parking
- A passenger boarding the wrong plane
- A delivery person dropping a package at the wrong house
- An emailer hitting "send" before the message is complete

In all these examples, the error originated from a mental state. Hitting "send" too soon can happen because your finger touched the wrong button or what you wanted to say got jumbled in your head. In either case, the result is that you got the action wrong. Slips, like other human errors, can be the result of the interaction between our brains and our bodies—important to remember as we find ways to improve our personal reliability.

Lapse: A lapse is an inadvertent failure to meet an expectation. You may have heard the phrase "acts of *omission* and *commission*." It's commonly used in law and refers to "respectively, things you have failed to do, and things you have done."[14] In this sense, we might call a slip an act of commission, or something we did, and consider a lapse something we failed to do.

Lapses can also be mental missteps involving memory, such as forgetfulness or a "lapse in judgment":

- A coach forgetting his team has one time-out left
- Leaving the house and forgetting to turn off the stove
- Oversleeping because we forgot to set our alarm clock
- Forgetting to pay our bills on time
- Leaving our homework on the kitchen table

What slips and lapses have in common is that they are *inadvertent*—we don't intend to do (or not do) what we shouldn't (or should) have done.

Mistake: A mistake is an "error whose result was unintended, as opposed to an action that was intended."[15] Like a slip or a lapse, mistakes can be physical and originate from a mental state or condition. Mistakes are often regrettable errors in judgment, whereas the action itself was intended. A few examples:

- An umpire calls a runner "out" when instant replay clearly shows the runner was safe.

- A driver takes the wrong freeway exit, believing it to be the correct route.
- Pilots fly to the wrong altitude because they misheard an air traffic controller's instruction meant for another plane.
- A child takes home the wrong lunch box because it looks identical to her own.
- An accountant enters the incorrect figure in a tax return and must file an amendment.

It's easy to get confused among slips, lapses, and mistakes, and there can be overlap. But the important thing to remember is that they all involve *inadvertent* actions, thoughts, or results.

We all make slips, lapses, and mistakes. But applying system reliability principles can help us manage our rate of human errors.

A simple task shows how this can work. Take a moment and do this operation in your head, without writing it down:

$$5 + 3 + 2 \div 2 = ?$$

Did you get five? Or nine? These are the two most common answers.

The correct answer is nine. How is that calculated? You may remember in elementary school you learned about *order of operation*. Numbers in parentheses and exponents are calculated first, followed by division, multiplication, addition, and subtraction. There is an order, or *sequence*, to the operations.

So, in our equation, start by dividing two by two, which equals one. Add that to five plus three, and the answer is easy: It's nine.

When you did your calculation, did you use your System 1 or System 2 brain? Was your thought process fast or slow? If your answer was five, you probably were thinking in System 1 mode—quick and instinctive. If your answer was nine, you likely were thinking in System 2 mode—slow and deliberate. In this situation, thinking slowly and remembering the rule about order of operations gives you a better chance of getting the answer correct—that is, being more reliable.

Figure 4.3 is another example. Which dog do you find more threatening, and why?

Figure 4.3

There's obviously no right or wrong answer. You'd have to know more about the details in each photo. People usually consider the first dog more threatening.

It might be the first dog's facial expressions look more hostile to you. But both animals are baring their teeth, although one dog's eyes appear closed. So how do we recognize the threat? It might be that we have a built-in bias, or preconceived perception, based on the breed of dog. In either case, you probably used your System 1 brain to make a snap judgment. You were thinking fast when you made your decision. After all, in real life, you're not going to sit down when you're faced with a dog that could bite you and do a detailed calculation as you would in solving a math problem. You must think and act quickly—do you flee, or do you stop and pet the dog? In this situation, by necessity, we use our fast mode of thinking—our System 1 brain—to keep us safe.

You might be thinking, *That's great. You've shown me a math calculation I didn't remember from grade school and pictures of dogs, but how does that help me prevent human error?*

You might really be asking, *How do I keep myself from doing what I never intended to do in the first place?*

MANAGING HUMAN ERRORS

There are two answers to that question, and both will help us improve human reliability. The first answer is that, in any situation, we should recognize the risk in what we're doing, and choose either our System 1 or System 2 thinking modes accordingly.

The challenge, of course, is seeing and understanding the risk if we have not previously had a bad outcome. We often choose the wrong mode of thinking, expecting the same results we've gotten in the past. Choosing the correct mode of thinking is a starting point for lowering the likelihood of a human error or adverse result.

But what happens when choosing the correct or incorrect mode fails us? The second approach is to apply the three strategies discussed in the System Reliability chapter: *barriers, redundancies, and recoveries.*

Consider the human error that leads to somebody pulling away from the gas pump with the nozzle in the car.

How would we prevent that? We could look to the factors shaping human performance and minimize fatigue, stress, and distractions in our lives. Good luck with that, right? It's not that we couldn't or wouldn't try, but the mathematical probability of getting it right *every* time is virtually zero. There are more than 222 million licensed drivers in the United States,[16] and it's just a matter of time before it happens to someone. This is a simple lesson in probability. We don't know precisely *when* someone will do it, but we know with virtual certainty that someone will.

So what other options do we have to improve our reliability at the gas pump? We could be deliberate in using our System 2 brain when we're filling the tank and remember to remove the nozzle. This strategy works like magic—but only when it's applied. The problem is that once we've mastered a particular task in life, our System 1 brains tend to dominate.

This is true in all walks of life and especially in occupations involving high degrees of skill and expertise. The better we are at what we do, the less time and effort it takes to perform a task using our System 2 brains. What was once a deliberate exercise becomes an automatic function, such as learning to crawl, walk, ride a bike, or run a business.

But being careful requires us to see and understand risk and look beyond our experience—in this case, we've probably never left the gas pump with the nozzle still attached. Relying on this recognition, and a willingness to change our behavior, can improve individual performance. It takes significant time and effort to change behaviors among large groups of people, each with his or her own challenges in seeing and understanding the risk and being willing to modify choices. But it can be done.

In the case of the dangling gas hose, engineers designed something to prevent a catastrophic outcome. There are two kinds of possible interventions:

1. Preventing the *act* of leaving the nozzle and hose attached to the car and driving away.
2. Mitigating the *consequences*.

This is where barriers (obstacles to prevent failure), redundancies (parallel or backup components), and recoveries (after-the-fact corrective measures) come into play.

We could design a barrier to prevent people from driving off with the nozzle still in the car. It might be a switch keeping drivers from starting the engine with the fuel door open. Or it could be a person—such as in Oregon and New Jersey,[17] where by law you can't pump your own gas. Theoretically, a trained attendant is safer. But remember, no human is 100 percent reliable.

Because the consequences of an explosion are severe, we realize that relying solely on humans to be perfect would be a less than optimal strategy. So we might consider a redundancy. If you had a passenger who did a double-check before you pulled away from the pump, you might be more reliable. But maybe not. What if the passenger caused a distraction? The effectiveness of this redundancy depends on how many people are traveling with you and how reliable they might be.

That's why a recovery feature is the primary strategy for lowering the risk at the gas pump. There's a clean disconnect joint located near the top of the hose at every gas pump. If you drive away, the hose detaches without damaging the pump. More important, inside the pump is a one-way check valve that keeps gas from spilling onto the concrete.

If our goal is to come as close as we can to eliminating the risk, we'd be challenged to make 222 million drivers reliable. But engineers designed a recovery system that has been successfully applied across the country. Is it 100 percent reliable? No. But it's close.

This recovery feature reduces the risk *after* things go wrong, or the human error happens. It doesn't prevent the human error itself, but it dramatically lowers the likelihood of gas spill and explosion.

That doesn't mean recoveries are the only, or best, solution to managing risk. All three strategies have benefits, they often overlap, and we may use two or all three to address the same problem.

Here are a few common ways we use them to manage human reliability:

- Grocery lists so we don't forget anything
- Alarm clocks so we don't oversleep
- Instant replay to correct sports officials' misjudgments
- Advanced driver-assistance systems[18] such as antilock brakes, lane-departure warning systems, and adaptive cruise controls to help manage driver error
- Multifactor authentication for financial and other online and in-person transactions[19] to prevent human error and fraud
- Two methods of patient identification in healthcare[20] to prevent misidentifying a patient
- Online requirements to enter passwords and/or email addresses twice to lower the likelihood of human error

All of these examples involve *system* strategies to help manage human performance. More accurately, they are *socio-technical* strategies since they require human selection or involvement.

For example, the grocery list is an effective strategy, but only if we choose to use it. The check valve at the gas pump, on the other hand, requires no human selection and is a pure system strategy.

To improve socio-technical reliability, we should look first to system performance and understand the failure points and probabilities. Then we should do our best to manage the quirky human component, recognizing it's a *combination* of system and human performance strategies that produces results.

The sequence matters. Focusing on human errors in a less-than-optimal system still gets us less-than-optimal results. But recognizing risk and building a reliable system first, then managing human performance, gets us stellar results. That's why you can't recall an explosion at a gas station in recent memory.

But preventing human errors—those inadvertent acts we never intend to do—is not our biggest challenge.

WHY WON'T HUMANS JUST FOLLOW RULES?

Our biggest challenge is managing our choices—actions we intend—without recognizing or believing the consequences will happen to us.

So why don't humans just follow rules? The circular answer is because we're human. Throughout millions of years of evolution, we've been running from the woolly mammoth and playing with fire, testing the boundaries of consequential behavior.

Have you ever ordered a dish served hot, such as fajitas, at a Mexican restaurant? The first thing the server says when bringing the food is, "Don't touch the plate. It's hot." We heard the rule. We understand the rule. But what will we do as soon as the server walks away? Within seconds, we touch the hot plate. Our System 1 brain says, "I'm going to test the rule to see if it applies to me."

It's deeply ingrained in us. And it sheds light on why we tend not to believe bad things will happen to us: We make choices based on direct experience. But this can be dangerous. We've all seen rules we didn't have confidence in or didn't think applied to us.

A complicated thing about human behavior is that we see rules differently, especially whether we're a manager or an employee. When you become a manager, you're taught to rely on the rule book. In managing people, we look to our policy or procedures manual as the system that gets us results.

But when you were a frontline employee, did you follow all the rules? We can hear an employee's bias toward rules in statements such as, "No one follows *all* the policies and procedures around here," and "My manager doesn't do my job anymore," and "It's different here on the front line."

It helps to understand a psychology term called the *fundamental attribution error or bias*.[21] That means we tend to see other people's behavior differently than our own. We often think our own at-risk choices are justifiable, but we're suspicious or critical of the same choices by others.

As a manager, you may expect your employees to follow all the rules, but do you follow all the rules of the road when you drive home? Do you get irritated when someone is driving the speed limit—following the rules—in the left lane?

Choosing whether to follow rules to manage our risk often depends on our biases (seeing our behavior as more justifiable), our nature to make choices based on our experience (often whether we've had an adverse outcome), and our instinct to obey only when we're being watched (such as when there's a police officer parked on the shoulder).

We must understand these challenges to become more reliable. If we expect compliance with the rules without understanding what motivates us and other people, we will get only the results we've gotten for years.

The better approach is to understand the nuanced influences on human behavior, learn how to make the rules optimal, then manage behavior in a well-designed system. It may sound complicated, but breaking it down into segments will improve reliability.

AT-RISK CHOICES

At-risk choice = a behavioral choice that increases risk
where risk is not recognized or mistakenly believed to be justified
(action taken without intent to cause harm)

At-risk choices are not inadvertent. They are not human errors, although mistakes could be included in this definition. They involve no intent to cause harm, even though the risk is considered unacceptable by people who judge them. The act is intentional, but the bad consequence is not—we choose to exceed the speed limit, but we don't choose to have an accident or get a ticket.

Perceptions of risk change over time, making at-risk choices the most challenging (and eventually rewarding) human behavior to manage.

Surely, you've noticed that something unusual seems to happen to teenagers' brains. Teenagers, for reasons related to human evolution, do things that at least begin to help us understand the origins of at-risk choice.[22] An article in *Scientific American,* "The Amazing Teen Brain," reports:

Neuroscientists have explained the risky, aggressive, or just plain baf-fling behavior of teenagers as the product of a brain that is somehow compromised. Groundbreaking research in the past 10 years, how-ever, shows that this view is wrong. The teen brain is not defective. It is not a half-baked adult brain, either. It has been forged by evolution to function differently from that of a child or an adult.

Teenagers make at-risk choices as a way of seeing and understanding risk in the world around them.[23] The article goes on:

People will better see that behaviors such as risk taking, sensation seeking, and turning away from parents and toward peers are not signs of cognitive or emotional problems. They are a natural result of brain development, a normal part of adolescents learning how to negotiate a complex world.

It's the same reason we touch the hot plate of fajitas—wanting to see if the rule really applies to us, or if we can ignore it. (Teenagers also are affected by raging hormones, of course.) But the social utility of testing limits, pushing boundaries, and adapting to the results continues throughout our lives. Understanding this astonishing facet of our human nature will help us manage these risks to greater reliability.

An at-risk choice could also be called "cutting a corner." Or "drifting"— we often see entire groups of people drift into at-risk choices, such as most drivers speeding on a highway. In many cases, a work-around can be seen as an at-risk choice—where people ignore or modify a system or rule to accomplish a task—such as standing on a chair instead of using a ladder.

Driving over the speed limit is perhaps the most common at-risk choice. US drivers speed about 72 percent of the time,[24] the National Highway Traffic Safety Administration reported in 2009.

But that's not the only at-risk choice we make while driving. How about drinking a beverage or eating? We rationalize that it's safe to do that, but it adds risk to our drive. We might laugh (and then be horrified) if we saw someone reading while driving, but texting or putting an address into a directional app aren't much different than reading a magazine, are they?

Some everyday at-risk choices we make:

- Turning our attention away for a moment while supervising a child in a bathtub
- Exercising on a treadmill and not using the red stop cord dangling from the control panel
- Grabbing hot food from a microwave without a towel or oven mitts

- Using public Wi-Fi while submitting bank account or credit card information online
- Not washing our hands after sneezing or before handling food
- Not washing fruits or vegetables before eating them

The common element in all of these at-risk choices is that, when we do them, we think either that we're safe and nothing bad will happen, or that it's justified.

Much of what we do in our everyday lives involves at-risk choices, usually with positive results. That's what makes them so difficult to manage—when the choices we make every day help us get results we've come to expect. Except when they don't, and tragedy happens.

STEVE IRWIN

To a generation of fans, the famous Crocodile Hunter Steve Irwin's death was devastating. For many people, the shock of the Australian's death wasn't that it happened, but *how* it happened. We wouldn't have been surprised if he had been maimed by a crocodile or bitten by a poisonous snake. But stung by a stingray? What were the odds of that?

But the lesson Irwin teaches us about reliability goes beyond how he lived his life and died. On January 3, 2004, Irwin did something appalling. He took his one-month-old son, Bob, to work. Literally. When Irwin walked into his zoo's crocodile pit carrying his infant, people watched in disbelief: *Crikey, Steve! You can't do that. We'll pay good money to watch YOU go into the pit, but not with Bob, who is too young to sign away his consent. What if something bad happens?*

By all accounts, Irwin was as reliable as they come in his life's work. Honed by years of dedication and experience, he grew up seeing and understanding the risks of wild animals. In his experience, driving his children to the zoo that day was far riskier than bringing Bob into the crocodile pit.

Irwin was not ignoring the risk. He calculated it and built a system of reliability around him and his son. His assistants were standing by, ready in an instant to help him recover from a slip, lapse, or mistake. And the event happened just as they had expected, without a hitch. Well, except for the public reaction.

For many, Irwin had gone too far. Media commentators denounced his act as reckless. Boycotts were threatened, and the Queensland State Families Department looked into whether he had breached workplace safety regulations.[25]

But Irwin was perplexed. He had never imagined any result other than a safe, successful one. Irwin felt so strongly about this that he agreed to an interview with Larry King on CNN.

He brought his father, who had owned the zoo while Steve was growing up; his wife, Terri, who supported his decision; and his two children, Bindi and Bob. He explained that he was a professional. That he had worked with crocodiles all his life. That he knew the crocodile chosen for the show, when it had last eaten, its temperament, and its past behaviors. What could go wrong? he reasoned. Then he had this exchange with King:

KING: You mean Bob was never in danger?

IRWIN: Not once, ever never. The funny thing is I've been doing it with Bindi for like five-odd years, and I would never endanger my children.

KING: Are you saying the croc was not close to the baby?

IRWIN: No, nowhere near it.

KING: But by the camera angle it appeared close?

IRWIN: Absolutely. My camera that was filming it and the other news camera's (*unintelligible*) the second film crew, they didn't even—they put it at the end of the news, good news. The other one didn't even show it. So this great stacked vision. Credit to them, credit to them, because that's—it's pretty scary-looking vision. So I made a huge mistake. I should have gone surfing that day. But I didn't. I wanted to show the world my beautiful baby.

KING: So when you went on the *Today* show and apologized, what were you apologizing for?

IRWIN: I was apologizing for scaring people. That was never my intention. My intention was strictly and only to show people, here's my little baby boy. I would never endanger my son, as you wouldn't yours nor any good father.

KING: Were you shocked at the criticism?

IRWIN: I wasn't just shocked, I was absolutely devastated. I was taken to the lowest point of my entire life. The Irwin family is steeped in tradition. I was born on my mom's birthday. She died in a car crash and from that moment on, we as a family gathered around each other, as you do when you lose someone very, very close to you and to have that take place was incredible. The interesting thing was that no one knows and now you're about to know, is that you can imagine, everyone who was involved, every family person on Earth was picking at it. The authorities came in, the relevant authorities came in. I did a thorough investigation, come in, please come into my life, come into my family, come into my house, have a look. They did a thorough investigation. There was absolutely no case. Bob was never in danger. You never hear about that, though.

KING: They didn't charge you with being a negligent father?

IRWIN: Absolutely not. In fact, it was said by them and others that my children are the most well-rounded, educated, and loving family they've ever met.[26]

In that instant, Irwin summed up the essential element of at-risk choice—the belief that *nothing bad will ever happen to me. I'm a professional, and every other time in my life that I've done this, the result has been positive.*

Arguably, Irwin may have been the best in the world at what he did. But it illustrates a powerful point about at-risk choices:

Sometimes the better we are at what we do, the less likely we are to recognize we have drifted into at-risk choice.

History is filled with catastrophic accidents—events that were unimaginable in the participants' minds until the disaster happened: ship and plane crashes, bankruptcies, wildfires, and explosions. The people involved—the men and women we seek to hold responsible—are caught often in a socio-technical web of systems and human performance, each mistakenly led to believe that the accident wouldn't happen to them.

You've heard this quote, often misattributed to Albert Einstein: "The definition of insanity is doing the same thing over and over again and expecting a different result."[27] But that is the central challenge of understanding our at-risk choices in a probabilistic world:

We MUST expect that, eventually, our repetitive at-risk choices will produce different, even catastrophic, results.

Why? Because the context, or conditions, surrounding our behaviors will change, producing a combination that results in a different outcome.

It's a fundamental law of socio-technical physics. Small disturbances in nonlinear, time-dependent equations can swing wildly, even chaotically, to produce unstable results. But to our human brains, these changing conditions are hard to visualize. Our recent experience dominates our consciousness, teaching us the wrong lesson. *I've done this so many times before, so why should I expect a different result?*

Sadly, this may have been Steve Irwin's last thought as he died on September 4, 2006, from the stingray's piercing parry. For Irwin, it wasn't a theatrical dance with a crocodile that we might have expected would end his life—he prepared extensively for that risk.

It was the sudden, unexpected result of an everyday choice.

MANAGING AT-RISK CHOICES

At-risk choice represents the greatest danger of all the human behaviors—and our greatest challenge in managing risk. Why? Because it's the most common risky behavior you'll see in any organization, by a wide margin.

Managing at-risk choice starts with identification. But here, too, we face a challenge. At-risk choice is, by definition, personal. What's considered at-risk to one person or group might be acceptable to another. So how do we stand in judgment?

Inside organizations—governments, businesses, teams, schools, families—we must establish the authority by which we determine behaviors. A judge has the authority to stand in judgment in a courtroom. So, too, does a manager, a coach, an administrator, or a parent, in their jurisdictions. Can higher authorities override these authority figures? Of course. That's a function of system design.

But to manage at-risk choice, we must identify it. To identify it, we need a standard:

Whether or not we consider a choice at risk depends on the views of those with authority to stand in judgment.

These views often vary by culture, organization, circumstance, and location. Accepted behavior in one group might be unacceptable to others outside the group. But we need a standard.

Once a choice is determined to be at-risk, the next step in managing it is to understand the behavior. Understanding it starts with looking at the reasons why we make such choices.

We often make at-risk choices because we get an immediate reward. Studies have shown that we get a jolt of dopamine when engaging in high-risk activities, such as skydiving or high-stakes gambling.[28] But what about the everyday risks we take, such as jaywalking, using a cell phone while driving, or speeding? In all these activities and more, there is a risk-reward tension.

Our brains are wired to respond directly to immediate results, which are powerful. If we need to reach something just beyond our grasp, the urge to stand on the top rung of the ladder—against the OSHA warning label—is irresistible in the moment. We perceive an immediate reward, something biologist John Medina calls "brain candy" in his book *Brain Rules*.[29]

There usually are competing priorities when we make an at-risk behavioral choice. Take the behavioral choice to drive over the speed limit. We might think we're more productive because we expect going faster saves time. If we're late to an important meeting, we might think speeding is justified. Or we might speed simply because it's fun.

Then there's the powerful reason we discussed earlier: *Everyone else is doing it, so what's wrong with me doing it?* We may even convince ourselves that speeding is safer. While driving too slowly can contribute to accidents, on average, the lower the speed limit, the fewer the fatalities and the less severe the injuries.[30] The theory has been tested and proved that slower speeds cause less severe injuries.

But the question is whether slower speed limits lead to fewer *crashes*, regardless of severity. Further research yields two opposing positions: They either save lives or they don't. Depending on the researcher and how the numbers are interpreted, correlations can be found in data that support raising speed limits to save lives. But this can be misleading. There's a difference between causing something to happen and merely being associated with the result.[31]

Most of us want to believe our choice to speed produces safe results because it aligns with our other incentives, such as saving time, being productive, and having fun. In much the same way, we want to believe that french fries and ice cream are good for our health, don't we?

This illustrates a common challenge to any study: Interpreting data to align with our self-interest has been a temptation throughout the history of scientific research. Whether it's the health benefits of red wine and coffee or the search for extraterrestrial life, there's always the potential for human bias. When it comes to driving, we must recognize the powerful incentives supporting our behavioral choice to speed, factual or otherwise.

There are two dominant reasons we might choose not to speed: the possibilities of a ticket or an accident. (Saving fuel may be a reason, but it's less influential.) Those are powerful incentives not to speed, but only if we think they're likely. But we usually don't get tickets every day, and we surely don't have accidents that often. So perhaps the most important question is, Which list of incentives, pro or con, has the most effect on our behavior?

The pros provide immediate results, while the cons are distant and often considered remote. When we make at-risk choices, the pros outweigh the cons, at least in our minds. Whether this is true isn't the point—it's the way we often think as humans. We must understand this to manage our behaviors more effectively.

The same is true with a simple choice such as whether to wash our hands properly. Just like speeding, there's an immediate perceived benefit to not doing it: We're in a hurry and saving time. On the other hand (perhaps literally), what would encourage us to engage in procedural hand hygiene by singing "Happy Birthday" twice while we wash our hands, as the Centers for Disease Control and Prevention recommends?[32]

There are two important reasons for doing it: preventing germs from invading our body's defenses and preventing the spread of germs to someone else.

We can't say which reason is more powerful without knowing more about the circumstance—whether an infant or immune-compromised person were involved, for example. But there's value in thinking about this with our System 2 brains.

We often think the first incentive, not getting ourselves sick, is a remote possibility. Our System 1 brains tend to rationalize that nothing bad will happen to us. Much like Steve Irwin, it's hard to imagine a remote possibility that hasn't happened to us. On the other hand, if we've been sick recently, our perception is different. The memory of how it felt to catch a cold or the flu may still be fresh. But this memory usually fades over time. We've evolved to learn best from direct, recent experience, which hurts our reliability.

In healthcare, infection prevention is vital and perhaps poses our most difficult challenge. According to the CDC, US hospital patients contract an estimated 722,000 infections each year. That's about one infection for every twenty-five patients. Infections that patients get in the hospital can be life-threatening and hard to treat. Hand hygiene is an important way to prevent their spread.[33]

Spreading germs to others poses a slightly different challenge, involving that old nemesis, the fundamental attribution bias—seeing our own behaviors differently than we see others'. When we choose not to wash our hands, we may rationalize that we aren't spreading germs because we're good people and we don't intend to get someone else sick. But when others don't wash their hands, we think it's a detriment in their character.

This human bias plays out in several other ways. As parents, we may be upset when other children attend school with runny noses and a mild fever, possibly infecting our children. But when our child wakes up with the same symptoms, we may shrug it off as merely allergies.

In addition to our natural attribution bias,[34] some research suggests washing hands too much reduces our exposure to germs and weakens our immune system. This is like the debate on speed limits. One study says washing hands is the best way to avoid getting sick. Another says washing them too much, and using antibacterial soap, hurts our body's defense systems. So which research do we believe?

What's missing here is our ability to see and understand the risk. With bacteria and viruses, we typically can't see, taste, smell, feel, or hear the germs. The critical feedback loop is missing. And the feedback we do get— getting ourselves or others sick—is often remote or untraceable back to us. So skipping washing our hands or using the five-second rule[35] to eat food off the floor sometimes takes precedence over the perceived unlikely possibility of getting sick.

There are many reasons a healthcare worker may not wash her hands: To save a bit of time. Believing it's other people passing along infections *(there certainly are no bugs on me)*. Cracked skin that the soaps won't soften. No one—the boss in particular—is watching. No one else is doing it, either. This is normal human behavior: We always look for a reason for not doing what we should.

Sometimes we drift into at-risk choices when our System 1 brains take over. It starts in childhood. When you learned to ride a bike, you probably did exactly as you were told and followed all the rules. But as you gained independence and experience, you began riskier behaviors, such as throwing up your arms and saying, "Look, Ma, no hands!" You may have been surprised when the inevitable happened and you took a fall.

Why do we drift into this pattern of at-risk choices? Once again, it's because we've evolved to learn from our most recent and direct experiences. Most of the time, our at-risk behavioral choices produce positive results—until something goes wrong and we see that a bad result can happen to us.

Like Steve Irwin, ironically, sometimes the better we are at what we do, the less likely we are to recognize when we have drifted into at-risk choices. We touch the hot plate, we play with fire, we step into the crocodile pit, not expecting tragedy because it's never happened to us. We learn from direct experience, and our recent experience seems to count most, often teaching us the wrong lesson.

So how do we counter this?

SEQUENCED SOLUTIONS

The best solutions to managing at-risk choices are technical-socio: addressing systems before behaviors. If we can make the system resilient enough—to protect us from ourselves—the behavior becomes inconsequential, and the risk may be acceptable without human intervention. (Think of the gas pump.)

We must use barriers, redundancies, and recoveries to help us manage our choices. Once we build system structures that lower the likelihood of bad things happening, our reliability improves dramatically. Then we must learn to make the rules meaningful by helping others understand why they exist, seeing the real risk hidden in front of them, and influencing their behaviors.

This is the key: Each of us can design our own strategies—within our own personal systems and the environment around us—to manage risk more effectively and improve reliability. This gives us the best chance of managing at-risk choices, for ourselves and others.

Improving the system requires us to apply our engineering strategies. But this may not always be possible or achieve the results we're looking for. So we must also influence people—their perceptions and behaviors—to achieve optimal results.

For example, what's the solution to crashes caused by drivers using cell phones? Will we be successful influencing 222 million drivers to put down their phones? Or will easily bypassed apps do the job?

Of course not.

The ultimate solution is clear: Autonomous vehicles will eventually replace us as drivers, so we'll be free to text and talk without causing an accident. Until then, our best system design is turning off our phones and putting them out of reach or handing them to a passenger.

But we shouldn't give up on humans just yet.

Our behavioral strategies for managing at-risk choices must engage our System 2 brains. Logically, we realize that our actions pose risk, but our System 1 brain is ever-present, encouraging us to cut the corner and grab the immediate reward.

Our System 1 and System 2 brains are like those cartoon characters with an angel on one shoulder and a devil on the other, each urging contrasting behavior.

We're often caught between the pressures of performance, at work and in our daily lives. It's easy to fall into the temptation of at-risk choices because, for the most part, we enjoy immediate positive results. On the other hand, taking the time and energy to resist the temptations of at-risk choices is hard work, and delays our gratification.

If our System 2 brain wins a debate with our System 1 brain—and we resist the at-risk choice we would otherwise make—how do we know that our choice to do the right thing prevented the accident that *didn't* happen? It's easy to dismiss our choice as unnecessary because the direct feedback loop is missing. Our brains are forgoing a reward.

The secret is providing immediate rewards, or incentives, to do the right thing, even when no one is watching. In other words, balancing our temptation with the same brain candy we get when we cut corners.

One way to do this is to enlist other people. Hand washing and hygiene compliance increase when people know they're being observed,[36] studies show. The presence of "watching eyes" can, in some situations, overpower our at-risk choices. Peer pressure can be a big part of the cultural or organi-zational influences on our behavior. But be careful. Peer pressure can swing two ways: positive or negative.

Inviting others to coach us when they see us make at-risk choices can be an effective personal system-design strategy. But we must be willing to be coached. And the coaches must see a benefit—otherwise, why would they do it?

There's another benefit when we ask people to coach us: They can see their own at-risk choices. When we invite coaching—especially when we're in leadership roles such as a boss, coach, or parent—we establish a culture of transparency, which can lead to greater organizational awareness of risk.

Influencing other people's at-risk choices—especially when they didn't ask for input—presents both a challenge and an opportunity.

Think how you might approach someone who is making an at-risk choice. It could be someone overloading a forklift, doing sensitive business on a laptop in an unsecure Wi-Fi hotspot, or routinely failing to properly log sales. If we don't like this person, we might have no reservation about point-ing out his risky behavior. But it's usually not that simple. How we approach the person, or whether we even say anything, depends on many things:

- Is our relationship a long-standing one? Is it a friendship? Or are they a stranger?
- Is there a power gradient between us?
- Are we worried they might take offense?
- How will others react if they see us?

Several approaches provide useful guidance on the art of coaching.[37] But there's a science to getting it right. Effective coaching starts with the relationship between two people, and their respective trust and receptive-ness to input.

Our central coaching challenge is to change another person's perception of risk enough to improve behavior. We're unlikely to improve behavior simply through education or telling someone what they should do. Most of the time, people are driven by perceptions of the consequences of their actions, rather than rules, policies, procedures, or other guidance.

Once we see the risk, and understand how it relates to our self-interest, our System 2 brains can overcome our System 1 brains. Coaching, then, becomes an effective strategy only when we've helped someone change how they see the risk.

Successful coaching requires the person being coached to see the risk sufficiently to accept the guidance. And here's the secret to doing that:

We must convince people how vulnerable the system is around them, exposing them to harm.

The hidden insight here is that by focusing on the system, not the behavior, we accomplish three things with the person we're coaching:

- Make them less defensive about their behavior.
- Allow them to see how a risky system puts them in jeopardy.
- Show them we understand and care about them in this situation.

The result is a self-interested desire to improve behavior. And while each conversation will vary, this strategy produces consistently favorable results.

But coaches can't be everywhere. For many of the at-risk choices we make in our lives, the chances of someone seeing us cut the corner are low. An environment with no one watching is fertile ground for at-risk choices.

Just how tempting is our System 1 brain when no one's watching?

WHEN NO ONE'S WATCHING

We often judge people solely on their results and give them autonomy in getting something done. We do this for many reasons.

In some situations, it's the best we can do because of limited resources, such as requiring employees to show up to work on time. We don't tell them *how* to get to work, we just expect them to be reliable in getting there. In other situations, we expect autonomy because we want to preserve personal liberties, allowing people to make their own choices rather than be constrained by an employer.

With many activities requiring specialized skill, we must rely on expertise beyond our own capability: a gourmet chef preparing a meal in a restaurant, a surgeon performing an appendectomy, or an IT professional developing software. If we don't get the results we want, we try remedies: We refuse to pay for the meal, we sue the doctor, we fire the IT developer. These are recoveries we hope function as barriers to deter risky behaviors and bad results. Sometimes they do; many times they don't.

And there's another hidden pattern to how businesses become more reliable: They often start out relying on autonomous-based expectations, then evolve toward policies, processes, and procedures to achieve product or service delivery goals.

Organizations must be careful when measuring human performance strictly on outcomes. Vulnerable systems and risky choices often produce positive results, until they don't. The unintended consequence of measuring human performance strictly by results is that we sometimes incentivize risk-taking. We may tell a pizza delivery driver that "Safety is job No. 1," but when we pay them by the number of deliveries they make in a shift, we're encouraging them to speed.

The level of system oversight and control we put on people should be proportional to the risk and the social utility of their activity. Our best strategies recognize this.

When the results are critical, we get prescriptive and build robust oversight systems: strict protocols for chemotherapy, three branches of government to guard against tyranny, a second medical opinion for a life-threatening condition, two pilots in commercial planes, an independent review of investment portfolios.

When the risk is tolerable, we provide occasional or no oversight of the activity and simply monitor the results: yard maintenance, postal delivery, compliance with driving laws.

Wait, you say. Aren't driving laws essential to our safety? Shouldn't we be watching all the time?

Yes. But at what cost? Both the risk and the social utility are high. This is where systems help us achieve reliability that would be difficult with police officers alone. Increasingly, technology lets us monitor human performance when results are critical.

Aviation advanced dramatically when the industry began proactively monitoring everyday flights, rather than waiting for "black box" readouts after a crash. We can apply this same approach to other high-consequence activities. Insurance companies work to understand individual driving patterns before a crash happens, which helps predict future performance. Digital security systems are becoming increasingly adept at monitoring homes and businesses before a break-in happens. Bodycams and dashboard devices monitor police and civilian behavior before injuries and deaths happen. And real-time monitoring will soon become our primary means of maintaining our health.

How we get results matters, especially when no one's watching. Our reliability solutions require a sequence, using systems to monitor human performance, whenever practical. But when technological monitoring and oversight systems don't exist or they fail, we must rely on other strategies to make us reliable.

This requires a shift in thinking.

THE MODEL PENAL CODE

Sometimes people will go beyond human errors and at-risk choices, with the intent (or at least knowledge) of causing harm. A bookkeeper may save her employer a lot of money with tax strategies but skim some off the top for herself. Or a disgruntled employee may make life miserable for his co-workers, hurting their production. How should we react in those situations? Do the engineering and behavioral science strategies we've discussed go far enough in making us reliable?

The Model Penal Code,[38] completed in 1962 by the American Law Institute and intended to standardize criminal-law terms and sentencing guidelines in every state, may seem like an odd place to learn about reliability. But we can better manage the risk of intentional harm if we understand the similarities and differences between socio-technical science and how we hold people accountable with our justice system.

The law tries to manage people and their behaviors only after there has been harm. Courts may impose penalties to deter behaviors, but harm must be shown to have happened to achieve legal standing.[39] In our everyday lives and workplaces, though, we shouldn't wait for an accident, or harm, before managing the risk—that's the essence of reliability.

We can learn from the law about how to classify harm and associated behaviors, but reliability begins well before harm, focusing on prevention through socio-technical science. That's why the central task of managing everyday risk and reliability lies beyond our judicial system.

The Model Penal Code ranks culpable behaviors—those that deserve blame—in increasing order of culpability. The first two are *negligence* and *reckless*:

> **Negligence:** A person *should be aware* of a substantial and unjustifiable risk that the element exists or will result, such that the failure to perceive it involves a gross deviation from the standard of conduct that a reasonable person would observe.

This description is problematic when seen through the lens of reliability. Both *human error* and *at-risk choice* could be negligent under this definition, depending on the circumstances.

Take, for example, running a red traffic light, which may be because of human error or choice. But a finding of negligence might tell us little about how that behavior led to this result, and more important, how to manage it.

If someone ran the light by human error, would it be negligent by the above definition if harm happened? Likely so. But by our definition of human error, the act is *unintended*. So how does being aware of the risk matter if the person never intended the act? When it comes to preventing human error, the law seems to try to deter what we never intend to do.

If someone runs the light by at-risk choice, the negligence definition gets us closer to managing risk. By our definition of at-risk choice, the person *should* be aware of the risk involved. But by punishing at-risk choice, there are unintended consequences. One is the "chilling effect" on people in organizations, who may be reluctant to report their at-risk choices for fear of punishment.

We wouldn't be in court unless the police gave us a ticket or we were involved in a crash. So the behavior itself is managed in court only if there is a bad outcome. But the behavior matters a great deal, independent of the result. We should manage human errors differently than at-risk choices—knowing these distinctions and what influences them are crucial to reliability.

To improve reliability, we'll reject the definition of negligence used in the law in favor of our more nuanced understanding of human behavior based on science. We'll substitute our definitions of human error and at-risk choice in place of negligence because these descriptions allow us to see, understand, and manage the risk more effectively.

The next behavior defined in the Model Penal Code, however, is pitch-perfect:

Reckless: A person *consciously disregards* a substantial and unjustifiable risk that the element exists or will result, such that its disregard involves a gross deviation from the standard of conduct that a law-abiding person would observe.

This definition fits in reliability science because it provides a clear distinction between reckless and at-risk choices. This distinction is key to our success in managing behavioral choices.

These three elements must be present for reckless choice:

1. Conscious disregard
2. Substantial risk
3. Unjustifiable risk

It's important to recognize that with reckless choice, there's no *intent* to cause harm even though the person consciously disregards a substantial and unjustifiable risk. For example, most drunk drivers aren't trying to kill. (Being sober would be more reliable in the act of killing.) But the choice represents substantial and unjustifiable risk of harm and is unacceptable by society's values.

A reckless choice can involve multiple values, such as safety—physical, psychological, or emotional harm. In healthcare, it could involve privacy, respect, compassion, or any of the other values the organization wants to live up to.

On a personal level, when we engage in a reckless choice, we usually have a knot in our stomach—this is a recognition that we're in an unsafe place, or we're doing something other people would consider unacceptable but we're doing it anyway. We've all exceeded the law, or cut a corner, or not followed procedure, but the reckless choice is when we take a substantial and unjustifiable risk, and we should know it by the knot in our stomach.

In healthcare, a reckless choice could be someone stealing a drug from the pharmacy or taking it from a patient scheduled to get it.

What do we do when we see a reckless choice? The answer depends on whether we see it in a group or organization and we have the authority to respond, or help manage the risk.

If we're tourists and we see someone dancing obliviously at the Grand Canyon rim, dangerously close to falling or possibly bumping into others and causing them to fall, our social expectation might be to report it to the nearest park ranger. If it's our own child and we have the authority to act ourselves, we probably would have a stronger response, possibly including punishment, to manage the risk in the future.

This is the first time we've introduced punishment as a considered response. Until now, we've concentrated on making *ourselves* more reliable, seeing and understanding the risks in our world, and managing our systems and human performance. But when we live or work in groups, managing risk involves accountability to each other for our behaviors.

This is true in families, where parents assume fiduciary and other responsibilities for our children. It's true in workplaces, where managers are responsible for managing people and the systems they work in. And it's true in associations where people hold each other accountable for adherence to rules, policies, and procedures, all designed to manage risk while living up to the organization's goals, objectives, and values.

So, what role does punishment serve? In the case of reckless choices, punishment is part of the "artificial danger," or consequence, influencing our behavior. The threat of punishment is why we often slow down when we see a police officer. In companies, human resources departments have guidelines for responding to reckless workplace behaviors, including termination. But all these have a common purpose: to deter future choices that add risk to us or our organization.

Reckless choices extend beyond specific laws, rules, policies, or procedures. What's important is how people see risks in their organization and how the organization responds to reckless choices that exceed its tolerance for risk.

BEYOND RECKLESS CHOICES

The Model Penal Code lists two behaviors of greater culpability than reckless: knowingly and purposely.

If reckless choices are uncommon in most of our society, these beyond-reckless choices are rare. And like reckless choices, they must be identified and stopped to effectively manage risk. They may be a little easier to identify because they stand out.

Although they represent a tiny fraction of the total risk, when they happen, harm is "practically certain" to occur:

Knowingly: If the element involves the nature of the conduct or the attendant circumstances, he is aware that his conduct is of that nature or that the circumstances exist. If the element involves a result, he is practically certain that the result will occur. Further, if the element involves knowledge of the existence of a particular fact, it is satisfied if he is aware of a high probability of the existence of that fact, unless he actually believes that it does not exist.

Purposely: If the element involves the nature of the conduct or the result thereof, it is his conscious object to engage in that conduct or cause the result. If the element involves attendant circumstances, he is aware of the circumstances or believes or hopes that they exist.

These two behaviors are slightly different but related.

Let's say a bank robber enters a bank to rob it, scuffles with a security guard, and shoots her. Although his purpose was to rob the bank, the robber *knowingly caused unjustifiable harm* to the guard. If shooting someone had been his main objective, he would have *purposely caused unjustifiable harm* to the guard.

In healthcare, if someone steals a drug, that's at least a reckless choice, but it could be an even more culpable behavior. It would be knowingly causing unjustifiable harm if the stolen drug were meant for a specific patient, denying that person a prescribed benefit.

Drug thefts where the purpose is to cause unjustifiable harm are exceedingly rare, but there have been cases where professionals did just that. Even though it almost never happens, the organization must realize that it *can* happen.

It's important that everyone in an organization knows to report these beyond-reckless choices—to top management, professional boards, oversight agencies, and law enforcement.

JUSTICE AND RELIABILITY

The reliability of the United States' (and other nations') criminal justice system plays a significant role in the well-being of society. Protecting the greater good is our main goal in becoming more reliable, but protecting— and punishing—the offender is sometimes key to doing that.

Everyday acts of unreliability are rarely crimes, so how can we best manage them? If we are in a position of authority or other influence, our effectiveness in helping someone become more reliable depends on two things:

1. Our ability to see and understand the behavior when it happens.
2. The response of the person we are managing or influencing, and their willingness to participate in the improvement process.

Every parent of a teenager knows this. If we don't know about our children's behaviors, how can we manage them? If our relationship is one of conflict, or based on punishment, what chance do we have of getting the results we want?

Reliability extends beyond mere "crime and punishment," especially in organizations. The proven strategy to becoming reliable is to design better systems and to make the best use of our positive influences on human performance. To do this effectively, we must recognize this:

Our response to human behaviors must be fair and consistent to achieve positive results.

If someone sees unfair or inconsistent treatment, our success at influencing their behavior diminishes. We may lose our ability to see, understand, and, therefore, affect their behaviors. And when we try, they are less likely to respond in a positive way.

Every parent learns this eventually. If we overreact or apply unfair punishment, our relationship with our children suffers. They simply won't confide in us. Our ability to guide and nurture them improves dramatically if our relationship is based on fairness and trust.

For these reasons, reliability science teaches us these general guidelines for responding to the behaviors we've discussed:

Human Errors: Support and encourage the person. Examine the system and personal factors shaping system performance around them. Examine any choices that may have increased the likelihood of their error. Then work with them to see, understand, and manage the risk, while examining the cultural and organizational factors shaping their performance.

At-Risk Choices: Support and encourage the person. Examine the system and personal factors shaping system performance around them. Examine any competing pressures of influences that contributed to their at-risk choice. Work with them to see, understand, and manage the risk, while examining the culture and organizational factors shaping their performance.

Reckless and Higher Culpable Choices: Consider punishment or discipline as a deterrent. Examine the system and personal factors shaping system performance around the person, and examine any competing pressures or other influences that contributed to their reckless choice. Consider any system redesign that may mitigate or prevent unintended harm associated with reckless or higher culpable choices. Then work with them to see, understand, and manage the risk.

Learning to react appropriately to all three of these behaviors will greatly improve our reliability. It's especially important to learn how to manage at-risk choices, which are the biggest behavioral contributor to risk in our lives. The key is this:

It's vital that we not punish at-risk choices. That lets us see and manage them when they happen, gives us the best chance of a positive response, and helps us manage future behavior.

HUMAN RELIABILITY SUMMARY

Humans are complex creatures with a wide range of emotions, talents, intellect, and capacity to survive. Our biology, environment, and experiences shape our perceptions and filter the way we see and manage risk, leading to the intended outcomes we often produce. But sometimes those influences cascade into less-than-expected results, or even catastrophes. Human reliability begins with an understanding of the forces shaping our performance: knowledge, skills, abilities, and proficiency; system factors; personal factors; culture; perceptions of risk and competing priorities; and our behavioral choices and human errors.

Managing these factors influencing human performance requires insight into their relative strength and proportion. Improving human performance and sustaining it over time requires an understanding of how these influences interconnect and how we react to them. At first glance, these influences may seem complex or even overwhelming. But like most complex challenges, we can break down these factors into simpler, easier-to-understand components. We find patterns in the complexity that we can manage more effectively.

By understanding these influences, we can train ourselves to think with both our System 1 and System 2 brains, and apply the system strategies we've learned to help us act differently, improving our reliability:

Reliable people employ reliable systems.

In the same way system design leads us to better management of the factors influencing system performance, one factor influencing human performance is vital to reliability: our perceptions of risk and competing priorities. Our perceptions are not static but change through individual experience.

A SPAGHETTI STORY

(How Our Perceptions of Risk Evolve Through Experience)

Carol, a nurse manager, was taking twice-monthly reliability training designed to help supervisors become proficient in managing the daily risks of running the hospital. During one practice session, Carol told her colleagues a story.

"It all began last night," she said. "I got off from work before my husband, picked up our kids from preschool, and brought them home. As I started to prepare dinner, I made sure my children were safely playing in the other room. My plan was to cook spaghetti. When my family eats pasta, I usually make a big batch so we'll have plenty for leftovers.

"I filled a large pot with water and put it on the front burner, where the large gas element is. I turned it on high.

"Our wall phone rang, so I walked across the kitchen to pick it up. I kept an eye on the stove to make sure everything was safe.

"On the phone was my husband, who was running late from work. I asked him to pick up a few things at the store for tomorrow's lunches on his way home. I had a list somewhere and tried to find it, but the phone cord wasn't cooperating.

"I happened to look up and saw my two-year-old had wandered into the kitchen and was climbing up the side of the stove trying to grab the handle on the pot of water, which was now boiling."

Carol then paused and asked, "How do you judge my behavior?"

Your first thought is probably, *What happened to the child?* But for our purpose of assessing Carol's behavior and understanding how she saw the risk, knowing the outcome biases our response.

Assessing human behaviors should be unbiased and seen in the context of the person acting in her environment, including both the system (the burner's position on the stove, the phone's location on the wall) and the culture (the family's habits and practices).

Why? Because if we're going to manage human behaviors effectively, we must be able to see and understand their influences. To do that, we must recognize how powerful the outcome bias is in our minds and how difficult it is to resist. We've evolved over millions of years to focus on the result. We must unlearn this inclination.

When Carol stepped away from the stove, it was not a human error; it was a behavioral choice. We must first establish this as a choice before we identify the type of choice or what happened after the choice.

After Carol chose to leave the stove unattended, distractions set in. Her attention was divided among at least two, and maybe three, tasks: watching the stove, having the phone conversation, and looking for the grocery list. She was multitasking, just like we all do at times. But after diverting her eyes, the moment she looked up she saw the risk clearly. Was it too late?

The first question we must answer is how to judge her perception of the risk when she chose to walk to the phone. Did she believe her children were safely in the other room playing? (Yes.) Did she expect to become distracted and take her eye off the stove when her children might enter the kitchen? (No.) This was the human error: becoming distracted and forgetting, for no more than a second or two, to keep her attention focused on the stove.

The two behaviors being assessed are these:

1. The choice to step away from the stove while leaving the pot of water unattended.
2. The momentary distraction that led to the lapse, or act of forgetfulness—a human error.

How did the group assess her behavioral choice? As we've discussed, one simple way to understand the difference between at-risk and reckless choice is to consider this: Did she have a knot in her stomach telling her she was taking an unacceptable risk but disregarded it and chose to step away from the stove anyway? Did Carol simply choose to step away recklessly, or did she believe her children were safe and that there would be no way she would not remain watchful?

In this case, her colleagues unanimously judged her as making an at-risk choice.

What happened next? The coaching began, of course. Someone immediately said to Carol, "Don't you know as a parent you can never leave a hot stove unattended for any amount of time when small children are in the house?" Carol's heartfelt answer was, "Yes, of course. I love my children and want to protect them. I clearly see the danger now."

But the story doesn't end just yet. After more coaching and "there-but-for-other-circumstances-go-I" discussion, Carol raised an important question: "Now that I've gone through this experience and everyone knows I clearly see the risk, how would you judge me if I made the same behavioral choice tonight?"

Without exception, everyone in the room agreed if she were to make the same choice tonight, they would call it reckless.

So, our question is: How can we expect an organization, much less any one of us as individuals, to manage our risk-taking behaviors if they're a moving target? If our perceptions of risk and how we choose to act change from one day to the next, from one person to the next, how are we to become reliable?

This is where the hidden science—segregated by specialties—comes together.

ORGANIZATIONAL RELIABILITY

WHAT ORGANIZATIONAL RELIABILITY MEANS

Leadership in business requires an understanding of how organizations see and understand risk, and the factors that influence their performance, as well as human behaviors. An effective business model is just the starting point. Reliability is determined not only by the behaviors of the leaders and workforce, but also by the systems in which they work.

Organizations are socio-technical combinations of people working within systems.

Let's consider an example. A professional baseball team is an organization, meaning a collection of owners, players, managers, coaches, scouts, trainers, analysts, groundskeepers, and so on. All these people are part of a system. In fact, we refer to the team's player development structure as a "farm system." Similarly, the manager, coaches, and players employ subsystems as strategies on the field. The number of pitches allowed each pitcher in an inning or game, the method of using gestures to signal which pitch to throw, the order in which each batter faces the opposing pitcher.

Each player in the organization is part of this collection of systems and subsystems. The players' human performance—their knowledge, skills, abilities, proficiencies, and behaviors (choices and human errors)—contribute to the success or failure of the organization.

Any baseball fan will tell you that this collection of systems, combined with players and their performance, adds up to a distinctive *culture*. This culture may exist for a long time, influenced by history and experiences of winning, or losing, championships.

Businesses have the same socio-technical structure: people working within systems. And as discussed previously, past performance is no guarantee of future results. If a company aims to grow, reliability is a key to gaining market share. If a company aims to hold on to market share after periods of growth, reliability is crucial to sustainable success.

We can extend this way of seeing organizations to any group of people working to achieve a common goal, including the following:

- Associations and clubs
- Government agencies
- The United Nations
- Families
- Schools

All organizations have imperfect systems and people—and both are vulnerable to risk. Seeing and managing these vulnerabilities before systems and people fail is critical to success.

Like systems and people, organizations' performance will change over time, meaning they will have good days and bad days. That's why *effectiveness* and *resilience* are important to organizations' reliability. In baseball, a team's overall reliability throughout the season directly determines its chances of winning a championship. Yes, it's true that a team can get hot during the postseason and win the World Series. But to be in a position for that to happen, the team must be reliable enough to reach the postseason. It must be good at bouncing back after a tough loss or an injury to a star player.

In business, too, sustainable success means managing the factors that shape organizational performance, such as weathering the economic climate or anticipating changes in customer demand and market forces.

ORGANIZATIONAL FACTORS

As we've done with system and human reliability, it helps to look at how the factors influencing organizational behavior are interconnected. These aren't all the potential influences, but looking at them side by side is a useful way of thinking about how to manage organizational reliability (see figure 5.1).

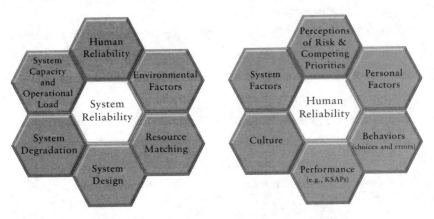

Figure 5.1

Trying to understand the complex interactions between factors influencing system and human performance can be daunting. But a general appreciation of these influences leads to a better understanding of how to manage organizational reliability.

A key point is that system reliability sets the stage for human and organizational performance. System performance can affect human performance, at the individual and group level. A few examples:

- The students in a school without enough qualified teachers and classroom capacity underperform on standardized tests.
- Multiple natural disasters overwhelm the Federal Emergency Management Agency's ability to respond.
- A mass transit system with aging equipment and inadequate route design can't meet the public's demand for transportation.

- An e-commerce business with inadequate web platform functionality and reliability can't support customer transactions.

We can improve our results if we can see, understand, and manage the factors shaping system performance. No matter how well we manage human behavior in our organization, investing time and other resources early to build effective and resilient systems will determine our organization's performance over time.

We shouldn't underestimate the effect that human reliability—people and their behaviors—has on our outcomes, for better or worse, because it's substantial. Take the following instances:

- A pro football player is suspended, and his team fined, for using illegal performance-enhancing drugs.
- The head of a household loses his job because of poor performance, and his family is evicted from their home because they can't pay the rent.
- A corporation's top executives are criminally charged with insider trading,[1] and its stock performance plummets.
- A government agency official is convicted of mishandling public money, and Congress subsequently cuts the agency's budget.

Of course, both positive and negative experiences shape organizations, just as they shape people. In each of these examples, we could just as easily think of situations where human performance and behavior led to positive results. So why focus on the negative?

It's counterintuitive, but the key to higher reliability is initially focusing on what can go wrong, as much as working hard to make sure things go right.

When we're about to do a task, such as hitting a golf ball or driving a car, we try to focus on a successful outcome. But to do this consistently, we must first see and understand what can go wrong to avoid negative consequences.

We must know that the green we're aiming at is surrounded by a water hazard that may cost us a one-stroke penalty. Or that just because the stoplight turns green for us doesn't mean cars coming from other directions will stop. Once we see and understand the relevant risks, *then* our focus shifts to behavioral choices most likely to produce positive results. It's like trying to cross a minefield: Success requires a mine detector or a map of steps to avoid.

For an organization, building a road map to reliability is a continuous journey. Seeing and understanding risk as an organization depends on individuals and their multiple perceptions of risk. As we've discussed, our individual perceptions of risk will change from one moment to the next, so how do we focus an organization's perception of risk? It takes a complex set of calculations, varying all the time. But patterns emerge, and we can manage them.

One advantage that organizations have over individuals is that, collectively, they can see and manage risk that individuals may not be able to detect on their own. No one can experience *all* the potential pitfalls that it's possible to encounter in a lifetime. But when seen from a larger perspective, experiences can be shared to influence our individual behaviors beyond our personal experience. While this might sound easy, the practical applications can be difficult.

Why? Because we've evolved to learn best through direct experience. We might read about someone crashing a car while speeding, but our fundamental attribution bias prevents us from believing that result will happen to us. We're wired to think positively.

But when those things happen to someone close to us, or we have a near-disastrous experience, the risk becomes relevant and our appreciation for the danger becomes acute. A central challenge for organizations is how to collect, organize, and make people consistently aware of the changing probabilities of risk.

All the factors shaping system and human performance that we've discussed affect organizational performance. But there's a larger picture to envision when trying to improve our organization's reliability (see figure 5.2).

Figure 5.2

As you can see, there are other influences on organizational performance, and they can be just as powerful.

Internal Influences: These may include the following:

- Cultural factors, including at the work unit, shift, departmental, and organizational levels
- Peer-to-peer influences
- Demographics
- Budgets and internal economic constraints

External Influences: Here are some examples:

- Societal, community, ethnic, religious, and other cultures
- News media and public perceptions
- Political climates
- Regulators
- Economies

Sometimes we can't directly control internal and external factors immediately, although internal influences often can be managed. But we can still work to become resilient—able to bounce back—when things go wrong.

Like the weather, while we can't always control it, we can monitor it and prepare (build shelters and stock up on supplies, for example) for stormy days ahead. Similarly, highly reliable organizations continuously try to see and understand risk, including the internal and external factors influencing their performance.

Perceptions of Risk and Competing Priorities: As with individuals, organizations must be able to recognize ever-changing risk as it evolves and to balance competing priorities.

And like humans, organizations tend to overvalue recent experiences, sometimes setting themselves up for failure by learning the wrong lessons. Managing organizational perceptions of risk can be daunting because it requires aligning leadership and engaging the entire workforce.

So how do we do that? We must first see the forces—competing priorities—influencing our perceptions. For example, airlines strive for on-time performance and baggage delivery, which the Department of Transportation measures and reports to the public. But, daily, internal and external factors—weather, illness, accidents, mechanical failures, and other schedule disruptions—compete for priorities in meeting those targets.

In hospitals, patient safety and satisfaction often compete with expectations for privacy and cost control. It's no wonder that organizations—like individuals—often drift into at-risk choices and consequences.

What are the at-risk incentives for organizations? The same competing priorities individuals face also confront organizations. A few examples of why organizations might cut corners:

- Production, financial, or time pressures
- Thinking the organization is in a safe place
- Past performance (learning the wrong lesson from previous successful results)

- No one's watching or the consequences seem remote or uncertain

Can we eliminate these competing priorities? No, but we can manage them if we understand what drives them.

MULTIPLE VALUES

Competing priorities exist because we have multiple values in our lives. The *Oxford English Dictionary* defines *values* as follows:

Principles or standards of behavior; one's judgment of what is important in life.

This definition fits our discussion precisely, because our focus is on the varied influences on human behavior. There are so many potential values that we often use the term *core values* to narrow the definition to a manageable size. But even this term offers seemingly endless possibilities, limited only by our imaginations and the constraints of the English language.[2]

So, let's conduct a short experiment, from a business perspective, and discuss the values important to us—those we aspire to live up to as an organization. We'll pick five values, in no particular order:

- Customer service
- Safety
- Privacy
- Cost control
- Diversity, equity, inclusion, and belonging

We normally wouldn't stop there, so here are a few more:

- Timeliness
- Excellence
- Teamwork

- Community service
- Equality

You get the picture. There's virtually no end to this. All these are values important to running a business. But does any single value stand above the others in all circumstances?

That's a complex question. If our business is in an environment where violence dominates our lives—a crime-ridden neighborhood or a region of the world with political and economic instability—safety takes precedence over all other values, at least until we know we're safe and can concentrate on other values and running the business.

At this point, psychologist Abraham Maslow,[3] who developed the hierarchy of needs, would say: *To focus on these other values, we must satisfy our basic needs of food, clothing, and shelter.* As Maslow pointed out, a *sequence* of core values is necessary, both in our personal lives and in business. But once basic needs are met, the values we care about expand dramatically.

Dozens of values are important to running a successful business. Think about what's important to us when we wake up in the morning. Does a single value dominate our thinking? (Other than, perhaps, the urge for coffee.) Most of us care about multiple values that become a balancing act throughout the day. These values may even remain embedded in our subconscious while immediate priorities dominate our attention: getting up on time, making coffee and breakfast, driving through traffic, dropping the kids at school, and getting to work. All of these priorities influence our behaviors, both our choices and our human errors.

In business, we want to make a profit. Or make a difference in our community. Or both. To accomplish these goals, we must establish a business model, then execute in an ever-changing market environment. We may want to introduce a new product, but to do that we must invest in research and development. So, we borrow money. Cost control is important to our ability to maintain credit, and we must expand our production and distribution capabilities to generate revenue.

But if our employees are not safe, or if the work environment is unfair or hostile, we jeopardize all these goals and objectives. How we get results matters. Multiple values and principles bond employers and employees. At the end of the day, our values become a complex array of competing priorities.

Competing priorities are a fact of life and business. We hope employees follow all the rules, policies, and procedures, but the reality is we're all good at noncompliance and work-arounds. We've evolved to manage the competing priorities in our lives. What drives us to act in each situation may change from moment to moment, as circumstances, priorities, and perceptions of risk change, even when our commitments to core values remain intact. Understanding this balancing act becomes crucial to becoming more reliable in our businesses and our everyday lives.

When we know the competing values and priorities we face, we can recognize the risks and manage them by designing better systems and influencing human behaviors. In running a business, that means recognizing the influences on our workforce—personal and organizational—will change throughout their employment. The core values of the company may remain consistent, but the many influences on human performance will not.

We may have conditions for employment, but they can't prevent us from being human. Our employees won't abandon their personal self-interests, nor should they. Each person's competing personal values and priorities has the potential to influence the organization.

Similarly, competing organizational priorities will affect individual performance. This complexity is unavoidable. A business may be dedicated to customer service as a top value, but stressful or hazardous working conditions will directly affect the organization's ability to deliver it. In healthcare, a hospital's commitment to protecting patient privacy competes for caregiver time and attention.

Our government institutions, designed as instruments of our democracy, are a framework for protecting our American values. So, it should be no surprise that the Declaration of Independence sums up our competing values with this eloquence:

We hold these truths to be self-evident, that all men are created equal, that they are endowed by their Creator with certain unalienable Rights, that among these are Life, Liberty and the Pursuit of Happiness.

The astonishing thing about these words is that we can put *all* our values—personal and organizational—into one or more of these three categories: life, liberty, and the pursuit of happiness.

In all aspects of life, government, and business, our strategies to improve must recognize our dedication to multiple values—and the natural pull of competing priorities they create. For example, respect for equal rights based on gender, racial, cultural, and religious differences has bettered the organizations managing them and paved the way for improvements throughout our society.

Commitment to competing core values—for individuals, organizations, and nations—defines our aspirations.

Reliability is our means of living up to them.

LEADERSHIP

Leaders lead. The challenge is twofold. First, leaders can lead in the wrong direction, as well as the right one.[4] Companies must employ *systems* to guard against errant leadership, applying checks and balances to ensure success.

Second, when leading in the right direction, leaders must understand how the systems and people they employ achieve reliability. Success requires vision and execution.

Organizations look to leadership to provide mission, vision, and values.[5] All are important. But they are merely aspirations. None of these guarantees success without execution, and that requires reliability.

This is where leaders earn their pay. Getting the best organizational results means providing the *means* to achievement by applying the Sequence. You must code reliability into your organizational DNA. By now, you know the first steps in the sequence well:

1. *Seeing and understanding risk*
2. *Managing reliability in this order:*
   a. *System performance*
   b. *Human performance*

Organizational performance begins only *after* these painstaking first steps. Why? Because optimal results require optimal approaches. Sometimes, you can lead an organization the wrong way easier than the right way. The trick is to ensure your organization is not only good at what you do well, but equally important, good at managing the risks of what you don't do well. It's the science of overcoming Murphy's Law.

Starting with the top of the organization, the primary function of leadership is to do the following:

- Inspire, guide, and support the workforce to achieve mission, vision, and values.
- Recognize and manage the multiple influences on organizational performance, especially competing priorities, and perceptions of risk.
- Promote and empower reliability in living up to all core values across the organization.
- Ensure organizational sustainment.

Take this hypothetical example: A start-up biotech company produces a neurofeedback device for home use. The product is innovative, and there are initially no market competitors offering anything similar. First-year sales are positive, and this leads to investment and expansion. As sales increase, the company splits production into two facilities to meet customer demand. This creates a quality gap between products made at different locations, and customer reviews begin to lower the product's ratings on social media and online distributors' websites. Eventually, the board of directors changes company leadership to halt the losses, which have extended over consecutive quarters.

What went wrong?

The company was founded on innovation, which was enough to create initial customer demand. But innovation alone isn't enough to ensure reliability, or sustained profits. The *mission* (to help customers better manage cognitive challenges at home), *vision* (to become the leading provider of in-home neurofeedback devices), and *values* (medical expertise and product innovation) didn't account for the unforeseen risks in manufacturing.

What could the company leaders do differently?

Begin by assessing core strengths (medical expertise and product innovation). Then look at what the company doesn't know how to do reliably:

- Build a business plan.
- Secure the right type of funding to match the plan.
- Identify missing strengths, such as manufacturing, quality control, auditing, and customer service.
- Understand external and internal market forces and evaluate the risk of start-ups in this sector.

Then continue with Step 2 in the Sequence:

- Design and manage reliable systems and processes, including production, distribution, marketing, and customer service, regulatory liaisons; apply ISO standards, and provide auditing and customer service training.
- Manage the workforce by aligning competing values and priorities, such as time pressures and cost constraints, and developing knowledge, skills, and abilities in the key areas identified above.
- Ensure organizational sustainment through reliable management systems and succession plans, requiring documented risk identification and management strategies across all departments.

Organizational alignment is key. It's not enough for a chief executive or president to lead the way. Like birds in a flock, alignment happens when *all* members are flying in unison. People are not birds, of course, and don't share the same innate instincts of migration. With humans, cohesive organizational alignment requires vision, planning, and execution, which depend on aligned leadership.

We sometimes refer to how organizations behave, personifying them as if they are individuals. But organizations are *collections* of individuals working together in systems, starting with leadership. Aligning leadership empowers individuals to apply the Sequence, resulting in a cascade of reliability across the organization, including systems and the entire workforce.

Learning the language of reliability, improving systems to become effective and resilient, focusing the workforce's attention on what should go right but also on what can go wrong, and building the organizational capacity for sustainment is no small challenge. But it's what organizational reliability requires. And it starts, but doesn't end, with leadership.

Given enough time, all organizational leaders will move on. In businesses and associations, whether by design, retirement, or death, all leaders are in transition. In the presidency, we have term limits; in the Supreme Court, lifetime appointments are limited by mortality; and in Congress, the will of the voters and life expectancy determine the tenure.

All organizational leaders move on, but:

The best organizations thrive beyond the personalities and styles of individual leaders.

Why do we emphasize this obvious fact? Because we must understand that long-term, sustainable reliability requires leadership and steerage beyond any single person. It's the proverbial "hit by a bus" scenario. What happens to an organization if the top leader is suddenly out of the picture? As leaders come and go, an organization's values and function remain, even though they may evolve in different directions.

In some cases, replacing leadership is a necessary recovery strategy when other strategies don't produce positive results. But seeing and understanding risk and improving systems should come *before* judging human behaviors—including those of leaders.

Succession plans, which often focus on who takes over a leadership role, require more than selecting the right person:

> *Succession planning begins not just with who the leadership is, but what it does, and how to sustain it.*

On our best days, leadership is a bellwether, inspiring and guiding an organization toward sustainable reliability. On other days, leadership must be a renewable resource, a replaceable component in a larger, evolving system.

As important as leadership is, it takes a combination of leadership, well-designed systems, a trained and reliable workforce, and an environment where all of this comes together to produce sustainable results.

And the sum of these elements leads us to culture.

CULTURE

But what is culture? Is it like the weather? Is it a gathering storm of impassionate variables or an unseen force acting with intention?

Perhaps it's all of that, and more.

The story of Uber serves as a cautionary business tale. Uber, founded in 2009, was an early pioneer in peer-to-peer ride-sharing, taxicab hailing, food delivery, bicycle-sharing, and other services. Using mobile apps and algorithms, Uber quickly became synonymous with the new gig economy, changing the way people live and work in the twenty-first century. By April 2019, Uber had raised $24.7 billion from twenty-four rounds of venture capital and private equity investors.[6]

But then the public began to see below the waterline. Reports leaked out of a culture run amok. A host of allegations surfaced, from predatory business practices and confrontations with regulators to internal claims of misogyny and sexual, gender, and racial harassment, and hostile labor relations.

What was the turnaround solution? The board replaced top leadership, hiring Dara Khosrowshahi as CEO in August 2017. In an interview with CNN Money ahead of his one-year anniversary as chief executive, Khosrowshahi said, "If there's one area that I would have liked to change faster, it is to execute more fully on our cultural transformation as a company internally, across all levels at the company."[7] He also said, "It will never be done. It's a continuous exercise. If I talk to you next year, I hope to be further along on the exercise than I am right now."

Every aspect of culture influences organizational performance, affecting everyone and everything, inside and around it. The challenge is to first recognize its influence, then manage it. But it's a moving target. Culture is dynamic, always evolving in time and place. Today's culture is different than yesterday's and tomorrow's.

Micro-cultures coexist with macro-cultures.

In all aspects of society—race and ethnicity, business, education, recreation, politics, and religion—diverse cultures arise whenever groups of people live, work, and play in groups. In business, culture will vary by company, region, department, work unit, and even shift. (Observe the expression on any manager's face when you ask how the night shift's culture compares to the day shift's. It's often what keeps managers awake at night.) In schools, students gather and interact in groups, developing cliques within classrooms and social relationships. In towns and communities, cultures arise through common bonds forged in daily life. Throughout the United States, every state's culture coexists with our national cultures.

Rather than being overwhelmed by cultural moving targets, you can tame the chaos:

To manage the cultures in your organization, it helps to understand that diversity is a system design advantage.

For example, in biological and ecological systems, there is strength in diversity, often called *hybrid vigor*.[8] In a meadow, the flowering plants thrive because of the variety of birds and insects that pollinate them, and the birds get prolonged sustenance from the variety of flowers that bloom at different times. In the same way, organizations—including businesses, military units, sports teams, and educational institutions—thrive when diverse thought and skills are harnessed into collaboration.

In the engineering terms we've discussed, cultural diversity provides barriers, redundancies, and recoveries to improve reliability. Diversity—intellectual, ethnic, gender, religious, and political—is a powerful counterbalance to *group think*,[9] one of the greatest liabilities to any business or organization.

Redundancies are most effective when they are independent, and cultural diversity gives us an advantage. Engineers, psychologists, and lawyers bring unique and overlapping perspectives to the hidden science of reliability.

Appreciating the role that culture plays in influencing organizations is crucial to reliability. We must see and understand culture (as we do with system and personal factors shaping performance) before we can manage its effects on organizational performance—all of which requires clear vision.

But sometimes biases can cloud our eyes.

BEWARE THE BIASES

Bias is a form of prejudice that affects us all. Hundreds of biases invade our thinking, for better or worse. Biases color the way we see the world, many times unfairly or inaccurately, and cause us to draw wrong conclusions. In some situations, biases can be dangerous.

The Outcome Bias: Remember the iceberg model? We saw how known adverse events or bad results can cause us to miss the everyday risk in system and human performance. This can be caused by hindsight bias, such as when something bad happens and people say, *I could have told you that*, or *I knew it all along*. At best, that's not useful. But one form of hindsight bias is even more dangerous—outcome bias.

Outcome bias is common and happens when we allow the level of harm, or the adverse result, to affect how we respond to systems or individuals. Often, our natural inclination is to address system or human reliability *only* when bad things occur, turning a blind eye to them when things go right.

On September 12, 2008, a Metrolink commuter train crashed head-on into a Union Pacific cargo train traveling the opposite direction in Los Angeles. If you remember anything about this accident, it's that the engineer was sending a text message while driving the train one minute and seven seconds before impact.

He ignored the company policy against texting while operating the train.

Before we reach any further conclusions about this accident, ask yourself: Do you believe this was the first time he had texted while operating a train? Was it the only time? Was he the only engineer who had ever done this?

Records show the engineer had texted several times in the past while operating a train.[10] But there's a more important question we should be asking: What lesson was the engineer learning every time he had texted and the train didn't crash? Was he learning the wrong lesson?

This is the challenge we have in managing at-risk choice.

The engineer had done this before many times without incident. Other engineers may have also done this routinely, without incident. But on this day, the train crashed.

If the engineer were your employee, how would you react?

Your first reaction might be to punish him, to hold him accountable. Thinking with your System 1 brain, you might have a strong desire to discipline the engineer because he didn't follow policy.

But thinking with your System 2 brain, you'll recognize what really upsets you is the *outcome* of the engineer's behavior. If the trains hadn't collided, it's likely no one would have known about the engineer's behavior.

We often react differently when the outcome is adverse because we have a strong desire to "fix" the problem. We'd like to believe that punishment works as a deterrent, and punishment may feel like we're holding people accountable.

But there's a problem.

We often don't see behaviors lurking below the surface unless bad outcomes happen. Rather than take the easier route of punishing behavior, we should take the time and effort to see, understand, and manage the risk more fully.

We can punish the at-risk choice to text and operate the train *after the crash,* but that's only because we know about it. Will punishment alone solve the problem of human distraction? No.

Clearly, punishment can have a deterrent, or preventative, effect. Every parent knows this. Before children fully understand the risk behind a parental rule, they understand punishment. A four-year-old may not recognize the risk of playing in a busy street but can appreciate how it feels when a toy or digital device is taken away.

Punishment *can* work with risk-based choices. But only up to a point. As the children grow older and begin to comprehend the world around them, their capacity to appreciate the risk evolves. A teenager's response to punishment is different from a toddler's. Our ability to see and understand risk—and our perceptions of the likelihood and severity of the consequences—drives our ability to manage it.

Reckless choices, along with more culpable behaviors, require a different approach. These behaviors are different in an important way: They involve knowledge, and sometimes intention, of substantial and unjustifiable risk likely to cause harm. We manage these behaviors best through system barrier design coupled with consistent punishment. But these behaviors are far less common than at-risk choices and human errors. At-risk choices are ever-present.

Punishing at-risk choices is sometimes impractical, or even impossible, because we may not know when they happen. As we've seen, punishing at-risk choices often diminishes our ability to see and understand them, and the response from the individual may be less than we had hoped.

Another reason we're compelled to react strongly when adverse outcomes happen in organizations is because we feel the pressure of external expectations. We believe that our customers or a regulator or the news media expect us to respond.

Remember the hospital story when the reporter asked whether the hospital fired the nurse? That's a common expectation because it may *feel* like we're holding people accountable, or at least trying to manage the risk. But the science of reliability teaches us a better strategy. Punishing human errors and at-risk choices when adverse outcomes happen is an instinct we must recognize and avoid.

There are two forms of outcome bias: when we overreact, primarily because the outcome is adverse, and when we *underreact* when nothing bad happens.

The sports world's "No harm, no foul" approach permeates our lives. It's why we speed when driving. It's why we don't always wash our hands according to CDC guidelines. It's why we cut corners throughout the day, believing nothing bad will happen to us. *No harm, no foul.* Then when the inevitable happens—there *is* harm—we overreact and cry foul.

We must be careful to see the full iceberg. The most dangerous form of outcome bias is underreacting when looking below the waterline. That's because positive outcomes happen much more often than adverse outcomes. The greatest risk we will see is when we don't react because nothing bad happened. In other words, we get positive outcomes with risky systems and behaviors, but we move on to our next priority without acting, wanting to believe that bad outcomes won't happen to us. "No harm, no foul" is a dangerous approach in our daily lives and can be catastrophic in organizations.

Outcome bias is only one of many biases that typically surface in organizations.[11] Many are individual biases, but groups of people can develop a consciousness, or collective awareness. It's important to understand how these biases influence an organization's behavior in responding to risk.

Professional bias: This bias often exists in organizations with strong hierarchies, or levels of power gradients. It happens in command-and-control organizations such as the military, or in businesses with strict reporting structures. It causes us to see and respond differently to individuals in different work groups or professions. For example, a hospital might respond differently to a physician who doesn't comply with hand hygiene protocols than it would to a nurse. Construction company officials might look at a CEO who doesn't follow safety rules at a job site differently than a laborer who does the same thing.

Professional bias can lead to perceptions of a "double standard." This bias is detrimental enough in individuals, but in organizations, it can spread virally into cultural perceptions that negatively influence the thinking of many people. Organizations with strong hierarchies often face strong challenges in overcoming this bias.

Fundamental attribution error, or bias: As we discussed earlier, this is our tendency to look at our own behaviors differently than how we look at others' behavior. With individuals, this thinking can prevent honest self-assessment of our at-risk choices and lead to diminished perceptions of risk resulting from our behaviors.

An example would be a race car driver who feels justified speeding on a city street, rationalizing that *I do this all the time on a racetrack, so why not here?* Or an airline pilot talking on a cell phone in heavy automobile traffic because it feels like flying a plane while communicating with air traffic control.

The fundamental attribution error is a very human bias that sometimes puts a higher value on our self-interests and behaviors than we do on people around us. When this bias creeps into an organization, entire groups of people turn a blind eye to risk, believing bad results won't happen to them.

Defensive attribution hypothesis: Related to the fundamental attribution error, this bias colors our perceptions when we witness or learn of mishaps that happen to someone else. When combined with outcome bias, we attribute more culpability to the people involved as the mishap's outcome becomes more severe, and as personal or situational similarity decreases.

In other words, when adverse events happen that involve people of political persuasion, skin color, or cultural mores that are different from ours, we often consider their behaviors more culpable than ours would be.

Again, when this becomes a group bias, it prevents an organization from accurately assessing risk.

Rule biases: There are two related biases toward rules, policies, and procedures in organizations: the **manager's rule bias** and the **employee's rule bias**. Managers can be biased toward rule compliance and tend to overvalue an employee's motivation to follow them. They often find themselves scratching their heads when employees don't follow the rules. In managing risk, managers often find comfort in knowing there's a set of guidelines they expect people to follow to keep them safe and live up to the organization's values and priorities.

The problem is humans don't reliably follow rules, policies, and procedures. And sometimes the more employees don't follow procedures, the greater the urge to escalate the penalties for noncompliance to "make an example" of someone and send a message to the entire workforce.

This thinking may make us *feel* like we're taking charge of the risks, but it's not supported by scientific evidence. Law enforcement studies have shown it's not the severity of punishment that has the greatest effect on our behaviors, but rather the likelihood of getting caught.[12]

Employees often show a reverse bias toward rules, policies, and procedures, tending to undervalue or not appreciate the risks involved in noncompliance. This thinking leads an employee to say, "My manager doesn't understand what it's like on the front line anymore. No one follows all the rules all the time." This mindset can be dangerous, especially when it leads to the next bias.

Normalization of deviance: This bias happens when groups of people drift into noncompliance that becomes accepted, or normal, behavior. It's why we typically speed on the road, rationalizing that everyone else is doing it, so it must be OK. Closely related to outcome bias, normalization of deviance reinforces the dangerous conclusion we often draw from at-risk choices: learning the wrong lesson when nothing bad happens.

Confirmation bias: This happens when we see, hear, or otherwise experience what we expect to see, hear, or experience. We tend to search for or interpret information or memories in a way that confirms our preconceptions. It could be a retail pharmacist asking a familiar customer his name and birth date as part of a required confirmation, not knowing he has an identical twin. The pharmacist "hears" the name she expects to hear, when in fact it's a new customer, the twin brother. Or it could be an airline pilot expecting to be cleared to land at a busy airport and responding to an air traffic controller's instruction intended for another plane. Or a physician marking a surgical site on a patient before an operation by asking, "We're operating today on your left knee, right?" and hearing what's expected to be heard.

Inattention or perceptual blindness: This is a common bias where we fail to notice an unexpected stimulus in our field of vision while we're focused on a task, distracted, or engaged in multiple activities. Returning to a familiar example, it's what happens when we don't remember our drive to work. Or a busy executive who can't recall what she had for lunch.

We find ourselves stuck in System 1 brain mode, thinking fast without stopping to assess our surroundings and situational awareness. Inattention blindness can happen in any setting in everyday life and can be deadly. In high-consequence industries, a moment's inattention can lead to catastrophic results.

Self-serving bias: This bias pops up when we react to positive and adverse outcomes. When good things happen, we tend to take credit for the desirable results. But when bad things happen, we may be loath to take responsibility for the undesirable ones.

Likability bias: How we respond to other people's behaviors sometimes depends on how much we like them. This bias can work negatively or positively. While this inherent bias may seem obvious, it's worth exploring how liking someone can influence our ability to respond to at-risk choices. An organization's managers must treat all employees with the same dignity and respect and respond fairly and consistently to workplace behaviors before mishaps happen.

Hindsight bias: We may think hindsight is 20/20, but it can be myopic when we focus only on apparent or immediate contributors. As we've discussed, it's common to have a bias toward behaviors after an event, not recognizing system or cultural contributors. Just as seeing and understanding risk is vital to managing risk before an accident, seeing the full picture of the causes afterward will determine our ability to manage the risk going forward.

Investigator's bias: This bias often influences people who investigate adverse events—and often includes managers and other members of organizations. Sometimes the more experienced an investigator, the more likely he may be to jump to a conclusion if he thinks he's seen something similar before. Or an investigator may be less inclined to make recommendations if those recommendations went unheeded in the past. This bias can alter our perception of the event and the recommendations resulting from our investigation.

Information bias: This happens when we look only at what appeals to us when seeking information. It may be a natural tendency to interpret data that confirms our expectations, much like confirmation bias.

Focusing effect: Like information bias, this happens when we drill down on only one specific aspect of a dataset and sometimes miss seeing the full picture in our analysis.

Normalcy bias: This is the tendency in all of us to want things to be normal. Sometimes we have a hard time accepting that bad things happen. It's true at the personal level and in organizations. We want to believe things are steady and solid. We're "wired" for normalcy, because it's the way we want things to be and because we may believe in the "power of positive thinking."[13]

While there may be many benefits to aspirational thoughts, the most effective way to see, understand, and manage risk is to anticipate when "normal risk" turns into risk beyond our tolerance. One way to guard against normalcy bias is to measure organizational risk using objective data, to the extent possible, but we must also guard against information bias and the focusing effect. Using indicators of increasing risk, or *precursors,* can counteract our human bias to believe everything is operating normally.

Bandwagon effect:[14] Humans tend to jump on board when groups of people engage in similar behaviors.[15] Sometimes, we rationalize that a group behavior is acceptable because we're "all in it together." Our System 2 critical thinking may give way to a System 1 acceptance. If people are waiting for the "walk" sign at a crosswalk and one person jaywalks, others are more likely to follow that risky behavior because someone else did it safely. By the way, whether people jaywalk is one attribute of culture.[16]

Understanding this bias not only helps us manage risk but also can help us create positive movements in our organization.

The Abilene paradox:[17] This story reveals how we sometimes "go along" with a group behavior without expressing concern or questioning the behavior's validity. The title comes from the Texas town, and the story is about an extended family sitting around on a hot summer weekend. They were bored, and the whole family—grandparents, parents, and children—decided to drive to Abilene, the nearest big city.

The drive was uncomfortable because the weather was hot and the car's air conditioner didn't work. The food in the restaurant wasn't as good as they'd expected. The whole family was miserable. So, they drove home, and the grandmother complained, "Who wanted to go? I never said I wanted to go anyway." Other family members said, "Well, Grandma, we went because we thought you wanted to go." They all went along with the idea of going, not knowing who really wanted to go. It turned out that no one really wanted to go.

Organizations have had adverse outcomes because groups of people in a work environment couldn't recognize how an unacceptable risk was normalized: a roofing company where workers ignore fall protection, or a police department where use of force becomes common during routine arrests.

That's the Abilene paradox—when individuals in a group come to accept risk without questioning. They often think to themselves, *This must be how it's supposed to be,* but don't ask aloud whether that's true. The Abilene paradox is a cautionary tale, warning us of the dangers of not speaking up when things don't look right or when we see an organizational risk.

JUSTICE WITH A PURPOSE

These biases are not the only biases influencing us at the individual and organizational levels. There is another bias that's important to recognize, because it can seep its way into our consciousness and invade our thinking process, for better or worse.

As a component of our culture, we develop *perceptions of justice* through our experiences that affect the way we think and act and have a powerful influence on our everyday performance. How? Consider our views on these authority figures in our lives:

- Our parents / custodians at home as we were growing up
- The teachers, coaches, principals, and professors when we were in school
- Our bosses and human resources department at work
- Law enforcement in our community
- The civil, contract, and criminal justice systems
- The Internal Revenue Service
- Our military service branches, commanding officers, and military systems of justice

Our direct experience influences our opinions and level of respect for the authority of these enforcers. If our experiences were positive, we're strong supporters of these individuals and institutions, as well as their authority. If our experiences were negative, or if we perceive unfair treatment, our respect for their authority diminishes and affects our behaviors.

Perceptions of justice, then, are crucial to the results we produce. Consider our discussion on punishment as a deterrent effect on behaviors. Punishing human errors and at-risk choices has a chilling effect on our ability to see and understand these behaviors. Similarly, the responses we get from people when we discipline them are often less than desirable.

Our motivation for ensuring and upholding justice in the home, school, workplace, and other organizations is twofold:

- Fair and equitable treatment is an intrinsic value supporting a basic human expectation.
- Justice improves individual response to factors influencing organizational performance.

Organizational justice is justice with a purpose—allowing us to manage risk more effectively while living up to our individual and organizational values.

Knowing that systems sometimes fail and that people don't always act as expected, we examine all the factors influencing organizational performance through the Sequence of Reliability. With the first step—seeing and understanding risk—in mind, *perceptions of risk and competing priorities* are the pivotal influences on organizational performance.

Is the picture coming into focus? The organizational results we produce, and thus our reliability, are a function of how well we manage the constantly changing influences on organizational performance over time. Our challenge is to see and understand these vulnerabilities and manage the risk. Our success depends on looking well below the waterline of adverse events and near misses that happened in the past and into the everyday socio-technical risks taking place today.

Seeing and understanding the present isn't enough. The highest form of reliability happens when organizations look to the future—predicting and quantifying risk ahead of catastrophe.

THE NASA SPACE SHUTTLE STORIES[18]

With the final return to Earth on July 21, 2011, NASA had flown 135 space shuttle missions, two of which ended in disaster.[19] The catastrophic failure rate over the life of the shuttle program was 1 in 67.5 missions. These offer lessons in organizational reliability.

Challenger: A Simple Demonstration

Richard Feynman was a member of the select team that investigated the *Challenger* space shuttle that exploded in midair in 1986. At the conclusion of its analysis, the investigation team announced its results at a news conference. In a famous demonstration, Feynman put a piece of shuttle rocket booster O-ring in a cup of ice water.[20] As you would expect with any elementary school science experiment, the piece of rubber contracted, demonstrating a lack of resilience. This was Feynman's elegantly simple explanation of what caused the accident.

Columbia: Culture or Complexity?

In a similar vein, NASA convened the Columbia Accident Investigation Board to investigate the destruction of the space shuttle *Columbia* during reentry on February 1, 2003. The panel determined that foam insulation broke off from the external fuel tank, forming debris that damaged the wing, causing the accident.[21]

They said the problem of "debris shedding" was well known but considered "acceptable" by NASA management. The panel also recommended changes to increase the safety of future shuttle flights. In its final analysis, the board concluded:

In Chapter 7, the Board presents its view that NASA's organizational culture had as much to do with this accident as foam did. By examining safety history, organizational theory, best business practices, and current safety failures, the report notes that only significant structural changes to NASA's organizational culture will enable it to succeed. This chapter measures the Shuttle Program's practices against this organizational context and finds them wanting. The Board concludes that NASA's current organization does not provide effective checks and balances, does not have an independent safety program, and has not demonstrated the characteristics of a learning organization. Chapter 7 provides recommendations for adjustments in organizational culture.

How did these system, human, and organizational risks escape the experienced engineers and leaders at NASA in both accidents? In a general sense, the answer is they didn't.

As an organization, NASA has long been a pioneer in socio-technical probabilistic risk assessments.[22] NASA conducted innumerable risk assessments and failure modes effects analyses and applied state-of-the-art techniques to evaluate the dynamic nature of the risks involved in human space flight. NASA knew about and even quantified many general and specific risks.

A NASA *Inspector General's Report*[23] published on July 1, 2002, a few months before the *Columbia* crash, revealed this:

The Space Shuttle is the only U.S. vehicle that can launch humans and payloads into space and safely return them from an Earth orbit. Since the Space Shuttle Challenger mishap [January 28, 1986] NASA has improved the safety of the Space Shuttle; the estimated risk of catastrophic failure during launch decreased from 1 in 78 missions in 1986 to 1 in 556 missions today. The continued safe operation of the Space Shuttle is a top priority and is essential in NASA's ability to support the assembly and operations of the International Space Station.

NASA recognized the risk involved in human space flight, even predicting an "improved" estimate of catastrophic failure. But the competing priorities of supporting the International Space Station while being good stewards of taxpayers' money undoubtedly pressured NASA as an organization. In space exploration, just as in everyday life, perceptions of risk and competing priorities often are pivotal influences on organizational performance.

We can examine all the factors contributing to the failures of these two missions through our model of factors influencing system, human, and organizational performance:[24]

Factors Influencing System Performance

- System design
- System degradation (O-rings and external foam insulation)
- Resource matching
- Environmental factors
- System capacity and operational load

Factors Influencing Human Performance (Engineers, Mission Control Specialists, NASA Leadership, Support Teams)

- System factors
- Culture
- Perceptions of risk and competing priorities
- Behaviors (choices and errors)

Factors Influencing Organizational Performance

- Leadership
- System performance
- Human performance
- Internal influences

- External influences
- Perceptions of risk and competing priorities

It's likely these factors did not contribute equally to the results, and their presence doesn't necessarily reflect poorly on NASA as an organization. All organizations will experience these influences at various times.

NASA was, and is, striving to be a *predictively*[25] *reliable* organization. It was working hard to predict where things might go wrong, not simply waiting for accidents to happen and learning from the failures. This is admirable, but easier said than done.

Investigative boards may criticize and the public will surely stand in judgment, but NASA was facing multiple competing priorities: political, economic, scientific, safety, and other imperatives leading to the decision to launch each mission. The only fair and accurate analysis of how well NASA performed must involve an apples-to-apples comparison with commensurate organizations facing the same competing priorities and removing hindsight and outcome biases. But at the time of these two catastrophes, which organizations could have provided this comparison?

Criticizing NASA's safety culture is an insufficient solution. There may be truth in how people in NASA generally viewed the risk in reporting perceived hazards, or in how leaders responded to available information about the technical risks of each mission. But pointing fingers and casting blame in this instance can be counterproductive. We should not expect tomorrow's challenges to be any easier than they've been in the past, and we must be careful to avoid the unintended consequences of our solutions.

The irony of the space shuttle catastrophes is that NASA was a pioneer in doing just that—becoming predictively reliable—and should serve as a model for us.

PREDICTIVE RELIABILITY

WHAT PREDICTIVE RELIABILITY MEANS

Successful business leaders see and understand risk, manage systems and people, and ensure organizational sustainment. But what if you could see beyond today's operations, market conditions, and economic climate? Are there clues hidden in the chaos, waiting to be discovered?

It's common to say that it's better to be proactive than reactive. Being proactive, however, requires more than guessing. There's a science to achieving it.

Organizations identify risk in many ways. The principal strategies below appear in increasing order of importance:

- Accident investigations and root-cause analyses
- Audits, surveys, making rounds, and inspections
- Customer and external reports
- Employee reporting systems
- Informal observations and experience
- Digital surveillance systems
- Predictive risk modeling and analysis

All of these have benefits, but let's assess the effectiveness/efficacy[1] and value of each strategy. Remember, it's the *totality* of the risks we're trying to manage that matters most. To do this, we must recognize this:

All methods of seeing and understanding risk have systematic limitations and are subject to human interpretation bias.

For example, plane crash investigations focus on a specific type of accident (such as wind shear–related crashes), but this may tell us nothing about other categories of plane crashes (such as controlled flight into terrain, midair collisions, or runway excursions and incursions) in the future. That doesn't mean we shouldn't investigate every fatal accident. We should. But we shouldn't expect more from these reactive responses than they can deliver.

Audits, surveys, rounding, and inspections can be effective strategies, but an audit or inspection is valid only for a specific time and place. If we can't see beyond what we observe during an audit or inspection, the information won't represent the risks below the waterline. So, we seek more information from external reports—from customers, regulators, or other sources.

Moving down this list gives us a clearer picture of the risks hidden in front of us. Employee reporting systems offer potential, but we shouldn't assume they provide complete visibility. Traditional employee reporting systems focus on thresholds above the waterline. You typically won't receive an employee report until something bad happens.

Near-miss reporting systems provide some visibility, but it's a mistake for organizations to overvalue them. Experience shows that humans don't reliably report near misses. This is generally true because of a *no harm, no foul* mindset, but also because employees are reluctant to do the following:

- Take time and effort to fill out and submit reports.
- Report when they have little confidence they'll get a meaningful response.
- Bring scrutiny, and possibly punishment, upon themselves and others.
- Be embarrassed if an investigation shows personal culpability.

There are positive reasons for employees to report risk, but we shouldn't expect these to outweigh the negative incentives without thoughtfully designing reporting systems and promoting a culture that encourages using them. In many industries, positive cultures and incentives inspire employees to report what otherwise is hidden from view. The Aviation Safety Action Program[2] (ASAP) and similar reporting programs have shown great value in seeing what's happening below the waterline.

But it took years for these programs to overcome a culture based on strict rule compliance without nuanced understanding of risk. Collaboration was the essential element of ASAP's success, aligning values and commitment to gain employee trust and confidence. The centerpiece of the program is a team committed to achieving unanimous consensus. The team is composed of representatives from the airline, regulator, and labor association(s).

In many places, we've turned to digital surveillance systems, which include devices such as body and security cameras. The airline industry led the way with sophisticated digital flight data–monitoring systems, providing trending data used for predictive analyses. These surveillance systems give us not only a snapshot of performance at a particular time, but also a picture of how the airplane is trending over an extended period. Aviation can infer, isolate, and improve system and human performance. Digital surveillance systems are powerful tools when applied and managed properly, helping us see and understand risk we couldn't identify otherwise.

Our goal is to develop as complete a picture as possible by combining the information gained from each strategy with that of complementary strategies. But we must recognize the limits of each. It's useful to keep the iceberg image in mind when considering strategies to identify risk. We rarely, if ever, have a complete picture of the risk below the surface.

But that shouldn't prevent us from investing resources in the best available *combination* of strategies. In a probabilistic world, perfection isn't in the cards. What matters is our ability to recognize our limitations, then make informed decisions about how to manage the known and predicted risks we encounter.

Predictive reliability means looking beyond what's happened in the past. Take the weather as an example. We wouldn't look at last month's weather patterns and assume next month will look the same. We wouldn't assume the weather next year—or decade, century, or millennium—will be the same as previous ones. We understand that as conditions change, so, too, does the weather.

By the same logic, all the strategies to identify risk we've examined on our list fall short of telling us about future performance—until we get to the last one: *predictive risk modeling and analysis.*

It's more challenging than looking at what's happened in the past and extrapolating to the future. Predictive risk modeling requires a synthesis of the hidden science and pulls together all the principles of reliability we've discussed: seeing and understanding risk, and managing system, human, and organizational reliability.

While Shakespeare may have been convinced that "what's past is prologue,"[3] in the hidden science of reliability, the future rarely, if ever, looks like the past.

But we can peer into the future to see what risks it may hold.

SIMPLE MODELS

The desire to explain the world using simple models is a powerful, if elusive, attraction. Early models in the field of organizational improvement were simple, such as describing accidents as "links in a chain."[4]

It's easy to visualize. But this is a dangerous oversimplification, leading us to believe all we must do is remove a link. But which one(s) do we remove, and in what order? There's often no rational basis for removing one link before or instead of another. And we rarely see them all.

In the 1990s, psychologist James Reason wrote two landmark books, *A Systems Approach to Organizational Error* (1995)[5] and *Managing the Risk of Organizational Accidents* (1997).[6] Safety professionals were enthralled, appreciating a theory explaining how accidents happen: the famous Swiss cheese model in figure 6.1.[7]

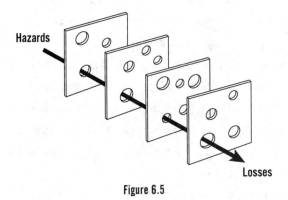

Figure 6.5

Reason's approach added a third dimension to the one-dimensional model. In his model, accidents are the result of latent failures and hazards in our system, like holes in Swiss cheese.

But if that's true, what's the solution? How do we prevent these undesirable outcomes? Do we just plug the holes and solve the problem?[8] Which holes do we plug first? All of them? Or, more accurately, all that we see? Slicing a bit deeper, the question becomes: Are latent hazards and conditions the result only of faulty systems? What role does human behavior play in this risk model?

PREDICTIVE RISK MODELING AND ANALYSIS

In the 1970s, concerns about nuclear power plant safety led scientists to adopt new approaches to identify and quantify risk.[9] Based on engineering principles used in building electrical circuits and mechanical devices, these engineers modeled system failures by designing "fault trees." These trees provide a picture of the ways things can go wrong, with multiple branches (known as cut-sets) leading to a top-level adverse event, or failure. Each branch provides mathematical estimates of fault rates that, when combined, yield probabilities and pathways to failure.

Think of the moving parts that make up your car: the engine, transmission, tires, headlights, seat warmers, and so on. Each part has a likelihood of not working, known as the mean time between failures.[10] Some components are critical to your car's reliability. When the engine fails or the car runs out of gas, or the charge runs out in an all-electric vehicle, the car won't run.

Sometimes a component, such as a headlight, fails and the car keeps running. But if the headlight fails at night, your ability to drive is diminished. If both headlights fail at night, you won't be able to drive safely. Generally, the combinations and probabilities are too much for our brains to comprehend without the aid of computers, but the general patterns are easy to grasp once the fault tree is complete.

So, too, with socio-technical systems. The problem is the mean time between failures for humans is much harder to predict than it is for electrical and mechanical parts. And since engineers don't think like normal humans, we need other experts, such as behavioral scientists, to help quantify and predict human behavior.

But the fault trees are illuminating.

Predictive risk modeling, like our ability to forecast the weather using computer models, gives us a clearer vision of risk than merely investigating adverse events. Yesterday's accident represents only one pathway out of hundreds of thousands (or possibly millions) of alternative pathways leading to most adverse events.

This approach starts by defining broad categories of adverse outcomes, then narrowing them to specific subcategories of risk. A few examples:

- A goal of preventing all vehicle traffic accidents is narrowed to managing the risk of accidents at a particular intersection or specific route, or accidents caused by a specific type of distraction such as cell phone use, or fatigue-related accidents.
- A hospital's goal of reducing adverse drug events—when patients get the wrong medication, or the right medication at the wrong time or by the wrong method—is focused on drugs incorrectly administered by infusion pump in the neonatal ICU.

- An airline's goal of reducing all plane crashes is narrowed to preventing crashes caused by pilot fatigue or distraction, a plane running off a runway, or a pilot flying a plane into the ground.
- A student's goal of improving her overall grade-point average focuses on raising her performance in Algebra II during the fall semester.

Doing this does not lower our expectations of improving in all areas of known risk. But before we assess where we should apply our resources using these methodologies to achieve the most success, we first must narrow our targets to show results. Then we start to build mathematical fault trees[11] by examining the ways bad things happen and assigning mathematical probabilities to the pathways that get us there.

Here's how it works. Let's say you hurt your back at work picking up something you dropped on the floor. The pain is excruciating, and you need medical treatment for a herniated disc that results in time away from work. An investigation reveals this:

- The way you reached down to pick up the object was ergonomically incorrect and put undue strain on your back muscles and discs.
- You committed a human error by dropping the object, which led to the act of reaching down.
- You dropped the object because you lost your balance.
- You lost your balance because you were wearing slick-soled dress shoes.
- You tripped because you stepped on a workplace hazard.
- You didn't see the workplace hazard because you were distracted by a coworker who needed help.
- The coworker asked for your help on an important project assigned by your boss.
- Your boss has a history of assigning last-minute projects.
- You have a history of being distracted.

- You have a history of poor posture.
- You have a history of not working out, leading to weaker core muscles and discs.
- The workplace is filled with tripping hazards.

All these contributed to hurting your back. But none of them, once addressed, is a magic bullet—a single solution to the problem of back injuries.

These contributors are more than links in a chain, however, and bear little resemblance to Swiss cheese. They are socio-technical interactions changing in real time. The good news is we can visualize and manage them.

In industrial accidents, the number of contributors expands exponentially beyond this simple exercise. The proportions—relative strengths and frequencies—of the contributors, and the cumulative effect of their combinations, can overwhelm even our System 2 brains. So, we must turn to mathematics.

The figures that follow are a better representation of adverse organizational events, illustrating a process called *socio-technical probabilistic risk assessment*. It's a method of building fault trees consisting of mathematical logic gates, or probabilistic pathways to specific classes of failures.

In these fault trees, there are two main types of gates (see figure 6.2).

Let's look at how these two types of failures combine in our back injury example. We'll start with the back injury and work our way downward to illustrate how we would build a fault tree.

Our top-level event (the back injury) starts with an AND gate (see figure 6.3), requiring two things to happen: First, you drop an object. Then you pick it up non-ergonomically. Remember, *both* must happen. Otherwise, your back feels just fine.

Here's how to estimate the probabilities involved:

- Probability of dropping an object in this situation = 1 in 100, which equals 1.00×10^{-2}, or .01, or 1 percent.
- Probability of using an ergonomically incorrect method of picking the object up = 1 in 2, which equals 5×10^{-1}, or 0.5, or 50 percent.

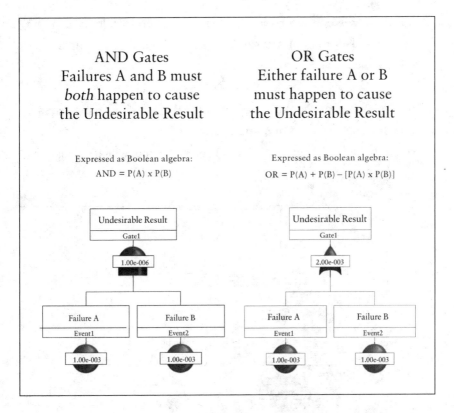

AND Gates
Failures A and B must *both* happen to cause the Undesirable Result

Expressed as Boolean algebra:
AND = P(A) x P(B)

Undesirable Result
Gate1
1.00e-006
Failure A — Event1 — 1.00e-003
Failure B — Event2 — 1.00e-003

OR Gates
Either failure A or B must happen to cause the Undesirable Result

Expressed as Boolean algebra:
OR = P(A) + P(B) − [P(A) x P(B)]

Undesirable Result
Gate1
2.00e-003
Failure A — Event1 — 1.00e-003
Failure B — Event2 — 1.00e-003

Figure 6.2

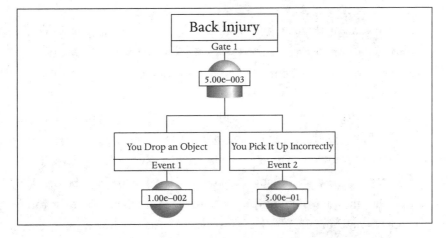

Back Injury
Gate 1
5.00e−003
You Drop an Object — Event 1 — 1.00e−002
You Pick It Up Incorrectly — Event 2 — 5.00e−01

Figure 6.3

But these were only "first-level" guesses. Our probability of dropping an object involves multiple possibilities (see figure 6.4), including (but not limited to) these two:

- Probability of slipping on a banana peel = 1 in 1,000, which equals 1.00×10^{-3}, or 0.001, or 0.1 percent.
- Probability of tripping on a briefcase = 1 in 100, which equals 1×10^{-2}, or 0.01, or 1 percent.

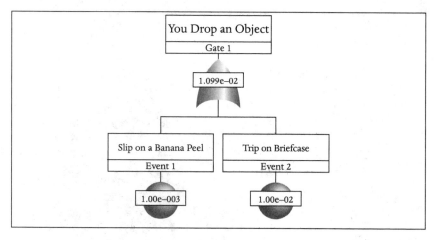

Figure 6.4

As you can see, there are many slipping and tripping hazards we could identify and estimate probabilities. So, we add more. Then, we adjust our estimates and improve them through focus group input and local experts familiar with the work environment.

Soon, the math becomes too difficult and we must use computer software to handle the calculations. Before long, our fault tree might grow into an elaborate forest of trees linked together by interdependent pathways to failure.

We start to see a quantifiable picture of risk we didn't have before. We realize that the way you hurt your back today is not likely to be the same way others may hurt their back tomorrow. Yesterday's adverse event represents only one pathway to another accident.

The result of this exercise is a picture of risk that highlights the *most likely* pathways to a specific type of accident. This gives us the opportunity to intervene in the most effective pathways—to plug the right holes—and manage the risk cost efficiently.

But this is not an exercise to conduct alone in a dark room. Fully seeing workplace hazards and understanding human behaviors requires collaboration. And because our human biases run deep, our best source of unfiltered information comes from those closest to the risk. To illustrate this exercise accurately, we would involve frontline workers to help us assess the environment more clearly.

In our example, the boss might not want to include the fact that last-minute assignments contributed to the distraction. Or the person who left the tripping hazard might not want to acknowledge his role in the event. But the combined picture we get from multiple perspectives is invaluable in our analysis.

In predictive risk modeling and analysis, our goal is to paint a picture as close to reality as we can, knowing that all models of risk are incomplete. But the pictures that emerge using these techniques never fail to bring clarity to our perspective.

In our back injury exercise, the pathways leading to this type of failure are local, meaning conditions will vary by location. But if we built additional fault trees in multiple locations, more patterns would emerge, showing commonalities in all locations. In this example, it's intuitive that wellness programs designed to strengthen core muscles and teach proper bending and lifting techniques would help prevent back injuries. Similarly, routine checks to remove hazards and coaching managers to assign projects sooner might help, too. But all these ideas stem from general observations and intuition, not science.

The power of predictive risk modeling and analysis is that often the fault trees show us something counterintuitive, a solution hiding in plain view. In some models, this approach works like magic, effectively eliminating accidents by providing a barrier at or near the top of the fault tree. We call these "capture opportunities," because they trap or capture the propagation of faults occurring in the lower portion of the tree. In other instances, the solutions lie lower in the tree, spread across several locations. These are harder to address because they occur with different people and systems in multiple environments. In all instances, probabilistic risk assessments paint a clearer picture of risk than we get from accident investigations alone.

The takeaways from this exercise are these:

- Our organizational data bank of adverse events and accidents—just like our data bank of personal experiences—falls far short of showing us all the risks. In some cases, they can be dangerously misleading, distracting us from other, more significant risks ahead.
- We must look beyond events—including our limited view of workplace hazards and behaviors—to see, understand, and manage risk more effectively.
- ASAP, and other similar voluntary safety reporting programs, are important in proactively identifying the "threats" that didn't result in "errors," and providing opportunities to address the risk before events occur. This is a new paradigm in safety and reliability.
- Probabilistic risk assessments—like forecasting the weather— require computational capability, combined with human experience and judgment.

Our goal is to build models of risk that give us the most complete picture, then make smart decisions about where to apply our limited resources. Developing this ability sounds complex, but it doesn't need to be. The key is to understand the limitations of traditional methods of managing risk— such as investigations, audits, and misleading models—and to invest in the capability of becoming predictively reliable.

It's simply a matter of applying the hidden science.

A TRAIN ACCIDENT STORY REVISITED

You may recall that after a Metrolink passenger train in Los Angeles crashed head-on into a Union Pacific cargo train on September 12, 2008, the National Transportation Safety Board discovered the engineer had been sending a text message while operating the train one minute and seven seconds before impact. Before we jump to the conclusion that this was simply a human-error accident, we should ask ourselves: Was this the only time this engineer had ever texted while operating a train? Was he the only engineer who had ever done it?

Records show[12] this engineer had texted several times in the past, but that raises more questions: What lesson was that engineer learning every time he texted and the train didn't crash? Was it the wrong lesson?

This is the simple challenge we have in managing at-risk choice. What you may not know about this accident is that it happened on a stretch of track where the engineer was supposed to stop at a signal. But, being distracted, he didn't stop. This was one of only two places in California where it was possible for trains to collide head-on. On all other tracks in the state except one, trains traveled only in one direction. If this track had been like that, the accident wouldn't have happened.

To examine the link between the behavior that led to this crash and a system that lacked resilience, let's use something we'll call a *contributory* map. This approach will show how we can become predictive.

Figure 6.5's elements are color-coded but are rendered here in black and white:

- Undesired outcomes: red
- System contributor: white
- Behavioral choices: orange
- Cause of the behavioral choice: yellow
- Human errors: green
- Cause of the human error: blue

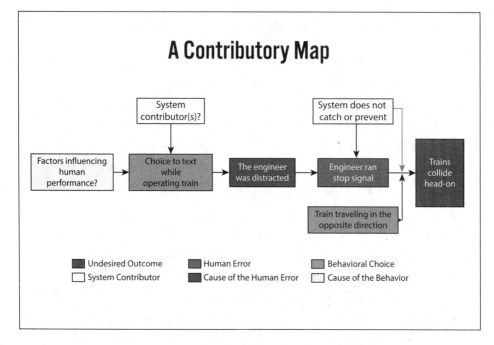

Figure 6.5

On the right side, you'll see the red block labeled "Trains collide head-on," which is the undesired outcome. Let's look at the connections between each block, moving *right to left*.

Next is "Engineer ran stop signal," colored green for human error. But before the human error is a behavioral choice: texting while operating the train. And before this behavioral choice may be several performance-shaping factors that influenced it, including, but not limited to, experience and the engineer's perception of risk, mistaken or otherwise.

At this point, let's examine some of the immediate contributors to this adverse event. It's easy to see the human error—running the stop signal—as a *direct* cause of the accident.

More important, the behavioral choice to text while operating the train was a *probabilistic* choice. That means texting while operating a train doesn't always cause human error but increases the likelihood of human error by distraction. Think about driving a car: We might text a thousand times or more before it leads to the running of a stoplight. We can run a stoplight lots of other ways, but texting is a primary cause of driver distraction.

This is where we must stop and assess ourselves and the limitations of all attempts to see and understand risk. As we've said:

All methods of seeing and understanding risk have systematic limitations and are subject to human interpretation bias.

It's important to remember there's something inside us that wants to concentrate on human behavior when things go wrong. As business leaders, parents, teachers, administrators, regulators, news media, lawyers, judges, and so on, we're tempted to focus exclusively on *holding people accountable* when accidents happen. We should, of course. But not to the exclusion of seeing and understanding the risk beyond the individual, or mistakenly thinking that correcting human behavior in one instance will guarantee success in the future with other human behaviors. With the Metrolink train accident, it would be a mistake to believe he was the only engineer who was texting while operating a train, or that a similar accident couldn't happen to other engineers.

If our primary purpose is to assess and hold people accountable for their human performance, focusing on the engineer's behavioral choices and errors fulfills that objective. But if our purpose is to fully see, understand, and manage the risk involved in this socio-technical activity, our investigation must look beyond human errors and choices and dive deeper into the interconnectedness of human *and* system performance. When we understand this as our goal, we can assess the engineer's behaviors in the *context* of the system in which they happened and have a greater chance of managing future socio-technical performance.

The engineer's behaviors—the behavioral choice to text and human error of running the stoplight—were consequential only because the system wasn't designed to catch or prevent the unintended result. The system— such as traffic recognition sensors, dispatchers, the stoplight, train pull-over space on the track—did not provide a sufficient barrier to stop the train in the event the human failed to perform as expected.

That doesn't make the railroad system a badly designed system, per se. It's just that, like people, systems evolve over time. When a system breaks, or fails to produce the results we intended, we measure the cost and may choose to redesign the system. In our everyday lives, we are surrounded with systems designed in much the same way. For example, a stove is a socio-technical system—a piece of hardware designed for cooking. But it relies on human input and activity. If a human turns up the gas burner and walks away, or leaves something flammable nearby, or doesn't see when a child is getting dangerously close, the stove itself can't be resilient, or prevent the potential harm from happening.

By contrast, many socio-technical systems in our world are improving, and we've discussed many examples: ground-fault circuit interrupters, one-way check valves in gas pumps, and overflow drains in bathtubs, to name just a few. All of these systems have improved over the years through engineering design. But for every socio-technical system with engineered resilience, there are many examples where the results we get still depend on human performance. In some cases, this may be by necessity; in other cases, it's because we didn't see and understand the risk fully and did not design resilience into the system.

In the case of the Metrolink train accident, we could add other elements of protection. Socio-technical contributors—texting, running the stop signal, the system not preventing the collision—are consequential only if another train is coming from the opposite direction at precisely the same time. This is why we describe the world as probabilistic. In most cases, the interconnected relationships between systems and people produce positive results, until variables change and disaster happens.

Records show the engineer had successfully operated trains his entire career despite choosing many times to engage in the risky behavior of texting while doing so. Did the management team at Metrolink know engineers were texting while operating trains?

The California Public Utilities Commission reported:

Some railroads—including Metrolink—prohibit operators from using cell phones on the job, but the commission's president, Michael R. Peevey, has said the rules are widely ignored.[13]

At the time of the accident, there was no federal regulation of cell phone use by railroad workers.

Can we see now what's meant by looking *below the waterline?*

Earlier, we examined a common pattern in accidents. Many adverse outcomes connect directly to human errors, which often connect probabilistically to behavioral choices. And with every behavioral choice, there are factors influencing human performance, such as experience, perception of risk, and many other potential contributors, including those originating in the system. Finally, systems that lack resilience will fail to catch or prevent the consequences of these combinations of human and system performance.

The contributory map we've presented is not a complete representation of the train crash. But it's useful to illustrate how socio-technical combinations contribute to adverse events. As we've seen, this is a common pattern.

With an eye to becoming predictively reliable, let's consider how we would respond to this crash. We'll start with how we likely would react after the accident, then consider how we would prevent future crashes.

The day after the accident, CNN reported a statement by Metrolink spokeswoman Denise Tyrrell. "It was human error," Tyrrell said, adding this was Metrolink's belief "barring any new information" from an investigation by the National Transportation Safety Board.[14]

So if the focus of our investigation began with human error, we would understandably try to put measures in place to prevent or manage the rate of human error. We might consider an intervention of some type. But to intervene, we would have to know when and where this activity happens, which requires more information than we would gather during our investigation into this crash alone.

Perhaps we could begin to monitor and try to reduce the amount of texting on trains with education or the threat of punishment. But remember, punishment as a deterrent works best when it's applied immediately and consistently. The challenge is to know when and where to apply it. We probably couldn't consistently identify and respond to cell phone use *every time* it occurred.

Alternatively, we could consider a device to block cell phone use. The downside would be that the blocker also would prevent operational and emergency calls unless we provided an override feature. You can see that trying this solution could work, but we'd have to be careful about causing unintended consequences.

We could go to great lengths to manage human performance, including education, threat of punishment, monitoring cell phone activity, and technological blockers. But by now we should have a sense that focusing on *only one* way in which the train might run a stop signal—because of cell phone distraction—might not prevent the other ways trains going in opposite directions can collide.

This reveals the limitations of relying on accident investigations to guide us in managing risk. In fairness to the professionals who conduct them, accident investigations often uncover many other organizational risks that may lie below the surface, but these insights are usually secondary to efforts to find and correct the probable cause of the event.

Our predictive approach would begin and end differently. We'd begin by asking: How many ways is it possible to run a stop signal and crash into a train coming from the other direction? There can be many answers, including the following:

- Engineer incapacitation (such as death, stroke, heart attack, sleeping, paralysis, debilitating intestinal pain, distractions, hallucinations, or alcohol- or drug-related impairment)
- Engineer distraction from causes other than cell phones (the possibilities are many)
- An engineer or hijacker intending to cause harm by running the signal
- A malfunctioning brake system

- A malfunctioning stop signal
- A weather-related event causing the train to run the signal

As you can see, focusing only on human performance limits our view and produces less-than-optimal results. Here's another way of framing the question that led us to this list: Do we fully see and understand the risk of a train running a stop signal and crashing? Continuing our reasoning, you can see how this list suggests other ways in which the train might crash differently from the one we examined, such as a train exceeding a track's speed limit, leading to a derailment.

The second step in our predictive analysis would be to examine system performance and reliability, how systems contribute to accidents, and how they fail to prevent accidents—lack of resilience. Our thinking shifts from how to control human behaviors first, to how to see the gaps in our systems that allow human performance to contribute to accidents.

Keep in mind that we are not expecting perfection, in system or human performance. This is what reliability scientists know: Perfectly reliable systems and people do not exist. But we can produce consistently better results by applying the hidden science.

Once we see several ways in which trains can collide by running a stop signal, we consider that at certain times trains traveled in opposite directions on this stretch of track. If trains were allowed to travel only in one direction, head-on collisions theoretically would not be possible, even though the engineer was texting.[15]

So far, we've discussed two possible solutions to the train crash, one during our reactive investigation that focused on managing human performance, and the other a system-based solution proposed during our predictive examination. Which of these two approaches and associated solutions will likely give us our greatest chance of success?

Well, if we could monitor and reduce, or even eliminate, all the human behaviors, we wouldn't have to look to the system for resilience. But that possibility is wishful thinking, at best. Preventing all engineers from using cell phones while operating a train with behavior management alone would be quite a challenge, if not impossible. (Just like getting drivers to remember to remove the gas pump nozzle from the car.) On the other hand, if we could apply a system solution, such as making the track one-directional, cell phone use would be inconsequential.

But system solutions often are cost-prohibitive. Converting all the tracks would cost a lot of money, no doubt. A cost-benefit analysis might convince us that the money to prevent this type of train crash is a good investment, but let's consider another system-based solution.

In the NTSB's final report,[16] finding No. 14 states:

> Had a fully implemented positive train control[17] system been in place on the Ventura Subdivision at the time of this accident, it would have intervened to stop Metrolink train 111 before the engineer could pass the red signal at Control Point Topanga, and the collision would not have occurred.

Positive train control is a system of sensors on board trains that's designed to stop them before an accident happens, such as a collision or a derailment caused by excessive speed.

So, here are the three solutions we've considered so far:

- Trying to monitor, reduce, or prevent engineers from texting while operating trains
- Converting the track to one direction
- Installing positive train control

Assessing these solutions and their effectiveness, we reach the following conclusions:

- Managing the human component alone gives us the lowest chance of success because of the number of people involved and the varying personal perceptions of risk and competing priorities.

- Applying a system barrier against texting could be effective but would prevent only accidents caused by cell phone–related distractions.
- Converting the track to one direction would be effective in preventing head-on collisions but would not prevent engine-to-caboose collisions.
- Positive train control would provide the most resilience where things could go wrong, likely preventing collisions of all types.

Once again, the hidden science reveals a pattern. Can you spot it?

UNCOVERING THE HIDDEN SCIENCE

Organizations often find themselves faced with tough questions about managing risk when catastrophes happen, and the decisions they make afterward are heavily influenced, or biased, by the severity of the outcome. Whether it's a business facing bankruptcy, a school system losing funding or certification, or a hospital responding to a wrong-site surgery, reacting to catastrophe after it happens is too late.

Long before things go wrong, we can apply traditional strategies of investigation, audit, reporting, and surveillance. But more important, we can apply the Sequence of Reliability by realizing the limits of traditional strategies and looking below the surface using predictive methods. In specific areas, predictive risk modeling and analysis strategies—such as socio-technical probabilistic risk assessments—provide superior solutions over traditional approaches. In all areas of risk, there's a trick to finding effective solutions.

When assessing risk and considering solutions, follow these steps in order:

1. Determine the probability that the recommended system design and human response strategies will effectively mitigate the risk.
2. Assess the operational effect on systems and human reliability to predict intended and unintended consequences.

3. If the corrective action plan is deemed effective and appropriate, provide operational and financial support for the design improvements.

A summary of how to gauge the strength of our solutions looks like figure 6.6.

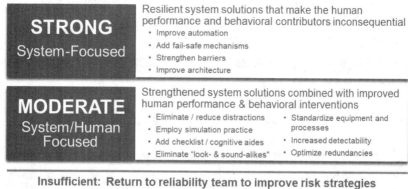

STRONG
System-Focused

Resilient system solutions that make the human performance and behavioral contributors inconsequential
- Improve automation
- Add fail-safe mechanisms
- Strengthen barriers
- Improve architecture

MODERATE
System/Human Focused

Strengthened system solutions combined with improved human performance & behavioral interventions
- Eliminate / reduce distractions
- Employ simulation practice
- Add checklist / cognitive aides
- Eliminate "look- & sound-alikes"
- Standardize equipment and processes
- Increased detectability
- Optimize redundancies

Insufficient: Return to reliability team to improve risk strategies

WEAK
Behavior-Focused

Behavior-focused attempts to manage risk solely through rule compliance, education, or the addition of procedural steps without strengthening systems
- Add documentation
- Train / educate
- Add double checks
- Reiterate warnings
- Add new procedures
- Change policies

Figure 6.6

The pattern is to look first to strong system-focused solutions. It may sound easy, but we must overcome our tendency to concentrate on human performance first. Human performance is important. But our ability to manage it increases significantly when we apply the hidden science in sequence.

Reliable organizations wrestle with managing risk, and the associated costs, long before tragedies happen. The shift from reactive to proactive response is more than a mindset; it's an investment in sustainable success. Your organization is likely very good at what it does—the reason you're in business. But staying in business—living up to your potential—also requires being good at what you never intend to do. This requires predictive reliability.

This approach works equally as well in our everyday lives, opening our eyes to ways we can make the world a less risky place now and for future generations.

A BIG TRUCKS STORY

In 2013, a gas and electric utility company operating a fleet of more than eight hundred large vehicles (bucket trucks, backhoes, tractors, and other service vehicles) needed help in solving a problem. Its drivers were backing into things. The rate of these accidents wasn't out of line with other businesses in their industry, but because the company operated such a large fleet, executives felt their risk exposure was higher than normal.

They installed various devices to help the drivers, including backup cameras, flat-panel and parabolic mirrors on each side, cross- and rear-view mirrors, and aural proximity sensors. They even added spotters to guide the trucks while drivers were backing up.

They trained their drivers and told them to follow procedures. As a reminder, they placed a sticker in the cab of each vehicle instructing the driver to *Look front, rear, and up as you back.*

But the drivers still backed into things. In one year alone, there were fourteen trucks-in-reverse accidents resulting in significant damage or injuries. The managers needed help. They called me to conduct a socio-technical probabilistic risk assessment.

The first thing I, along with my reliability team, did was to meet with executives, who were frustrated by the problem: "We don't understand how this keeps happening. We pay our drivers well. We give them the best equipment and training. They all have commercial driver's licenses. Why can't they be more careful and not back into things? How hard can it be? Why can't they be more *professional?*"

Before we started our analysis, we met with dozens of drivers, even going on ride-along trips to watch the drivers in action. We wanted to see and understand the risk we would model.

After the first day of observations, before we started building fault trees, we reported our first finding: The drivers *were* professionals—just not *driving* professionals. They were gas and electric experts, reliable in what they did once they arrived at a customer's residence or business. But when they went home at the end of a long workday, they didn't say to their loved ones, "Boy, I really drove safely today."

Their pride came not from how they drove; it came from what they did when they arrived at their job in the field. Driving a truck was just a means of getting them to the work they took pride in doing.

One day at the end of my last ride-along, as the driver was about to park the truck in the company parking lot, this exchange took place:

DRIVER: OK. Now I have to park in the lot, and the procedure requires me to back into the parking space. I need you to get out of the truck and guide me as I back in. Understand?

ME: I think so. But can we go over the hand signals so I know how to guide you? I'm not sure I remember them.

DRIVER (laughing): That's not necessary. You don't think I'm actually going to look at you, do you? I wouldn't trust you as far as I can throw you.

ME: What?

DRIVER: I just need you to stand there in case my boss looks out his window. I want him to know I'm following procedure, even though you and I know it makes no sense.

When our team had completed its observations, the company safety officer offered to show us the accident rate history for trucks in reverse, to give them an idea of the magnitude of the problem. I declined. The safety officer was perplexed. I explained that knowing the numbers wasn't important before the exercise. The reason was that their numbers were undoubtedly too low and might bias the analysis. Long before any driver reported a significant damage event, there would be several other minor collisions and near-misses they wouldn't report, because the damage wouldn't be noticeable.

To illustrate, we walked out to examine a few trucks. As everyone looked along the bumpers and side panels, each vehicle showed signs of minor collisions—with curbs, trees, concrete posts, and so on—none of which had been reported.

My point was that the fourteen reported events in the past year were merely the tip of the iceberg. If we focused too much on investigations of these events, we might miss the underlying system and human performance contributors leading to other collisions.

Then we started to model the risk. One of my employees sat down in a chair, pretending to drive a truck. He closed his eyes. He wasn't a professional driver, so he imagined he was backing his own car out of his garage. He thought to himself, *How can I run into something?*

He thought about all the ways he had come close, or nicked something while backing up in the past: being in a hurry, being distracted, or going too fast. Then he realized something.

In all cases he could imagine, the collision resulted from the car being in motion without his brain having precise knowledge of the car's location. *He would have to have the wrong mental picture in his head for the collision to happen.*

How does this happen? Our System 1 brains are wired for fast thinking. We move. We make decisions. We multitask, all while believing we're in a safe place. But we have an imprecise mental model in our heads.

We do this throughout the day—when driving, certainly, but also when performing other tasks. Our System 1 brains don't perceive time and space accurately all the time. We lack *situational and position awareness.* When we're distracted, or task-focused, or consumed with something we're trying to accomplish, secondary inputs can cause problems.

In the cockpit of commercial airplanes—at critical times during a flight—warning and cautionary alarms and lights are inhibited or repressed. This is known as "load shedding."[18] For example, on a low-visibility landing below a specific height, the warnings are blocked so as not to distract the pilots from the most important task—landing the airplane. They won't even know if there's a fire in the engine or elsewhere until the plane touches down. Why? Because focusing on too many things at once ensures none of them will be taken care of.

Then it hit me: I realized that a fault tree wasn't necessary. Instead, I came up with this:

> Our analysis shows sensory multitasking to be a common cause of vehicle-in-reverse accidents. Neurological studies have proven when humans attempt to perform multiple tasks simultaneously, the time it takes to complete the combined tasks while multitasking is generally twice as long as it takes to perform the total tasks in sequence, and the error rate increases by 50 percent for each task involved.[19] Consider the common driver sensory inputs in figure 6.7.

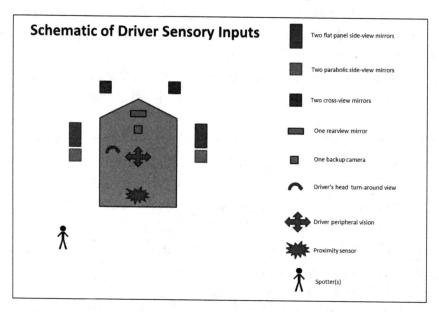

Figure 6.7

This model illustrates the mental state of mind present when a driver believes she has clearance but does not have precise visual, aural, or verbal confirmation of the location of the obstacle. In other words, the vehicle is in motion and the driver is distracted by *too many* sensory inputs.

The report described what happens when you're backing up a car or truck and looking at too many things at once. Say you start by looking at your left-hand mirror. But as you back up, you're now worried about what you might hit on the right-hand side. So, your brain decides to stop looking at the left-hand mirror and look at the right-hand mirror. But this doesn't happen instantaneously. Your eyes must disconnect from the left mirror, transition to the right mirror, then focus on what you're seeing and interpret it. This takes microseconds. But our brain believes it to be instantly when it's not. While this is happening, the vehicle is moving.

In your car, there might be up to six sensory inputs. But at this utility company, there were at least twelve sensory inputs competing for the drivers' attention in most trucks. And the procedure required them to *Look front, rear, and up as you back.*

We provided a table like this to illustrate normal and predicted driver error rates, based on the number of sensory inputs (see figure 6.8).

n = # of sensory inputs	Q = failure rate	Comment
1	0.0005	Estimated professional driver error rate
2	0.001	Target driver error rate post intervention
3	0.01	
4	0.02	
5	0.03125	Current estimated driver error rate
6	0.07	
7	0.1	
8	0.135	Distracted driver error rate
9	0.17	
10	0.2	
>10	0.5	Reliability team members' driver error rate when thinking about risk modeling

Figure 6.8

Our conclusion was this:

Focusing on a primary sensory target produces higher reliability (i.e., a lower error rate) than trying to visualize multiple targets simultaneously.

We then made a small number of recommendations based on our observations and analysis. But the main one was this:

KEY SYSTEM IMPROVEMENT

- Remove selected sensory inputs from the vehicles
- Provide a better system of backing up for employees
- Train to proficiency

KEY EMPLOYEE IMPROVEMENT

- Adopt a "Stop, Scan, then Primary" method of backing up
- Reduce "multitasking" while vehicle is in motion; Plan strategic stops

KEY ORGANIZATIONAL IMPROVEMENT

- Ensure the systems and training program continues for all employees, both new hire orientation and continuing proficiency training

---

When I reported our findings and recommendations to the company's executive team, a top operational leader took me aside: "Not many people know this, but I only have one eye. What you recommended is precisely what I try to do whenever I back my car out of the driveway at home. My daughter asked me why I do this, and I told her it's because I'm trying to compensate for my handicap. I suppose what you've suggested here is that this same approach works even better for those who have two eyes. Is that right?"

"Well, yes," I said. "But be careful. What appears intuitive to you now wasn't apparent to your organization yesterday."

The company accepted all the recommendations. The result?

Zero reported accidents the first year and two the second.

The problem wasn't eliminated, but the organization was on the path to sustainable reliability in this area of risk. They became predictively reliable—not through accident investigation or focusing on human performance.

They applied the hidden science, in sequence.

7

BIG CHALLENGES

In the last century, technological advances (i.e., systems) had a powerful impact on our lives. Similarly, individuals and organizations dramatically shaped our world. In the future, our capacity to preserve our planet, improve our health, and manage the dynamic, evolving global risks will likely be even more challenging than in the past. The Sequence of Reliability gives us a framework to meet those challenges.

WAR

Military history is littered with strategies gone awry. Malcolm Gladwell, in his book *David and Goliath,* offers fresh analysis on an old tale:

> Why has there been so much misunderstanding around that day in the Valley of Elah? On one level, the duel reveals the folly of our assumptions of power. The reason King Saul is skeptical of David's chances is that David is small and Goliath is large. Saul thinks of power in terms of physical might. He doesn't appreciate that power can come in other forms as well—in breaking rules, in substituting speed and surprise for strength. Saul is not alone in making this mistake.

Gladwell goes on to say this:

But there's a second, deeper issue here. Saul and the Israelites think they know who Goliath is. They size him up and jump to conclusions about what they think he is capable of. But they do not really SEE him.

He then explains that Goliath may have had a medical condition limiting his ability to see his opponent. And the result?

David came running toward Goliath, powered by courage and faith. Goliath was blind to his approach—and then he was down, too big and slow and blurry-eyed to comprehend the way the tables had been turned. All these years, we've been telling these kinds of stories wrong.

The extension of Gladwell's logic to the US involvements in Vietnam, Iraq, Afghanistan, and at the time of this book's writing, Russia's invasion of Ukraine, is irresistible.

In Vietnam, for example, the United States believed it could bomb the North Vietnamese into submission but underestimated their enemy's ability to mount sophisticated air defenses, rebuild infrastructure at night, and disperse troops and supplies underground. Not seeing and understanding these risks proved fatal for many.

Whether we're discussing conventional, cyber, or nuclear war, seeing and understanding the risks is the critical first step. Otherwise, no system (such as battle plans, training, and equipment) or human behavior (such as heroic acts of bravery) will win the war alone.

PEACE

By any measure, US government military spending consumes an enormous amount of national resources—in lives and money. Our best use of resources will always be reliable prevention. The benefits exceed any results achievable through war. Since the advent of nuclear weapons, sustainable peace is the only way of ensuring the future of life on our planet.

After World War II, the Allies prosecuted some German and Japanese individuals for war crimes and created the International Criminal Court.[1] But the primary strategy was a system-based approach to keeping peace, including establishing the United Nations in 1942, and economic and political plans for rebuilding the defeated nations devastated during the war. That's a big reason those two countries have been at peace with their neighbors, and the world, for the longest period in their modern histories.

Which illustrates an important point about preserving peace:

To prevent war, we must understand the influences on system, human, and national performance.

The change to figure 7.1 from earlier chapters is replacing "Organizational Reliability" with "National Reliability." But the ramifications for preventing war are significant.

Figure 7.1

Yes, punishment works as a deterrent, but only up to a point. Unfortunately, we often apply it only after the fact when it's too late. Predictive reliability allows us a better chance at preventing atrocities before they happen.

An example is the US reaction to the 9/11 terrorist attacks. The initial focus was on tracking down Osama Bin Laden and holding him accountable. But after his death, the challenges in fighting terrorism didn't go away; they merely shifted to other locations and individuals. Here, too, the ability to see and understand risk, followed by system-based interventions, is far more effective than the deterrent effect of punishment alone.

Since World War II, a buildup of the US nuclear arsenal has been a primary strategy for keeping peace. But what began as a unique show of strength, and the most powerful deterrent the world had ever known, soon became an existential threat to all civilizations.

A reliable peace process requires more than nuclear deterrence; we need a nuanced approach to identify and manage the cultural, socio-economic, and socio-technical influences on nations and other groups of people with the capacity to cause harm.

Consider the factors influencing organizational performance, adjusted now to a national level. Nations, like organizations, consist of both systems and people. Systems include government institutions (such as the three branches of the US government), regulatory agencies, voting systems, economic and currency systems, and so on. In other countries, these systems may look very different. We can group the factors influencing system performance for any nation into the categories listed in the diagram. As we've shown, these influences do not represent all the factors, but these major categories will always apply.

These factors will combine in various ways to influence the peace process, depending on the unique circumstances and history of each nation. Just as biology, environment, and experience play a cumulative role in our personal lives, these factors and their histories will play a combined role in national performance.

Perhaps the clearest example—and most challenging problem to solve— is peace in the Middle East. Home to the cradle of civilization, this region has experienced many of the world's oldest cultures and civilizations and has been in conflict since 3150 BC.

You might be wondering if we're going to propose a solution to the Mideast peace crisis here. A solution is undoubtedly beyond the scope and expertise of this book. But as with any complex problem, if we break it down into components, a clearer picture emerges.

Throughout Middle East history, and on all sides of the disputed territories, influences have shaped national performance and contributed to the crises. Understanding these forces, and the relative strengths and proportions, can help world leaders not only see and understand the risks, but also manage the results. There are patterns in the conflicts, and the hidden science gives us the opportunity to tame them.

The strengths and proportions of these influences will vary over time and location. The history of a country recently at war will have significant influence on the nation's collective perception of risk. As history has proved, these influences run deep. Stability today is no guarantee of peace tomorrow. We must focus on sustainable reliability in the peace process.

If we see and understand the factors influencing the risk of war for each nation, whether allies or adversaries, then the steps in our sequence of reliability provide potential for improved, more peaceful results.

The stakes are high. A sustainably reliable peace process offers one of the most beneficial returns on investment the world can expect to achieve. But there's another risk that poses an even greater threat to our long-term survival.

CLIMATE INSTABILITY

Humans have been researching climate change since at least 1895, when Swedish chemist Svante Arrhenius[2] discovered we could enhance the earth's greenhouse effect by making carbon dioxide, a greenhouse gas. He kicked off one hundred years of climate research that has given us a sophisticated understanding of global warming. But how much closer are we to minimizing the risks?

Reducing greenhouse gases will help protect our lives and livelihoods, and those of our children and grandchildren, from more powerful storms, hotter temperatures, flooded coastlines, and other effects of climate change. But global success depends on *how many of us* become reliable in managing this risk. Much like getting a COVID-19 or other vaccination, the more people who participate, the better our chances of protecting all of us. This requires seeing and understanding the risk at the individual, organizational, national, and international levels.

Meeting goals on reducing greenhouse emissions requires aligning individuals, businesses, regulators, and nations to common strategies and actions. This takes commitment and collaboration on a global scale, enjoining climate scientists, economists, politicians, legislators, regulators, business and association leaders, and citizens.

But if we expand our model from organizational to national to global performance, something interesting happens: A breakdown occurs. While we can examine nations as organizations, applying all the factors contained in our model, we cannot say the same for concerted global action.

Why? Because there is no current *system or organization* governing worldwide performance. Several multinational entities are bound together by treaties and common goals, of course, such as the United Nations, the World Health Organization, North Atlantic Treaty Organization, the World Bank, and others. But a single governing body overseeing the world's 195 countries does not exist. So how should we proceed?

The optimal approach to the challenge of global warming is an aligned multinational effort.

The rational path for the United States is to focus on optimizing our national performance and try to influence other nations and associations in positive ways. This approach should work both ways—other nations and associations must also influence us.

The scientific approach is to take the best of all the demonstrated solutions and first translate, then replicate, those results in various locations under differing conditions, cultures, and environments, measuring the combined effects. This is where our organizational performance model applies. Each nation approaches the challenge by marshaling systems and human performance–shaping factors, using our knowledge and experience in managing these to improve organizational performance at the national level.

Like many everyday risks, the fact that our results may not be optimal does not prevent us from applying the science with the information and resources we have on hand.

The book *Drawdown*,[3] edited by environmentalist Paul Hawken, modeled and ranked one hundred solutions to reverse global warming. One Earth[4] summarized the top ten:

1. Refrigerant management
2. Onshore wind turbines
3. Reduced food waste
4. Adoption of a plant-rich diet
5. Tropical forest restoration
6. Educating girls
7. Family planning
8. Solar farms
9. Silvopasture (combining trees, plants, and livestock)
10. Rooftop solar

On December 12, 2022, a new, revolutionary discovery jumped to the top of our list to reverse climate instability:[5] At Lawrence Livermore National Laboratory in California, the Department of Energy announced scientists had reproduced the power of the sun, a massive milestone that opens the door for the kind of fusion found in stars to one day power the world's homes, businesses, cars, and economies.

The holy grail behind this achievement came in the form of "net energy gain," the creation of a nuclear reaction that yielded more energy than what was needed to initiate the reaction. Livermore scientists did this by blasting a pencil eraser–sized capsule containing hydrogen with 192 lasers. That produced 50 percent more energy than the laser beams had delivered.

This has the potential to safely produce clean, renewable energy from water with a valuable by-product: helium. It could make petroleum-based energy sources a relic of the past. Now that physicists have demonstrated the breakthrough, it will be up to engineers, economists, business leaders, and politicians to bring this planet-altering solution to production.

None of these strategies is a silver bullet. But their combined effect has the power to improve our chances of survival. There are no guarantees in a probabilistic world. But if we do our best with the boundary conditions, recognize our limitations, and align our efforts in sequence, we improve our chances of survival. Our existence as a species depends on how well we apply a more sequenced, systematic approach to taming climate change.

And as in other areas of life, to ensure our survival is sustainable, we must pass along our reliability skills to the next generation.

PARENTING

We're all mentors and role models for the next generation, whether we have offspring or not. Through our actions and experiences, we leave behind a path for others to follow. Passing along the hidden science can help them.

Everything in life involves risk—from dangers during childbirth to sudden infant death syndrome to the multiple ways children can be hurt as they grow into adulthood. To parents, these challenges can seem overwhelming.

Our perspectives on child-rearing often change as we grow and reflect. Think back to the everyday risks you were exposed to as a child, and compare them to how we manage those risks today:

- Causes of sudden infant death syndrome
- Dangerous household contaminants, including paint, water supplies, cleaning products, building materials, and clothing
- Foods known to cause fatal allergic reactions
- Carcinogenic compounds and hormone disruptors in environmental and dietary products[6]
- Car accidents

To prevent harm from these risks, we must first recognize them. As our children grow into adulthood, every parent knows it's the risk we *don't see* that keeps us awake at night. There's comfort in seeing, and while we're watching them, we feel secure. But managing risk involves both seeing *and* understanding, which requires more than merely a watchful eye.

As children grow, we try to pass along our perceptions and strategies in managing risk. This is much harder than looking out for them ourselves. Our central challenge becomes this:

Mentoring children to see, understand, and manage risk on their own is a key indicator of parental success.

Because we can't always be with them, our greatest gift is to prepare them for life on their own, navigating their experiences. Preparing them for the future requires predictive reliability—the ability to anticipate the risks they'll face down the road.

We recognize multiple values and priorities will compete for our attention as parents, balancing our focus on our children's rights to life, liberty, and the pursuit of happiness. Our priorities with them include not only health and safety, but also compassion and respect; teamwork and collaboration; morality and spirituality; and instilling in them an appreciation for education and a strong work ethic, as just a few examples.

From prenatal care to adulthood, seeing and understanding risk is the crucial first step to parenting success. The subsequent steps in the sequence depend on the first step. Everything we do in the sequence improves when we get the first step correct.

When focusing on health and safety, much of the science often lies outside our personal expertise. But being aware of the most current recommendations from the CDC and other reputable organizations helps us see and understand risk beyond our direct personal experience.

What should we do when we see conflicting advice? We turn to the principles of the scientific method. Studies may contradict each other, leading us to scratch our heads. One reason for this is that variables will change from one experiment to another. Be careful not to confuse causation with correlation. Pay attention to the authors' recognition of these differences. Be mindful when studies are based on individual *perceptions*—often employed in surveys—rather than fact. Remember, too, that we all have biases, and they can alter how the authors perceive and report on findings.

One helpful strategy when trying to comprehend health-related studies is not to rely on only one source of information. Independent observations and conclusions improve our ability to effectively see and understand risk, which is crucial to the scientific method. This concept also applies in other areas of risk beyond health and safety.

Typically, a single measurement of reality—whether it's presented by the news media, a scientific study, or our personal experience—is rarely comprehensive. In many instances, the data will be insufficient to prove cause and effect. Independent verification is the system strategy of redundancy applied at the personal level.

From the moment of conception, we put our children in systems. The prenatal conditions in which they originate, the home where they live after birth, how we feed, clothe, and shelter them, the schools we choose for them, the cultural, political, and socio-economic environment around them throughout their lives, are all systems. Some of these systems are by design or our choosing, and some are beyond our direct control. All the influences on system performance apply in parenting. Putting our children in these systems requires insight and the ability to manage these systems, at least to the extent that the system affects human performance.

Take, for example, a child who is not meeting expectations for making passing grades in school. Rather than simply punish the outcome, our best strategy is to first see and understand the risks inherent in learning:

- Are there factors influencing the school's performance as a system?
- Does the child have the tools needed for human performance success?
- Does the child show signs of perception or learning disabilities?
- Is the child in an environment where we recognize the risks in not learning and can identify factors and influences that contribute to performance?

- Are we working with the teachers collaboratively to see and understand the risks, and applying systematic strategies to design the best approach for each child?

We start to realize the powerful influences that systems have on human performance, and work to manage our children by seeing these influences first, before focusing on human behavior.

After we've seen and understood the risks and thoroughly examined the system influences, we would appropriately turn our attention to the factors our child can control, where strategy *and* effort become critical. All the factors influencing human performance in our model apply: from knowledge, skills, abilities, and proficiencies at the appropriate grade level; to cultural influences (including peer pressures); to personal performance-shaping factors; to perceptions of risk and competing priorities. All these influences will combine and manifest themselves in our children's behaviors—the choices and the errors they will make. Understanding these influences, their strengths and proportions, will allow us to parent our children more effectively, guiding them to their best chance at success.

Every parent knows, of course, that perfection is only an aspirational goal. But we try to design and manage systems that allow our children to thrive in the environments we put them in. We can best guide and manage human reliability when we see that academic results are a mutually dependent, or symbiotic, combination of systems and human performance.

The last step in our sequence is devoted to sustainment, at the individual and group (family) level. For people with multiple children or extended families, it's easy to recognize parenting can be a trial-and-error approach to managing risk, with each child providing a feedback loop on how we're doing. We recognize that each child is a unique combination of biology, environment, and experiences, of course, and we learn that what worked well for one child might not work well for another child.

But the *sequence* matters. If we look at each child as unique, we undoubtedly will see and understand their risks differently than we do for others.

Although different children may live in the same system or family environment, the way they respond to these influences will vary.

Within groups—families, schools, and other organizations—applying the hidden science yields consistently better results. Guiding our children along this sequence at an early age helps prepare them for success in other areas of their lives.

SURVIVING A DANGEROUS WORLD

We live in a dangerous world. Many of the things you and I do in our everyday lives—fly in an airplane, get treated at a hospital, or drive a vehicle, for example—come with inherent risks. The pilot could misinterpret a cockpit warning signal, the nurse could give the wrong dose of medication, or we could back our car into a fire hydrant. There are also global risks we didn't anticipate, such as the COVID-19 pandemic. And who knows what else lies ahead as our world becomes more complex?

But rather than labeling unexpected events as Black Swans or lying low because the gods must be crazy, there's a better way to see, understand, and interact with the world around us. We can manage our limited resources—governmental, organizational, and personal—to achieve optimal outcomes.

Predictive science suffers from an age-old dilemma: How do you prove you prevented the accident that didn't happen? By applying the Sequence of Reliability, then documenting, measuring, and monitoring to produce scientific results. Let's turn our attention back to aviation to learn how an entire industry went from waiting for accidents to happen to the proactive management of risk. We'll then show how any business or organization can achieve similar results by applying these principles.

FLIPPING THE ICEBERG

AFTER FLIGHT 191

I came to aviation by way of my father, who was an airline pilot. A former Army Ranger, he learned how to fly on the benefits of the G.I. Bill after his service in World War II and the Korean War. He told me that before the wars, as a farm boy in Texas, he used to look up at the sky and imagine himself flying like a bird, free of the constraints of a sharecropper's life. After he left the service, becoming an airline pilot was the fulfillment of a lifetime dream.

Looking up to my father as I grew up, I imagined he might have some wisdom to impart to me about what it's like to soar above the clouds and "reach out and touch the face of God," as the poem goes.[1]

One day when I was twelve years old, my father came home from a flight in his captain's uniform, and I asked him if I could take flying lessons. His response: "Son, never forget that an airplane is nothing more than a piece of machinery waiting for a chance to kill you."

So much for the romance of flight, I thought. The next day, I asked him again. This time, he told me to wait while he left the room. When he returned, he was carrying a stack of NTSB accident reports. "Read these, and we'll talk about it again when you turn sixteen," he said.

For the next four years, I read each NTSB report my father gave me— scores of reports he received in the mail. I found each one fascinating, but time after time, the conclusions left me with more questions than answers.

I didn't understand the board's focus on "probable cause," which seemed to me an arbitrary selection from multiple contributors. If accidents are "links in a chain," I asked, "why do we always seem to focus on the last link?"

My personal path to uncover the hidden science began in earnest shortly after witnessing Fight 191's fatal crash. By coincidence, I discovered a few days later that the captain of Flight 191, Edward Connors, was a friend and classmate of my father's during their primary aviation training. My search became personal.

When the details of the flight became public and it became apparent that a weather-related phenomenon—wind shear—contributed to the crash, I reached out to my former graduate professor Dr. George Kattawar,[2] in Texas A&M University's physics department. I had an idea. It seemed logical that our work in light absorption and scattering[3] might be helpful in predicting wind shear. He agreed.

The next step was to request a leave of absence from my employer, American Airlines. They also agreed. It wasn't long before I headed to Boulder, Colorado, to meet with Dr. Sammy Henderson, a brilliant Texas A&M alumnus who had recently completed his physics PhD dissertation. He was working at Coherent Technologies, Inc., in Boulder. Dr. Henderson introduced me to the company's founder and president, Milton Huffaker.

Huffaker was a modern renaissance scientist: quirky, perpetually disheveled, and consumed by the intellectual pursuit of science. And he was convinced there was a business opportunity. Huffaker, along with Dr. Henderson and Dr. Michael Kavaya, had recently won a small-business grant cosponsored by NASA and the FAA to study atmospheric phenomena. Their vision was to advance the practical applications of laser radar—known as lidar, the acronym for light detection and ranging.[4] Through our work as a public-private partnership, Coherent Technologies taught me the importance of science and business contributing to good government.

Soon I was working with Huffaker, Dr. Henderson, and Dr. Kavaya to design and build a prototype airborne lidar wind shear–detection system. My role was to model and optimize design specifications to measure invisible wind.

Here's how it works: A pulsed laser beam is shot into the atmosphere ahead of the plane, colliding with tiny aerosol particles. The beam scatters and refracts off these particles, and a small portion bounces back directly to the plane. The frequency of the beam that bounces back is wave-shifted—something called the Doppler effect[5]—and from that wave shift, the radial velocity of the particles can be determined. Because these particles are riding on the wind, we now know the wind's velocity relative to the plane.[6]

The key advantage this system had over existing radar equipment was that it could measure wind, not just rain and other forms of precipitation. This means pilots could now see dangerous winds and take avoidance and recovery action. Our lidar system was the first truly *predictive* wind shear–detection system for airborne applications.

Over the next eighteen months, several leading experts—giants in their fields[7]—were kind enough to contribute to the project, which I used to complete my master's thesis. Among them was Dr. Theodore Fujita, the renowned severe storms researcher widely known as the father of the Fujita Scale, or F-scale.[8] An enhanced version of this scale is still used today to designate the rotational strength of severe storms. Dr. Fujita surmised there was evidence of a microburst—an intense downward wind shear—in the Flight 191 crash.

This information became our primary design specification. We developed our airborne lidar to measure the presence of microbursts ahead of the aircraft. The system works in dry and wet conditions.

Aviation is a socio-technical endeavor, and pilot training and technology go hand in hand. Through this experience, I learned the importance of integrating system and human performance. Wind shear prediction and detection systems are valuable tools, but optimal results required human involvement. Our goal was to improve both system and pilot performance.

The results of the NTSB investigation of Flight 191 and our combined research and development efforts led to an overhaul of how the aviation industry detected and responded to microburst wind shears. Later, after a successful space shuttle test of our lidar system, the applications for lidar technologies continued to evolve. Today, lidar is indispensable in detecting wind shears[9] caused by weather and by airplanes' wakes at airports around the world. It's also used in obstruction surveys[10] to make sure the glide path is clear for airplanes to land. Lidar systems are growing in other areas, such as integral components of autonomous vehicles.[11]

THE ASAP STORY

Flight 191 became a central metaphor propelling my career. When I returned from my leave of absence to my job as a pilot at American Airlines, I became involved in professional flight safety activities. The Allied Pilots Association appointed me to the National Safety Committee, which I eventually chaired.

In 1994, American Airlines' chief operating officer, Bob Baker, and vice president of flight, Captain Cecil Ewell,[12] invited me to become managing director of flight safety. I accepted. My role grew into managing director of corporate safety and quality evaluations. Historically, the American Airlines safety department's primary function was to investigate accidents and conduct regulatory compliance audits. Although I recognized these were required functions, my objective was to shift the airline industry's priorities to the collection of accident *precursor* information.

The Flight 191 crash stuck in my mind. I wanted to see and understand the risk ahead in all areas, not just react to it.

During these years of safety advocacy, the founding director of the NASA Aviation Safety Reporting System[13] (ASRS), Bill Reynard, invited me to become a member of its board of governors.[14] This NASA program, a landmark safety program, was established in 1976 as a safe-haven national reporting system for pilots, dispatchers, mechanics, and air traffic controllers. They called it a safe haven because aviation professionals didn't trust the regulator—people feared losing their licenses through punitive action. The reporting system was designed to shield the reports from the regulator responsible for overseeing aviation safety.

I thought this posed a problem.

So, one day during a board of governors meeting at NASA Ames Research Center, as I was sitting alongside former FAA administrators and other aviation notables, I asked a simple question: "What percentage of the risks in the national airspace system do we believe is reported under the ASRS?"

The silence made me uncomfortable. *Did I say something wrong? What if they kick me off the board for asking dumb questions?*

Then Donald Engen,[15] a former FAA administrator, turned to me and said, "That's a great question. The obvious answer is it must be quite low. But it begs a better question: What should we do about it?"

"I think we have two challenges," I said. "First, the number of reports the ASRS receives must be a small fraction of the everyday risks in the system. Our second problem is that the ASRS is a *research* organization, not a fix-it organization. I propose that we create a new program where aviation professionals report into a partnership committee involving the FAA, the airline, and the labor association. If we can develop trust in this committee, people will report more, and we just might have a chance to fix the problems identified."

Engen spoke again: "You do realize the FAA has legal enforcement-related authority over those airmen who would report and the airlines they work for, don't you? And you want the FAA to be a part of this committee?"

"Yes, sir," I said.

"You may be onto something," was his unexpected reply.

Shortly after this meeting, I found myself in FAA administrator David R. Hinson's[16] office at their Washington, DC, headquarters. I proposed a new confidential reporting system I called ASAP, or Aviation Safety Action Program.[17] The administrator was interested but questioned whether the airlines and labor associations would agree to participate. We both knew that pilots, mechanics, and dispatchers would never agree to turn in reports—much less admit mistakes—if the program were run by the FAA. Civil penalty actions—that is, fines and license suspensions—were too great a risk for individuals to report directly to the regulator. The airlines, too, were not likely to support employees identifying instances of regulatory noncompliance, which would expose the airline to fines and suspensions as well.

There were precedents, though they seemed like long shots. First, the NASA ASRS had proven that licensed professionals would report when the right incentives were in place. The most powerful incentive was in *not* losing their license. In other words, the guarantee of protecting a reporter's livelihood and reputation outweighed all other considerations. A report would offer the benefit of not having to undergo the nerve-wracking investigative process of FAA legal enforcement. This exchange—a candid and complete disclosure in return for the waiver of sanction against the airman if they were found to have violated a regulation—was priceless. For the first time, the industry was getting a peek below the surface, though the full extent of the iceberg remained mostly hidden.

While the ASRS collected information that likely would never have been disclosed otherwise, the problem was that, as a research organization, the program did very little to achieve corrective and preventative actions. But ASAP would be different, focusing on getting to the heart of the reported risk and managing it in a collaborative fashion.

So, I made two additional visits while I was in Washington, DC, one to the Air Line Pilots Association, the nation's largest pilot union, and the other to the Air Transport Association,[18] the trade group for the major airlines in North America.

Interestingly, the response from each was similar: "This sounds too logical," the union president, Captain Randolph Babbitt, said. "Do you think the FAA and ATA will buy it?"

Later that afternoon, Al Prest, vice president of operations at the trade association, said, "This makes perfect sense. But will the FAA and ALPA buy it?"

However, it didn't take long for the attorneys to get involved. The next week, Administrator Hinson phoned to invite me back to DC. "The FAA chief counsel and the inspector general at the Department of Transportation would like a word with you," he said. "Don't worry," he continued, "stick to your guns. There's nothing else like this on the horizon. Lawyers serve an important purpose here in government, as they do in business. But these folks don't know how to keep planes from crashing. Your program will do exactly that."

Our meeting began. The attorneys stated their position up front: The FAA would not compromise their statutory authority to enforce the regulations, as I expected. The most vital element of the program was the triadic Event Review Committee, composed of labor, airline management, and the FAA, requiring a *unanimous* consensus—not just a *majority* consensus.

Authorizing a program like I was proposing was fine, they said, so long as the FAA remained above the process and reserved the right to overrule the consensus of the Triad committee. They argued that requiring a unanimous consensus wasn't possible under FAA regulations.

I knew this would kill the program before it ever got off the ground. I swallowed hard. I had no legal background and wasn't prepared to debate them on the regulations. But I had been an English major in college and had years of experience investigating plane crashes. I had only one card to play.

"Oh, really?" I replied. "Then help me understand this." I pulled out a large book of federal statutes, marked with a yellow Post-it Note on the relevant page:

> The FAA has broad authority to regulate under 49 U.S.C. 44701. In particular, section 44701(a) grants the FAA authority to prescribe regulations and minimum standards in the interest of safety. Subsection (c) grants the Administrator the authority to regulate "in a way that best tends to reduce or eliminate the possibility or recurrence of accidents in air transportation."

I continued. "If this program can demonstrate a more effective way to prevent accidents, wouldn't the FAA be seen as negligent in not supporting it, as designed?"

The attorneys called for a break in our meeting. When they returned, they offered exactly what I had hoped: an eighteen-month Demonstration Program authorization to prove our assertion.

On June 1, 1994, the American Airlines Aviation Safety Action Partnership program was established as a collaborative endeavor between the FAA, American Airlines, and the Allied Pilots Association. It took not one, but two, eighteen-month demonstration periods to convince the FAA and DOT legal counsels of its validity. But by the end of 1997, the FAA agreed to formalize its commitment by developing an Advisory Circular as guidance for other airline programs.

In 1998, the FAA established an Aviation Rulemaking Committee (ARC) and appointed me as the industry chairman. Pulling together leaders from the airlines, labor associations, and the FAA, the committee expanded ASAP to include other work groups beyond pilots: aircraft mechanics and technicians, air traffic controllers, dispatchers, flight attendants, and eventually ground workers responsible for loading and unloading the planes. Any professional contributing to the operation of an aircraft would become eligible.

It's worth noting that prior to ASAP, pilots and other licensed aviation professionals reported at a modest rate. In fact, it's been said many times that pilots reported only what they could not hide. Why? Because they were fearful of the FAA. Routine inspections, known as line checks, could cost an individual their livelihood. If an air traffic controller reported noncompliance with an altitude or heading assignment, a two-year investigation could follow, resulting in a series of sleepless nights and license suspension or, worse, revocation.

Similarly, airline employees were reluctant to report mistakes and errors to management. After all, who in their right mind would voluntarily report risk where blame could be assigned, resulting in punishment? It would be like flagging down a police officer to let them know you had been speeding just minutes before you passed their squad car while observing the speed limit.

But all this changed. Before the first ASAP program began, the parties negotiated a detailed letter of agreement specifying the rules and conditions of participation. Criteria for acceptance, exclusion, and completion of satisfactory corrective and preventative actions were required to be in

place. Rigorous adherence to the terms and conditions of program operation were necessary to gain acceptance and participation. Standardization
was key to success. Each program required training, standardization, and
independent review and audit by the FAA every two years.

Critics called ASAP a "get-out-of-jail-free" card, a derisive reference to
the Monopoly game. But the critics couldn't argue with the program's success. Once the programs became formalized, the floodgates opened, and
aviation professionals reported at exponentially higher rates than before.

Much has been written about ASAP and the positive effect it's had on
aviation safety. Perhaps most important, it's a visible demonstration of the
power of collaboration. ASAP exceeded the earlier results of the ASRS by
providing collaborative solutions to identified risk, not just collecting data.
ASAP became a hallmark success because of the combined commitment of
the airlines, the regulator, and the labor associations. All three were necessary in building trust to make it safe for professionals to report. This trust is
the reason ASAP provides a clearer picture of the risk below the waterline
than existed previously.

In 2000, Sandia National Laboratories conducted an independent review
of ASAP, and concluded in a final report:

> With the Aviation Safety Action Programs (ASAP), the Federal
> Aviation Administration (FAA) is developing a nonpunitive collab-
> orative approach that supplements traditional regulatory actions. An
> ASAP team is a triad composed of air carrier (corporate), pilot asso-
> ciation (union), and FAA (regulatory) personnel who meet to review,
> discuss, and analyze event reports submitted voluntarily by flight per-
> sonnel. The team is required to reach unanimous consensus on the
> event report and the corrective actions to be taken. Our analysis sug-
> gests they do so through a hierarchy of shared values, a working buffer
> to exclude distractions, and sideband communications that build trust.
>
> ASAP appears to be a highly effective cultural mechanism for
> identifying novel and subtle hazards, and designing rapid, mutually
> acceptable corrective actions.

ASAP is an important and promising demonstration of FAA leadership and its willingness to work collaboratively with industry for the public good.[19]

In the years following the industry-wide adoption of ASAP, something astonishing happened: A picture began to emerge below the waterline, making accidents look less mysterious than before. The industry began identifying precursors, those everyday warning signs that eventually lead to adverse events. We learned about pilots falling asleep on long, late-night flights. We saw instances of confusion and distraction caused by automation; risky choices induced by competing operational pressures; rushing to make altitude assignments and airport curfews; and hundreds of thousands of other conditions and risks pilots dared not report otherwise.

The industry was taking the first steps to becoming *predictive*.

AVIATION'S DRAMATIC IMPROVEMENT

The lessons learned from the US aviation industry's astonishing safety improvements over the past several decades have advanced reliability science. Applying those lessons to other industries and our daily lives can achieve dramatic results, too.

The advent of the jet age in the late 1950s marked the beginning of a precipitous drop in the number of fatal plane crashes per year—from approximately thirty in 1959 to a reduction of almost half in just a few short years.

Coincidentally, in 1958 Congress authorized reorganization of US aviation oversight. The previous regulatory agency, the Civil Aeronautics Board, gave way to the Federal Aviation Agency, later renamed the Federal Aviation Administration,[20] setting up an enforcement-focused approach to protecting the public. In 1967, Congress consolidated all transportation agencies into a new Department of Transportation and established the National Transportation Safety Board as an independent agency within the department.[21] In 1974, Congress reestablished the NTSB as a separate entity, outside Transportation, reasoning that "No federal agency can properly perform such [investigatory] functions unless it is totally separate and independent from any other . . . agency of the United States."

The FAA and NTSB continue to serve different functions, with separate roles and responsibilities and distinct lines of reporting. The FAA oversees air commerce and is responsible for licensing, certification, and regulatory oversight. It reports to the Department of Transportation. The NTSB investigates transportation mishaps and recommends safety improvements to the FAA and Congress. It reports to Congress. The effect on reliability is this: One agency oversees the business of and the public's access to aviation, the industry's *effectiveness*. The other responds when things go wrong and recommends how to improve *resilience*.

The two agencies were not solely responsible for the dramatic reduction in US aviation deaths. It takes time for regulatory agencies to hit their stride, and measuring success typically takes decades, not years. So, what caused such significant improvement in reliability?

The initial cause of the big drop in fatal aviation accidents from the early 1960s to today was the widespread adoption of the jet engine to replace reciprocating engines, aviation experts agree. Fewer moving parts led to greater reliability, which led to fewer crashes caused by engine failure.

But there were other contributors causing fewer accidents. Here's a list of key improvements:

- Transition to jet engines
- Use of simulators
- Ground Proximity Warning Systems
- Presidential Commission on Two-Pilot Aircraft
- Crew Resource Management
- Extended Range Operations (ETOPS)
- Traffic Collision Avoidance Systems (TCAS)
- NASA Aviation Safety Reporting System (ASRS)
- Air Carrier Voluntary Disclosure
- Flight Operations Quality Assurance (FOQA)
- Aviation Safety Action Program (ASAP)

- Air Transportation Oversight System (ATOS)
- Safety Management Systems

Technological advances generated more system improvements. Advanced use of simulation in pilot training, ground proximity warning systems, weather radar, inertial guidance, and, later, global positioning systems and traffic collision warning systems all added layers of reliability. But as these systems were adopted, the fatal accident rate began to improve more slowly because technological improvements were becoming harder to find.[22]

In that partial list of improvements, you may have noticed that only one is tied to human performance: simulator training. For the first time, pilots could see risks—and train to manage them—in a safe environment. They could practice emergencies, make mistakes, and get feedback without the danger of crashing a plane, which improved pilot performance.

Even with the big increases in aviation system reliability, accidents still happened. Why? One reason is that humans were still involved, and improving human performance was a bit more complicated than issuing a software update or replacing hardware. Rewiring the human brain to manage an increasingly automated cockpit is no easy task. So behavioral psychologists were brought in to help improve pilot performance.

United Airlines was the first airline to provide crew resource management, known as CRM, for its cockpit crews in 1981.[23] For the first time, pilots were trained to understand the interactions between crew members, and strategies were adopted to help them better manage advancing cockpit automation. The FAA later mandated periodic CRM training for every licensed commercial pilot.

But what's little known is this: *The first classes were utter failures.* Senior pilots stood up and walked out of the room.[24] Why? Because the initial classes were taught by psychologists, not pilots. The perception was that the classes were too "touchy-feely." CRM was a big advancement in effective communication and crew reliability, sure. But at first, pilots didn't see and understand it. In a classroom setting, pilots couldn't tie the subject matter to their real-world experiences.

But over time, CRM classes evolved from a focus on "getting along" to the stark realities of how to prevent fatal plane crashes. The content and method of teaching became a better way to see and understand risk in a safe environment. By the 1990s, CRM had become a global standard.[25]

Yet accidents still happened, and the NTSB continued to cite "human error" as the most frequent probable cause in fatal crashes.

ZERO ACCIDENTS?

From January 9–10, 1995, after public concern over seven fatal commercial airplane accidents claiming 264 lives the previous year, more than a thousand industry, government, and union aviation officials met in Washington, DC. Never had these aviation industry officials gathered in one place. Their objective? To assure travelers that US airlines were safe to fly. Secretary of Transportation Federico Peña, FAA Administrator David Hinson, and NTSB Chairman James Hall led a clarion call to action. In the words of Secretary Peña, "The industry must make it clear to the public we will not settle for anything less than zero accidents."

Senior industry leaders from all sectors, including manufacturing, labor, airlines, air traffic control, and regulators, looked at each other in disbelief. Was Peña setting a realistic goal? Was *zero* attainable? Almost everyone in the room had an engineering and technical background. And every Engineering 101 course that teaches system design—mechanical, electrical, civil, software, or otherwise—punctures the myth of 100 percent reliability. Or was setting this unattainable goal the surest way to achieve a commitment to try?

Two years later, when the White House Commission on Aviation Safety and Security issued its final report, the answer became clearer. Without fanfare, the goal was revised: "Aviation safety experts at the FAA and at NASA are confident that a fivefold reduction in the fatal accident rate could be achieved in the next decade given the right resources and focus."

That equates to an 80 percent reduction over ten years. By 2005, a decade after Peña's announcement, the fatal accident rate had been reduced by 78 percent.

That reduction was no accident, so to speak. Was it the direct result of human factors and CRM training? Was it a determined effort by the FAA and the NTSB? The partial answer, unsurprisingly, is that all of those efforts likely had some effect. But the more complete answer is that an entire industry came together to collaborate—including airlines, labor, regulators, and manufacturers—to solve a common problem. The focus turned to safety management systems, integrating our knowledge of engineering system design, human behavioral psychology, and the regulator's rules and procedures. Then something magical happened. This collaboration led to a different approach to seeing and managing risk.

In response to the White House Commission report, the Commercial Aviation Safety Team was established. This group, composed of experts from all areas of aviation, began a consensus-based, data-intensive review of worldwide accidents. They grouped them into broad categories of adverse events and assigned teams of stakeholders to analyze them. They proposed joint solutions to regulatory agencies, airline operators, airplane manufacturers, and air traffic control facilities. They took measurements.

The problem was that outcomes in aviation take decades to measure effectively. But the teams doing the analyses didn't want to wait that long for results. So, do you know what they did? They didn't stop analyzing. They dove even deeper. That sea change in thinking eventually led to a level of success that had eluded aviation since the days of the Wright brothers.

They were solving the first piece of the reliability puzzle: finding what you can't see.

There's no doubt the NTSB's role—determining what caused an accident and what might prevent it from happening again—has helped improve aviation safety. But the Commercial Aviation Safety Team learned that alone isn't enough to successfully manage risk. Why? Because what happened to any plane that crashed may be only one of many possible outcomes. In other words, analyzing what happened shows us just the tip of the iceberg of risks.

That approach means we can see only the adverse and near-adverse events—bad outcomes that happened or almost happened. We miss the proportion of risks that are beneath the surface in any organization and in our daily lives. One area of these risks is the performance of our systems, which may not be resilient enough to keep us safe when things go wrong. The other is the fallible human performance and behaviors that happen every day.

The NTSB typically investigates outcomes as if they were the dominant risk in the organization involved. The fallacy in that approach is that what happens yesterday may not represent the most likely, or even the most severe, outcomes tomorrow. So that kind of investigation diverts us from seeing risk below the surface. It's natural to want to investigate accidents as they happen, and we're compelled to do so for legal and ethical reasons. The NTSB has its place. But if we are to manage risk optimally, we must take a deeper dive into the realities of socio-technical risk and think differently. The Commercial Aviation Safety Team proved that. Looking below the iceberg's waterline is what produced the dramatic 95 percent reduction in fatal aviation accidents, a trend that continues.

It may sound simple, but recognizing that there's much more than meets the eye is only the first step in managing risk more effectively.

APPLYING THE SCIENTIFIC METHOD

As we've seen, there are four important reasons why the US aviation industry has achieved dramatic improvements in reliability since 1959:

- An initial focus on advances in technology and engineering system design
- A gradual shift toward examining and retraining the human component
- A deeper recognition that we must see and understand risk below the surface, instead of merely reacting to adverse events

- Implementing standardized and collaborative safety management systems

Much like the history of science,[26] our understanding of reliability evolved by trial and error. If you look at the historical steps of aviation's path earlier, the puzzle pieces nearly fit. Almost.

Let's move the third bullet to the first, and the result is our Sequence of Reliability:

I. See and understand risk
II. Manage reliability in this order:
    a. Systems
    b. Humans
    c. Organizations

The reason for this rearrangement is simple: The Sequence of Reliability helps us optimize results.

Learning from experiences and translating the lessons from one industry to another is like using an analogy. But as we know, all analogies break down eventually.

If we view an analogy as an experiment, we can apply the scientific method[27] to test its application in other areas (see figure 8.1).

As you can see, the scientific method is a continuous process. There's a good reason for that. Scientific advancement requires iteration—educated guessing, failure, measurement, and further attempts at solving the puzzle. Whether we solve the puzzle one piece at a time or start with the whole, the process involves a sequence, a method. This lesson is critical if we are to translate aviation's reliability success into other industries, and into our everyday lives.

Richard Feynman—noted Nobel laureate physicist, member of the NASA *Challenger* crash investigation team, and enthusiastic bongo player—understood this principle. As he succinctly put it:

It doesn't matter how beautiful your theory is, it doesn't matter how smart you are. If it doesn't agree with experiment, it's wrong.[28]

Figure 8.1

There are many examples of well-intended but flawed applications of aviation solutions to other industries. Take checklists, for example. Their success in aviation led to healthcare professionals using them in operating rooms. You might think operating-room checklists would improve certain outcomes, such as lowering the rate of wrong-site surgeries, but results have varied widely from their use in aviation.[29] Studies show that how we make the translation is important. How we train the professionals to understand the design and function of checklists during operations, and the role of leadership, flexibility, and teamwork in adapting checklists to the dynamic conditions of surgery, are critical to the results.

What's the best way to adapt someone else's success? Use the scientific method: observe, question, hypothesize, experiment, and analyze, then conclude. The conclusions should come only after identifying the different conditions and variables in each experiment, and clearly seeing and understanding the results.

PREVENTING EMPLOYEE BURNOUT

The phone rang. Caller ID flashed the name of one of the nation's most prominent businesses. The caller identified herself as an executive. She asked that our conversation be strictly confidential, a standard request.

"I don't know what to do. I've been put in charge of employee well-being, and we've instituted several wellness programs. But none seem to be working. None of my management colleagues will admit what every frontline employee knows: It feels like no one cares. I could be fired for saying this, but I don't think the organization recognizes the depth of the problem—or wants to. They expect staff to do their jobs and not complain. As you know, our reputation is world-renowned. They act like everyone is replaceable, which I suppose we are. But it's disheartening. It's affecting me personally, and I'm the one charged with fixing it!"

She said she'd heard of my work doing risk modeling. "Would it be possible for you to model employee burnout and offer solutions? It seems we're putting all the responsibility on the employees. There must be better solutions than taking yoga classes and petting comfort dogs."

"Wait," I said. "You're actually doing that?"

"Oh, yes. And more. Our newest program is forest bathing."[30]

I have no doubt that forest bathing offers benefits beyond the scope of this book, but it was the chance to model the socio-technical contributors to burnout—from systems to the environment to culture to the organization—that got my attention.

Organizations often avoid the difficult task of analyzing and revising their systems to reduce the contributors to burnout. Instead, workers are left to believe they must better manage their own wellness and be more personally resilient. Coping mechanisms are vital to mental and physical health, but if all we do is try to build a better canary in the mineshaft, we are continuing to risk the well-being of each canary even as the mineshaft becomes more toxic. Making humans more resilient without seeing, understanding, and managing the causes of burnout is, at best, an exercise in frustration.

The effects of burnout on individuals are staggering and include widespread feelings of frustration and inadequacy, diminished morale and job satisfaction, and increased symptoms of depression and risk of suicide. For businesses, this translates into risk of the following:

- Decreased safety
- Reputational harm
- Financial loss
- Higher employee turnover
- Disrespect toward coworkers
- Reduced operational performance and teamwork
- Diminished employee morale
- Customer dissatisfaction
- Loss of trust in leadership
- Other, hidden effects

Although most people would agree that "burnout" means a diminished capacity to perform a job, the World Health Organization defines burnout like this:

A syndrome conceptualized as resulting from chronic workplace stress that has not been successfully managed. It is characterized by three dimensions:
- feelings of energy depletion or exhaustion;
- increased mental distance from one's job, or feelings of negativism or cynicism related to one's job; and
- reduced professional efficacy.[31]

But this definition doesn't go far enough. Notice the phrase *chronic workplace stress that has not been successfully managed*. Without describing who is responsible for managing workplace stress, it sounds like the WHO is saying the canary just isn't strong enough, doesn't it?

If we hope to prevent burnout, the key is to first see and understand the risk. This requires an understanding of workers' perspectives on burnout. Gaining a better understanding of context in the work environment may help reveal the systems, environmental factors, and culture that affect human performance. (This is the model we examined in the chapter on Human Reliability.) The list of contributors is long: stress, fatigue and distractions; lack of equipment and training; customer demands; excessive work hours and conditions; cultural biases and discrimination, to name a few.

Seeing and understanding the risk of burnout means more than providing annual surveys. Such surveys may be well intentioned but usually fall short.

First, employees are often reluctant to report burnout, afraid of being seen as not up for the job. In one instance, a business administered an online burnout survey to a group of employees, and one of the questions was to rank the level of burnout on a scale from one to five. If the employee rated their burnout at a three or above, a pop-up message would appear advising them to seek psychological counseling. Most employees did what you would expect: They lowered their score so as not to draw their employer's attention.

Second, even if a survey were to provide an accurate indicator of the *level* of burnout and go so far as to identify the *symptoms* of burnout, it would invariably fail to identify the *causes*. Telling an employer you're experiencing burnout is not the same as shining a light on what causes it and how to prevent it.

Furthermore, even if a periodic survey were well designed enough to identify the system, environmental, cultural, personal, and organizational contributors to burnout, it would fail to keep pace as conditions change. The causes of burnout will vary over time, location, employee group, and environments.

Businesses across the globe saw this during the COVID-19 pandemic, creating a cascade of new challenges contributing to burnout. For frontline employees without work-from-home options, staying safe during the pandemic became the dominant, daily challenge. And while work-from-home options worked for some people, for many others hybrid workplaces became the norm and created new challenges in juggling responsibilities. For those with children, access to childcare and uncertainties about their school attendance added complexities to even small changes in work schedules. And the rising costs of food, housing, and energy added further pressures to employment. No annual survey could have kept pace with the changing conditions during this crisis.

What if we could replicate the success of Aviation Safety Action Programs (discussed earlier in this chapter) by including employee burnout as a primary risk to be reported? Most importantly, what if we could identify the myriad *contributors* to burnout present in everyday operations to allow for trending and collaborative organizational response? Wouldn't it be desirable to see a more accurate picture of the contributors to burnout and gather the right resources to manage them, knowing that conditions change and must be accounted for in real time? Wouldn't this be a shared responsibility between management and labor, providing an opportunity to work collaboratively toward a common goal? Wouldn't this be a data-driven, logical, and more engaging approach than just having individuals focus on wellness?

These goals are not unrealistic. ASAP is evidence-based, meaning we have clear documentation of its success. The challenge is adapting what worked in aviation to other environments with different external and internal conditions. But it can be done. After all, humans—despite varying cultures and working conditions—have common traits and motivations. Let's examine a few necessary conditions for success.

A trusted reporting system: Documenting a risk is a first step in being able to monitor and measure results. Without documentation, anecdotal evidence can lead us in the wrong direction. (One executive said they always listen to their employees at the annual holiday party and that if there were a problem, surely someone would tell him.)

A trusted reporting system must be the following:

- *Simple and easy to use, not time-consuming.* Some reporting systems are complex online forms with drop-down menus and required form fields. As consumers, we've often been frustrated with an online product or service request or a menu of telephone options asking for redundant information unrelated to our needs. Imagine how this feels if it's your employer asking for such information. Many people report frustration with burnout surveys and reporting systems, believing these well-intentioned efforts add to their burnout.

- *Confidential and anonymous—encrypted, if possible.* Let's make a distinction between confidential and anonymous. Confidential means your identity is required but is revealed only on a need-to-know basis. The reason should be obvious: If you can't verify the source of a report, anyone could conjure up a false record.

  But trusted systems must have ironclad guarantees of how this confidentiality is provided. In most cases, this means not providing your identity to your supervisors or colleagues. In other words, your report must be anonymous to those who could potentially disadvantage you, whether it's a boss who might discipline or reprimand you or a coworker who might think less of you.

  Data encryption[32] is a practical means to satisfy this requirement from a system perspective. But by now we know that most systems are socio-technical and require human reliability, too. The encryption system is only as confidential as the people interacting with it.

- *Protected from legal discovery, if possible.* Why is this important? Because anyone who could be disadvantaged by external access to a report would likely think twice before exposing themselves, even if the likelihood is only remotely possible. Think about healthcare workers, airline employees, and others doing work in the public sector. These professionals often face strict regulatory oversight and/or the possibility of lawsuits. Why would they take a chance by exposing themselves to additional scrutiny and possible loss of their livelihood? For most, there must be a clear and powerful incentive to report to overcome this danger.

Employees must feel validated when they report. We must understand the mindset of our employees and that not acknowledging a report leaves them feeling that their opinion doesn't matter. They'll wonder if anyone even cared to read the report. Why would someone stick their neck out or bother to take the time and effort to make a report, only to be left wondering if it made a difference? It's the "what's in it for me?" question we must answer.

While blind altruism certainly exists, for most of us being able to see the positive results of our actions plays into our decision-making. An effective way to encourage reporting is to provide positive feedback and validation. It is important to acknowledge receiving a report even if the organization can't make any changes or decides to take a different action. In situations where the organization is trying to gather more information and can't take corrective action yet, knowing that the issue is under consideration can provide some measure of comfort to the worker. When system issues contributing to the risk of burnout are not being addressed, workers feel helpless. When their reports of contributors they see are not acknowledged, their sense of helplessness becomes hopelessness.

Acknowledgment of their concerns could simply be a generalized note saying a report will contribute to making the environment or business better, or a more detailed recognition of the value of the report. If the risk being reported rises to a specific level of concern, a best practice approach is to provide the reporter the option of requesting a personal reply on the organization's eventual response.

Transparent and equitable representation in how the report is handled. Knowing how the report will be managed often determines whether an employee will turn in a report. Providing clear visibility about who sees the report and how they will analyze it helps build confidence in reporting.

It's important to know that all reporting systems—both technological- and human-based—contain bias. A digital camera is limited by the number of pixels it provides as well as the field of view and angle of capture. A human's recollection of what she saw may be influenced by trauma, surprise, or other emotions during and after the event. It's important to account for potential biases and recognize their value and limitations.

Many factors can bias employee-based burnout-reporting systems. These biases may be the most important information an employer can collect to fully understand the challenge of preventing burnout. Knowing that the people analyzing an employee's report understand and share similar perspectives on the risk being reported goes a long way toward instilling employee confidence in reporting. For example, both the scientist in a research lab and a worker on an assembly line want to know the people reading their reports understand the complexities of their jobs. While an employer's risk tolerance may vary from their employee's, understanding the difference in perspectives is key to managing the gap.

Collaborative analysis and response process. Perhaps the most important factor in getting employees to accurately report contributors to burnout is the organization's commitment to a collaborative response. It might sound like Employee Relations 101, but addressing the challenges of burnout requires an *esprit de corps*, a belief "we're all in this together."

Vital to this employee–management bond is recognizing that while only frontline workers can identify the many contributors to burnout, only the organization has the authority to respond to most of them. A partnership must exist to manage burnout effectively. Collecting accurate data is only the first step in the Sequence of Reliability. Managing systems and people are the next steps, all of which require collaborative organizational response.

ASAP provides one example of evidence-based success, specific to a highly regulated, labor association–driven industry. Now let's look at how any business in any industry can achieve similar results by combining the key elements of ASAP with the Sequence of Reliability and principles of a just culture.

COLLABORATIVE JUST CULTURE®

In 1997, Professor James Reason first coined the term *just culture* in his book *Managing the Risk of Organizational Accidents*.[33] By 1999, the Institute of Medicine's report *To Err Is Human: Building a Safer Healthcare System*[34] encouraged healthcare professionals to embrace a philosophy intended to remove the stigma associated with human error and mistakes. At the same time, an algorithmic approach used to categorize human behavior grew into common practice in healthcare.

To the disappointment of healthcare leaders, just culture training has not led to measurable improvements in patient safety.[35] Variations in reliability among individuals using behavior-based algorithms and a lack of definition and standards for organizational adoption persist. While the core principles showed promise, just culture proved to be an incomplete approach. Inconsistent training, individual certifications without proficiency evaluations, and lack of standardization have yet to yield evidence of improved outcomes in healthcare.

When I trained just culture in high-consequence industries in the late 1990s, I noticed certain concepts always resonated—for example, not punishing human error, agreement that reckless and higher culpable behaviors should be punished, and so on. Over time, I recognized many managers and supervisors held strong confirmation biases, each one seeing just culture in ways that confirmed their personal experiences:

- Risk managers recognized the importance of examining systems.
- Human resources professionals supported the need to document and manage human performance and human behaviors.
- Attorneys appreciated the parallels between the model penal code and a hierarchy of culpability.

But there was a problem. By its title, the term biased its focus on people and the organizational response to human behaviors. (After all, have you ever heard someone say a system wasn't treated fairly?) Managing risk, along with the factors that shaped system performance and human performance, was an afterthought, to be examined only *after* the organization labeled and responded to the behavior. Was it human error, at-risk, or reckless? The answers to these questions require more than an algorithm; they require sequence and collaboration.

Why sequence? Because if we don't understand the risk, the system, the performance-shaping factors (including KSAPs, system and personal influences, the environment and culture, as well as competing priorities, and other factors), not only will we risk being unfair to the people whose behaviors we evaluate, but we'll miss valuable opportunities to manage the risk more effectively. Despite our best intentions, our efforts will fall short.

Why collaboration? Because we're human and subject to bias. In our legal justice systems, both civil and criminal, as the impact of our judgments rise, the courts require juries to decide. Most importantly, when the stakes really matter, we require unanimity to help ensure reliability. All this points to the need for collaboration as an important system design, bringing diversity of viewpoint. When employment decisions are involved, a just culture shouldn't depend solely on one manager's perspective. A balanced, diverse process is required.

In the early days of just culture, managers were enthusiastic to learn new strategies to manage people. The term *just culture* became a buzzword, and organizations spoke of *implementing* it, as if it were as easy as installing software. Over the next two decades, this led to thousands of organizations hiring consulting companies to train their people—often just a select few managers and supervisors—in just culture principles, such as distinctions between human error, at-risk choices, and recklessness.

But something was missing. It seemed that few people could grasp all the concepts associated with just culture without time, effort, and practice. A problem with this education was that there was no training standard to measure against. People who were trained often gained valuable insights and methods, but organizations lacked the discipline to determine how these individuals performed when managing people and systems. One manager might be very skilled in applying just culture principles, while others performed far less reliably. For example, one manager might determine a behavior was at-risk while another would see it as reckless—and often both managers would ignore the performance-shaping factors that contributed to these choices.

The result was that just culture training failed to improve organizational outcomes and remained an aspirational philosophy. We were missing a complete description of just culture and a standard to measure it against.

With this vision in mind, I developed a model combining everything I had used in designing the Aviation Safety Action Program, aligned with the Sequence of Reliability, and based on the principles of a just culture. Any organization that claimed to embrace the model would be required to prove its adoption and show results. I call this the Collaborative Just Culture (CJC) program.

The goal was to define Collaborative Just Culture as an evidence-producing program based on high reliability principles and quality management standards.

Collaborative Just Culture: a documented program to assist the organization in achieving sustainable reliability through workplace justice and collaboration. CJC supports the multiple attributes that make the organization highly reliable.

The program is:

- Documented, monitored, and measured
- Independently audited by an external, accredited audit organization

Without these standards, any business or organization could claim they had a just culture with no objective, verifiable proof. But by embracing CJC standards, just culture is more than an aspirational philosophy; it's an evidence-producing program that can be standardized, improved upon, and replicated.

The documented elements of a Collaborative Just Culture program include these:

- **Executive Leadership and Governing Body Responsibilities:** Written policies demonstrating organizational commitment.
- **Employee Involvement (including labor associations):** Engagement promoting collaboration and guarding against managerial biases.
- **Policy:** Written guidance on program policies, processes, and procedures.
- **Training Requirements:** Educational requirements supporting engagement and proficiency.
- **Tools:** Fact-gathering processes identifying risk and guiding organizational response.
- **Sustainment Plan:** Organizational strategies to maintain commitment, educational proficiency, and engagement.

These elements are just the starting point. Imagine a workplace where everyone is treated fairly and consistently, regardless of professional role, race, gender, sexual and/or gender orientation, or religion. Imagine, too, that this organization recognizes the many internal biases in systems, and the ones humans carry through their experiences, and guards against all forms of bias by acknowledging their existence and eliminating their influences.

A Collaborative Just Culture program follows the Sequence of Reliability, focusing on risk, systems, human performance, behaviors, and organizational response, in that order. A CJC organization refuses to tolerate reckless and higher culpable behaviors and embraces accountability as a set of mutual expectations between employees and the employer.

A Collaborative Just Culture program recognizes that variation will exist in how leaders manage employees, even when trained to proficiency. To guard against unjust employment outcomes, a CJC requires a Triad process to ensure a balanced organizational response to risk and events.

Based on the ASAP model and applied inside the business or organization, a Triad review helps ensure management actions involving employees are consistent with the CJC policy and program. Like ASAP, a CJC Triad requires unanimous consensus and provides an escalation process, as needed.

The Triad review is a partnership that depends on the balanced participation of diverse participants with independent perspectives and areas of expertise. Only qualified individuals who have been trained to proficiency in the Sequence of Reliability will participate in the review process (Triad Team members need not be members of the Reliability Management Team). Triad review members and their roles include:

- **Management Representative:** Provides the management viewpoint responsible for managing the system and human performance of the work environment(s) being reviewed. When multiple departments are involved, the management representative may collaborate with multiple other operational individuals, but only one management viewpoint may be documented in the final determination of unanimous agreement on each of the findings and recommendations.

- **Human Resources (HR) Representative:** Provides the HR perspective to ensure workplace fairness and to monitor culture and team member relations throughout the review process. The HR member may collaborate with multiple other HR individuals, but only one HR viewpoint may be documented in the final determination of unanimous agreement on each finding and recommendation.

- **Safety/Quality/Risk Representative:** Provides a system-based perspective, independent from the views of the operations and HR members. It is recognized that Safety, Quality, and Risk are often represented by different people—the Triad must choose a person to represent these views. The Triad Team member may collaborate with multiple other Safety/Quality/Risk professionals, but only one member viewpoint is documented in the final determination of unanimous agreement on each finding and recommendation.

A Collaborative Just Culture program flips the iceberg by requiring a confidential risk reporting system—rather than an event or incident reporting system. A CJC risk reporting system is used to see and understand all risks affecting the organization, employees, customers, and other stakeholders.

A Collaborative Just Culture program recognizes employees will face multiple values and competing priorities in the workplace. When such circumstances occur, a CJC program sets the expectation that individuals must escalate their concerns in a timely manner, up to and including the highest-ranking authority available at the time, whether that authority is in proximity to the circumstance or not. Each department is responsible for establishing the processes and procedures supporting such escalation. A CJC pledges to support any employee who escalates a concern in good faith, free of retaliation.

A Collaborative Just Culture program seeks to see, understand, and manage risk associated with multiple organizational values, including safety; privacy; customer satisfaction; diversity, equity, inclusion, and belonging (DEIB); operational integrity; and financial stewardship.

A Collaborative Just Culture program embraces the proactive management of risk, including employee burnout. A CJC program acknowledges the internal and external contributors to employee burnout and invests in identifying and managing it through collaboration. A CJC recognizes the existential benefits of improving employee morale and retention and, as a result, producing greater operational outcomes.

So, what's the purpose of a Collaborative Just Culture program? The simple answer is to help the organization achieve sustainable reliability through workplace justice and collaboration. Is it enough to guarantee high reliability? No. In mathematical lingo, it's a necessary but not sufficient condition for success. Organizations will not achieve high reliability without it. But having a Collaborative Just Culture program is the first step.

Now let's turn our attention to the remaining steps—including developing an internal team of subject matter experts and building a system to see, understand, and manage risk—and show how any business can build on CJC success to become highly reliable.

COLLABORATIVE HIGH RELIABILITY®

Edwards Deming's pioneering consulting work in the mid-twentieth century inspired organizations to higher levels of performance. His quality management philosophy revolutionized automobile manufacturing and established a path for other industries to follow by balancing the competing priorities of customer expectation, product delivery, and cost. Quality methods guided organizations to document, monitor, and measure, which produced better results.

But all industries are not the same. Hospitals, airlines, emergency medical services, firefighting, law enforcement, and energy production, to name a few, are not automobile manufacturers. These high-consequence industries grappled with unique challenges requiring siloed solutions. They needed specialized operational, regulatory compliance, risk management, information technology, performance improvement, and safety departments to stay in business and maintain a competitive advantage.

Since all organizations engage people, the human resources function arose to address the challenges of managing the workforce. In the late 1990s, just culture gained popularity as a human resources philosophy, using an algorithm to categorize employee behaviors with an aspiration to improve culture. However, just culture came with its own challenges: how to ensure consistent organizational response using a complex tool subject to unreliability. Sometimes cultures improved; many times they did not.

Subsequently, industries turned their attention to the term *high reliability organization,* or *HRO*, in hopes of achieving improvement. Curiously, consultants advised organizations to compare themselves to aircraft carriers and nuclear power plants in hopes of achieving similar levels of reliability.

But naval ships and power plants are the products of sophisticated engineering system design. Arguably, the focus of their reliability is technical, or system-based, defenses-in-depth. Healthcare, by contrast, evolved separate from the engineering sciences and requires many more individual points of delivery, each carrying a potential for harm. Healthcare requires human-centered care, on the delivery and receiving ends. As a result, healthcare poses a different set of challenges. All industries do.

Adding to these challenges is a lack of consistent definitions: *What is just culture? What is high reliability?* Without answers to these questions, organizations have struggled to achieve and replicate results. One-and-done training, individual certifications without proficiency evaluations, and an array of unaligned activities have led to inconsistent outcomes from one industry to the next.

To answer these questions and challenges, I applied the hidden science and developed a new model and taxonomy called Collaborative High Reliability (CHR). CHR is based on my work in high-consequence industries, including aviation, healthcare, railroads, emergency medical services, firefighting, law enforcement, and energy. This evidenced-based approach draws heavily from the following:

- Aviation Safety Action Program (ASAP) and other safety management system programs
- Collaborative Just Culture
- The integration of engineering and behavioral sciences with legal and ethical systems of justice
- International Standard for Organization[36] (ISO) 9001 and quality management principles

Building on quality management principles, I combined the lessons learned in multiple high-consequence industries to produce a model and taxonomy representing the latest advances in socio-technical science.

This approach can be documented, monitored, and measured—consistent with quality management principles. Most important, CHR can be aligned and integrated into an organization's quality management system to produce sustainable, high reliability results.

I needed a set of terms describing how organizations function. I assigned simple classifications to differentiate these functions:

- **Activity:** actions that are usually not documented (e.g., practices)
- **Process:** a documented set of activities (e.g., procedures, checklists, methods, etc.)
- **Program:** a documented alignment of related processes and/or other components
- **System:** a documented alignment of programs, processes, and/or other components
- **Integrated System:** a documented coordination of aligned systems, programs, policies, processes, and/or other components

These terms form a foundation on which to evaluate high reliability. Building on this taxonomy, I defined the following:

- **Documentation:** Written or other recorded and visible record of an organizational requirement, such as a process, program, system, or integrated system. A policy may serve this purpose. Documentation is required to meet a standard.
- **Alignment:** Occurs when all documentation between programs, systems, or integrated systems does not conflict and generally supports an overarching purpose or goal.

  It helps to understand alignment by contemplating its opposite. Think of a car with mixed components, some with parts built using the metric system (meters, liters, and grams, for example) and others on the imperial system (inches, gallons, and pounds). The car would be difficult to work on if the parts were incompatible, affecting the vehicle's functionality.

  Similarly, imagine an organization where departments have conflicting policies on how employees would be investigated, evaluated, and disciplined. You might expect differences in cultures, departmental performance, and difficulty in achieving a cohesive workplace. An aligned organization, however, provides the framework on which to build reliability.

- **Integration:** All components function in relation to the other components to support the purpose of the system. Integrated components coordinate and overlap with other system components.

The car analogy works here, too. Just because a car's parts are all metric and don't conflict doesn't guarantee they integrate in performing a function. For example, an aftermarket radio can be installed in almost any vehicle but may not integrate with other features in a digital audiovisual system, such as Bluetooth[37] functionality, displays, or voice commands linked to navigation and vehicle control.

On the other hand, an *integrated* system would perform all these features seamlessly by design. For this reason, automobile manufacturers build proprietary parts customized for vehicle, make, model, and year.

Likewise, organizations must design integrated systems to match specifications. Processes, programs, and systems must integrate well to optimize organizational reliability. For example, policies describing finance, risk management, quality, safety, performance improvement, and human resources programs should align and integrate, each one supporting and enhancing the organization and its goals.

Once we have these definitions and taxonomy in place, we can start building on this foundation. Have you heard the analogy of the big rocks in the jar?[38] As the story goes:

An expert on the subject of time management was lecturing to a group of business school students, and to drive home a point he used an illustration those students will probably never forget.

Standing in front of a classroom filled with self-motivated overachievers, he pulled out a one-gallon, wide-mouthed Mason jar and set it on a table. Then he produced a half-dozen fist-sized rocks and carefully placed them, one at a time, into the jar.

When the jar was filled to the top and no more rocks would fit, he asked, "Is this jar full?"

Everyone in the class said, "Yes."

He said, "Really?"

He then reached under the table and pulled out a sack of gravel. He slowly began dumping the gravel in, pausing to shake the jar as he did so the gravel could work itself down into the spaces between the big rocks. Then he smiled and asked the group once more, "Is the jar full?"

Some in the class were starting to catch on. "Probably not," one of them called out.

"Good!" he replied. Next he reached under the table and brought out a bag of sand. He started shaking the sand in, and it sifted down into all the spaces left between the rocks and the gravel. Once more he asked the question, "Now is the jar full?"

"No!" the class shouted.

"Excellent!" he said, and finally he grabbed the pitcher of drinking water off the desk and began to pour it in, until the jar was filled to the brim.

Then he looked up at the class and asked, "What is the point of this illustration?"

One eager student raised his hand and said, "The point is, no matter how full your schedule is, if you try really hard, you can always fit some more things into it!"

"Nice try," the speaker replied, "but that's not really the point at all. The truth this little Mason jar illustration teaches us is simple but powerful: If you don't put the big rocks in first, you'll never get them in at all."

The point of this story is that two big rocks must be in the jar before an organization can become highly reliable:

- **Collaborative Just Culture:** a verifiable program, documented, monitored, and measured according to quality management principles
- **Reliability Management Team:** an internal team of subject matter experts (SMEs) who guide the organization toward sustainable high reliability

Once you have the big rocks in the jar, the next step is to build a Reliability Management System, or RMS. The RMS integrates the processes, programs, and systems needed to run an organization and become reliable.

Every business starts out by establishing a financial system to support its operations. But smart financial management is only one attribute of a highly reliable organization. In the CHR model, we define the following additional attributes:

- **Safety:** encompasses the physical, psychological, and emotional well-being of customers/patients, staff, and visitors, as well as the protection of property.
- **Customer Service:** aligns with customer expectations, balanced against available resources. In healthcare, this attribute includes compassionate care; in aviation, customers may expect on-time performance and baggage delivery. In emergency management services, response time is critical in meeting customer expectations and business requirements.
- **Privacy:** protection is important in all business endeavors—for customers/patients, staff, and visitors. Examples include personal financial and employment records, Health Insurance Portability and Accountability Act (HIPAA) information, and other forms of personal data.
- **Quality:** the relationship between customer expectation, product delivery, and cost. Quality management principles include the requirement to document, monitor, and measure organizational performance.

- **Financial Responsibility:** all organizations—for-profit and not-for-profit alike—require financial responsibility to operate.
- **Operational Integrity:** includes staffing, supply chain management, information systems security, as well as other infrastructure requirements to complete an organization's mission.
- **Equity:** equitable treatment of customers, staff, and visitors—including diversity, equity, inclusion, and belonging (DEIB) initiatives—is essential to organizational reliability.

These attributes are universal in free and in regulated markets, where customer demand, competition, and government oversight may influence organizational performance. Every business striving for high reliability in today's world must pay attention to them.

While mission, vision, and values statements remain important, achieving high reliability requires additional steps. If we look back on the evolution of the airline industry's dramatic reduction in the fatal accident rate, one of the key drivers of this success was the evolution of safety management systems, or SMS. Initially, SMS was a collection of disparate activities designed to prevent plane crashes, including activities and processes such as accident investigations, training records, inspections, and audits. As the industry became more proactive and flipped the iceberg, programs such as ASAP, flight data monitoring programs, line operation safety audits, and crew resource management were added to the list.

Aligning these activities, processes, and programs into a system was challenging. Like most large organizations, airlines were siloed into specialized departments. Flight and maintenance departments were typically aligned according to FAA regulations, but other departments, such as ground operations, customer service, flight attendants, marketing, and other business operations, marched to different drummers. The cultures varied widely. As a result, even today, the airline industry's SMS programs are not fully aligned and integrated across all departments and specialties.

High reliability is not as simple as replicating the success of SMS. The challenge—and rewards—are much greater. So, with CHR, I developed the concept of a Reliability Management System, or RMS, to support all high reliability attributes.

The foundation of RMS is the Sequence of Reliability. A visualization of this concept looks something like figure 8.2.

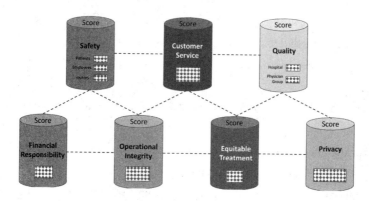

Figure 8.2
Reliability Management System

BUILDING THE RELIABILITY
MANAGEMENT SYSTEM (RMS)

The following steps can guide how an organization builds the Reliability Management System:

1. Examine industry best practices for each Attribute Management System (AMS).
2. Evaluate all current organizational initiatives for each RMS Attribute System:
   - Qualify each initiative according to RMS inclusion criteria below.
   - Score each individual component of the Attribute Management System(s).
   - Sum the RMS components for each Attribute Management System(s).

3. Develop **RMS Dashboard**: Continuously monitor and measure results in each AMS.

4. Prepare for external audit.

RMS INCLUSION CRITERIA

Evaluate all organizational initiatives deemed necessary for organizational high reliability, in support of the CHR attributes. For each initiative:

1. Describe the purpose of the initiative. What risk(s) is the organization trying to see, understand, and manage? What are the specific outcomes and goals the initiative is expected to produce?

2. Beyond the primary goals, are there ancillary benefits to the initiative? If so, list them.

3. Is the initiative *evidenced based*? If so, what source documentation supports its application in this environment?

4. If not, can the initiative be *evidence-producing*? If so, how will it be peer-reviewed?

5. Classify the initiative according to the hierarchy of terms (activity,[*] process, program, system, or integrated system) and assign it a Priority Ranking (1–10, where 1 is highest) based on its impact on operational reliability.

6. Is the initiative:
   a. Documented? (Where does this documentation reside? Who has access to it?)
   b. Monitored? (How, how often, and by whom?)
   c. Measured for effectiveness and resilience?

7. Can the initiative be aligned with other components of the RMS? Is this alignment documented?

8. Can the initiative be integrated with other components of the RMS? Is this integration documented?

---

*Note: Activities are not included in the RMS.

9. Monitor and measure performance of each component supporting the CHR attributes, as well as the combined result of the integrated system.

INITIATIVE CATEGORIZATION WITHIN EACH RMS ATTRIBUTE MANAGEMENT SYSTEM

Each element in an RMS must be aligned and integrated, forming a holistic way of seeing, understanding, and managing risk in support of CHR attributes (see figure 8.3).

- Does this initiative help us better **See and Understand Risk?** What kinds of risks can it reveal? How can the risks it identifies be reported and recorded for use in the RMS?
- Will this initiative help us manage **System Reliability?** Will inclusion in the RMS help make systems more effective and/or resilient? How will the organization quantify this improvement?
- Will this initiative assist our human resources staff and help our leaders and supervisors better manage **Human Performance** and **Human Behavior?** In what ways could this initiative be included in performance management systems, and what would be measured?
- Will this initiative support **Organizational Sustainment?** Will it help the organization become predictive? How will the organization quantify this improvement?

CHR means more than basic compliance with rules and regulations and exceeds Deming's vision for quality management. Achieving the next breakthrough in organizational performance requires commitment to the hidden science of reliability—mastering the topics presented throughout this book. And there's one essential element you've already learned that makes all the difference.

1. See and Understand Risk	2. System Reliability	3. Human Reliability	4. Organizational Reliability
Organizational Values & Risks: • Safety (patient, employee, visitor) • Quality • Operational Integrity • Diversity, Equity, & Inclusion • Finance • Customer Service	**Evaluation and Design:** • Are there macro- and sub-systems? • Are the systems effective when used as designed? • Are the systems resilient when things go wrong? • Can these systems be improved by elimination or re-design?	**Performance Management:** • Knowledge, skills, abilities, & proficiencies • System influences • Personal influences • Culture, perceptions of risk, and competing priorities **Behavior Management:** • Are choices and errors managed consistently?	**Measurements:** • Is the organization measuring this risk effectively across all departments? **Sustainment:** • Is the organization managing this risk on an ongoing basis? Is documentation provided?
Initiatives: • Risk Reporting • Risk Register • Collaborative Risk Review • Investigations • RCAs, FMEAs • Safety Huddles • Audits • Customer Experience • Feedback loops • Others?	**Initiatives:** • Resilient design • Lean practices • Team-based care • Equipment • Others?	**Initiatives:** • Collaborative Just Culture Program • Leadership training • Employee support • Critical communication • Online and classroom training • Employee support • Others?	**Initiatives:** • Reliability Management Team • Collaborative Risk Reviews • Triad process • Objectives & Key Results (OKR) • Dashboards • Policy integration • Board accountability • Predictive Reliability Systems • Others?

Figure 8.3

QUALIFICATION AND CERTIFICATION

As illustrated in previous chapters, independent verification—a type of redundancy—is a key component of reliable systems, people, teams, and organizations. In fact, all activities involving humans are limited by the reliability of the people involved. Without independent verification, the following tasks would not meet societal expectations:

- Physicians diagnosing a potentially fatal illness
- Pharmacists dispensing and nurses administering chemotherapy medications
- Accountants preparing key financial results
- Engineers mission-planning for space flights
- Government officials inspecting nuclear power plants
- Executive office and military personnel use of nuclear weapons

As organizations struggled to integrate just culture and high reliability without success, it became clear they lacked the discipline to meet even basic verification standards. In many instances, consulting companies training organizations in just culture offered individual certifications, with no independent or proficiency-based verification. But these certifications lacked scientific rigor.

There's an important lesson for us here: Companies that blur the line between consulting and auditing have contributed to disastrous ethical, financial, and operational results. Consider the cautionary tales of accounting firm Arthur Andersen and its work with Enron and the more recent fall from grace of the cryptocurrency exchange FTX.[39]

The solution to this problem is transparency and a commitment to independent verification. Recognizing this, I searched for an independent audit organization capable of this task. My research led me to DNV (Det Norske Veritas), one of the world's leading certification bodies. DNV helps businesses manage risk and assure the performance of their organizations, products, people, facilities, and supply chains through certification, verification, assessment, and training services. DNV combines technical, digital, and industry expertise to empower companies' decisions and actions.

In alignment with principles of high reliability, I granted DNV permission to use the CHR model for the purpose of independent, conflict-free verification. Collaborative High Reliability is the world's first high-reliability model to be independently audited to a standard. DNV CHR audits are the following:

- **Independent:** A key principle of reliability requires independent, third-party verification of the organization.
- **Proficiency-based:** Audits shall verify proficiency, (i.e., competency sustained over time). To demonstrate proficiency, audits shall occur repeatedly at defined intervals.

The first level of DNV's auditing applies to our first big rocks in the jar, described as qualification audits.

Qualification Requirements

- Collaborative Just Culture Program Qualification
- Reliability Management Team Qualification
- Following qualification, organizations are eligible to apply for the first level of a three-tier organization certification.

Certification Requirements

Tier 1 Certification requires the following:

- **Collaborative Just Culture program qualification** as a prerequisite
- **Reliability Management Team qualification** as a prerequisite
- **A Learning Management System** documenting:
  - CHR education and proficiency
  - Ongoing targets, measurements, and key results
- **An Integrated Reliability Management System** documenting:
  - All components (activities, processes, programs, and systems) contributing to organizational high reliability
  - The primary purpose for each component
  - Ongoing targets, measurements, and key results for each component
  - A risk management plan for each component
  - Ongoing evidence that the Integrated Reliability Management System is sustainable and adaptable to changing conditions

Tier 2 Requirements

An organization shall have sustained organizational reliability over at least two years following successful Tier 1 certification.

Tier 3 Requirements*

An organization shall:

- Achieve previous Tier 1 and 2 certifications.
- Demonstrate advanced predictive reliability in at least two distinct areas of organizational performance.

* Note: Organizations may achieve Tier 2 and Tier 3 certification requirements concurrently.

EPILOGUE

In 1998, after ASAP had been in operation for four years, Nick Sabatini,[1] the FAA's associate administrator for regulation and certification, called upon me to chair an industry aviation rule-making committee to establish the voluntary collection of critical aviation safety information. He said, "I don't care where the information resides, only that the FAA be allowed to access it in such a way that the industry and labor find appropriate. I want it to be a partnership, like ASAP, and I want us to analyze the information together."

Within two years, Sabatini's vision of joint industry-labor-regulator information sharing was a reality. The Aviation Safety InfoShare[2] forum became a bedrock gathering of aviation safety experts across the world. Behind the scenes at this widely anticipated semiannual event, vital aviation safety data was collected, aggregated among airlines, regulators, labor representatives, and technical experts. The forum presents key results of trends and solutions for industry review and action.

In those pivotal years, the FAA transformed itself from a compliance-based enforcer of rules and regulations to an effective oversight agency guiding the proactive, predictive management of risk. The FAA sees and understands risk first, then takes action to improve system, human, and organizational performance.

Around this time, Bob Francis, vice chairman of the NTSB, and Dr. Bob Helmreich, father of aviation's Crew Resource Management that later was applied to healthcare, were exploring how other industries and the public might benefit from aviation's success. They referred me to Surgeon

General David Satcher, who asked me to speak at a Department of Health and Human Services Advisory Committee meeting on Blood Safety and Availability on April 25, 2000. They asked me to describe the history and development of ASAP, and to explain how healthcare could embrace a similar path to improvement.

I didn't realize it at the time, but my speech to the committee shifted my professional path. It became clear when I described the history of ASAP that aviation was only a small experiment in a cohesive industry that had evolved toward collaboration and was overseen primarily by one regulator. Aviation leaders were early adopters, then pioneers, in synthesizing lessons from many disciplines. Healthcare, on the other hand, was more complex— vastly larger, with many regulators and state and federal oversight systems that didn't have a standardized approach to managing risk.

In 2006, I left American Airlines to join a friend and colleague, David Marx, in building a company called Outcome Engineering, which later became Outcome Engenuity. We focused on developing and demonstrating our approach, which involved using a proprietary algorithm to guide managers and supervisors when responding to human behaviors. We called this early approach just culture, and applications began to appear worldwide.

In 2013, I started a new company, SG Collaborative Solutions, LLC, with my friend and colleague Paul LeSage. LeSage, a nationally recognized paramedic and fire service executive, was co-author of *Crew Resource Management: Principles and Practice*.[3] Our goal was to synthesize all we had learned into a more sustainable approach to improving organizational performance.

Soon it became clear that previous algorithmic approaches to managing human behavior fell short of organizational success. So, we set about developing a more collaborative, sequenced set of methods to help organizations become more reliable.

One day, I was working with Lisa Ramthun, vice president of risk management at a large healthcare system in California. She asked me to build a new algorithm to help her organization identify and manage risk. I came into the conference room with a prototype I had worked on most of the night. It was an overly complex, symmetric jumble of lines, Yes/No questions, and response boxes. Lisa was blunt in her response:

"What's this?"

"It's a balanced approach to managing system and human performance," I said.

"But where do I start when trying to work my way through all of this?"

"That's the beauty of it," I said. "It doesn't matter which way you go—on the human side or the system side—because you'll be forced to loop back to the other side eventually."

"But that won't work, Scott. You don't understand. This isn't aviation. In healthcare, we're *system illiterate*. If we don't start with the risk and the system, we'll never see it."

That realization led us to explore the advantages of managing risk and systems before trying to manage people. The order mattered, and the Sequence of Reliability started to crystallize.

LeSage and I agreed: No algorithmic approach would work until we could teach the entire *organization* how to become sustainably reliable.

The Sequence of Reliability came into focus.

Afterward, we invited Michael Coffin, an entrepreneur and technologist, to join us as our partner. Coffin taught us that classrooms weren't enough. Together, we built a learning management platform optimized for cognition, retention, and proficiency. We realized that teaching and applying the Sequence of Reliability required collaboration, along with the hidden science. Our approach soon became standard practice with our clients.

While aviation's path to the hidden science was a crooked line, other high-consequence industries—such as healthcare, energy, law enforcement, fire service, railroads, and cybersecurity—each took a different path to managing risk, often with less-than-hoped-for results.

But all of these industries are now evolving in positive directions. The iceberg metaphor—seeing and understanding risk—is universal. The challenge lies in applying the scientific method to aviation's success and translating it to other industries. What we learn in one industry helps us get ahead in the next. Each failure, each success, informs us and helps us improve. The hidden science continues to evolve.

Each of us is on a unique journey through life—for better, and sometimes for worse. Our hope is that others might learn from our experiences. Richard Feynman, again, perhaps said it best:

> We are at the very beginning of time for the human race. It is not unreasonable that we grapple with problems. But there are tens of thousands of years in the future. Our responsibility is to do what we can, learn what we can, improve the solutions, and pass them on.[4]

Probabilistic risk fills our lives. Randomness and entropy lead to disorder, and Murphy's myth still tempts us. Yet there's a pattern in the sociotechnical chaos. We are constantly evolving—stumbling at times, but getting back up, learning from our mistakes, and passing on our solutions to the next generation. Feynman's hope is becoming an everyday reality, at the system, individual, and organizational levels. The challenge and the joy of success align:

> The science is no longer hidden. The sequence matters. Positive results are sustainable.

KEY TAKEAWAYS

A Better Business Model

To successfully manage risk, you first must see and understand what may not be obvious. Then you must improve your systems, manage your people and organization, and sustain your success through commitment and resources.

Seeing and Understanding Risk

Experience alone won't let you avoid risk. It doesn't give you the tools to see and understand what hasn't happened to you yet. You must develop the vision to identify unseen catastrophes before they occur and the intelligence to assess their potential dangers.

System Reliability

Understand that systems will fail because of influences on any number of interconnected factors. The most important of these factors is system design. Building in barriers, redundancies, and recoveries will improve your system reliability.

Human Reliability

The biggest risks come from choices people make, not simple human error. Many subtle, constantly changing factors influence those choices. Learn to understand these influences and design a resilient system, including optimal rules, coaching, and consequences, to manage risky behavior.

Organizational Reliability

Identify and understand the competing priorities, biases, and other factors that can harm organizational performance. Use this knowledge to design effective, resilient systems and influence human behaviors. Recognize that these risk factors change over time, requiring consistent leadership and strong culture.

Predictive Reliability

Yesterday's accident provides limited visibility in preventing accidents tomorrow. Use multiple complementary strategies to give you the most complete picture of the risks you face, seen and unseen. Collaborate with all stakeholders, including employees, to create systems that help you foresee dangers and achieve sustainable reliability.

Big Challenges

The challenges we face are not insurmountable but require applying the Sequence of Reliability to achieve optimal results.

Flipping the Iceberg

Managing risk—in business and everyday life—requires seeing below the waterline and applying the Sequence of Reliability. For businesses and other organizations, Collaborative High Reliability provides independent validation of sustainable success.

ABOUT SG

COLLABORATIVE SOLUTIONS

Scott Griffith Collaborative Solutions, LLC (dba SG Collaborative Solutions, LLC), founded by the author, is an enterprise risk management firm specializing in reliable performance in high-consequence industries and organizations. The firm developed the world's first independently-audited high reliability standards—Collaborative High Reliability® and Collaborative Just Culture®.

Website: https://sgcpartners.com/

ABOUT DNV

DNV is one of the world's leading certification bodies, helping businesses manage risk and assure the performance of their organizations, products, people, facilities, and supply chains through certification, verification, assessment, and training services. DNV combines technical, digital, and industry expertise to empower companies' decisions and actions.

With the addition of the DNV CHR Qualification and Certification Requirements, DNV expands their service offerings to organizations in industries worldwide.

With origins stretching back to 1864 and operations in more than one hundred countries, DNV experts are dedicated to helping customers make the world safer, smarter, and greener.

SG Collaborative Solutions grants authorization to DNV as the independent audit organization of the Collaborative High Reliability® and Collaborative Just Culture® standards.

FURTHER READING

A few books among many that have influenced this book:

Absorption and Scattering of Light by Small Particles, Craig F. Bohren and Donald R. Huffman

The Black Swan: The Impact of the Highly Improbable, Nassim Nicholas Taleb

Blink, Malcolm Gladwell

The Bonobo and the Atheist, Frans de Waal

Brain Rules, John J. Medina

Chaos: The Making of a New Science, James Gleick

Command and Control, Eric Schlosser

David and Goliath, Malcolm Gladwell

The Design of Everyday Things, Don Norman

The Devil Never Sleeps: Learning to Live in an Age of Disasters, Juliette Kayyem

The Downburst, Theodore T. Fujita

Fate Is the Hunter, Ernest K. Gann

The Feynman Lectures on Physics, Richard Feynman

Outliers, Malcolm Gladwell

Six Easy Pieces audio recordings, Richard Feynman

Thinking, Fast and Slow, Daniel Kahneman

Tipping Point: How Little Things Can Make a Big Difference, Malcolm Gladwell

ACKNOWLEDGMENTS

I began writing this book in my head immediately after the Flight 191 plane crash, although putting pen to paper would take more than three and a half decades. Throughout my life, my father has been the first important influence in how I have seen, understood, and managed risk. There have been many more.

I am grateful for my mentors at American Airlines, including Bob Baker and Cecil Ewell, both now deceased, but with legacies lasting generations to come. I am indebted to Rich LaVoy, who was president of the Allied Pilots Association during the years I developed ASAP, and who saw the vision and gave me the full support of the association. And I'm also grateful for my friends Joe Oyler, Don Wilson, Chris Zwingle, Shawn Kilgore, Rhett Tucker, Hugh Schoelzel, Ken Jenkins, Brad Brugger, Candra Schatz, Tim Ahern, Peggy Sterling, John Holmes, Tommy McFall, Curt Lewis, John Darbo, Christa Hinckley, and hundreds more, too numerous to list.

I am indebted to Milton Huffaker, Sammy Henderson, Michael Kavaya, George Kattawar, Roland Bowles, and Dave Hinton for their guidance—all of them giants in their respective fields of physics—and to Alex Thompson and Russell Targ, who still intimidate me with their knowledge of the universe.

I thank many current and former government officials, starting at the Federal Aviation Administration, especially Nick Sabatini, Greg Lander, Dave Bitonti, Wayne Williams, Ken Kadey, Bob Talmadge, and Robert Neumeier. I also thank my friends who served as officials at the National Transportation Safety Board, starting with Bob Francis, John Overton, Robert Sumwalt III, and Chris Hart.

I am indebted to Bob Helmreich and Bruce Tesmer (both deceased), Fiona Lawton from the land Down Under, Pedro Bustamante in Buenos Aires, and countless other aviation friends and colleagues from around the world.

I am indebted to Chief Chuck Gruber (deceased) for introducing me to law enforcement and describing our work as justice with a purpose; and to Outcome Engenuity and David Marx for inspiring me to embark on a personal journey assisting high-consequence industries.

Many other friends encouraged me in my quirky quest, including Marc Dickinson, David Hearne, and Alix Buckley. Whatever literary leanings I have are the result of my mother's genetic and environmental influences, as well as Texas Christian University professor Betsy Colquitt's nurturing inspiration. Both taught me the power of poetry.

I am grateful to my brilliant Renaissance business partners and associates at SG Collaborative Solutions. Each of them has enriched my understanding of collaboration. In particular, starting with Paul LeSage, whose heroic, first-responder experience and broad operational insights have made every product and service offering we developed together better and more reliable; to Michael Coffin, whose business acumen, entrepreneurial spirit, understanding of adult learning, and engineering/technological expertise have helped build a business greater than the sum of its parts; and to Dale Oda, who has combined engineering know-how with a physician-sensei servant's heart. And to Lisa Ramthun, who is simultaneously the most strategic and tactical healthcare visionary I know.

I'm appreciative of DNV and the shared vision of building an independent auditing program for our model, first with Patrick Horine, then with Geir Fuglerud and Kelly Proctor, and most of all, Tammy Allen and Maureen Washburn, who led the development of the independent audit qualification program for Collaborative High Reliability and Collaborative Just Culture. Their combined experience, vision, dedication, and sense of humor were the perfect mix of ingredients to develop the world's first independent qualification and certification of its kind.

I am especially grateful to my exceptional agent, Wendy Keller, who had faith in this book and the expertise to guide me in writing the proposal and in promoting our vision to publishers and potential clients. She is a unique blend of clear-eyed pragmatism combined with eternal optimism and charming, dynamic interpersonal skills. She is the proverbial force of nature.

This book would not have been possible without Pete Lesage, retired senior editor at *The Oregonian*, who kept me laser-focused on making the material accessible to the public, as well as to business leaders, regulators, labor unions, and scientists. The narrative shape of this book bears his mark as well as mine.

And to the great folks at HarperCollins Leadership, starting with senior acquisitions editor Tim Burgard, who more than lived up to his reputation as a skilled developer of business books while making the publication experience fun and productive.

I am most indebted to my stunning mystery companion, Farhin Ali, whose beauty, intelligence, and compassion have brought joy and love to my life every day. I'm looking forward to spending the rest of our lives together as we blend our life's journeys. I'm also inspired by her two exceptional sons, Joey and Omar, who amaze me with their unique talents and intelligence. And finally, I am eternally thankful for and grateful to my children, Sean, Sam, and Sophie, and their mother, Amy. Combined, all five children are our greatest achievements. They are fulfilling every dream I could have imagined for them. Their empathy, intelligence, love, and compassion give me hope that the probabilistic arc of human evolution bends toward a brighter, more equitable world.

ENDNOTES

Introduction: Blind Spots

1. Erika Hayasaki, "Could the Experiences of Our Ancestors Be 'Seared into Our Cells'?" *Slate*, June 27, 2018, https://slate.com/technology/2018/06/science-journalist-erika -hayasaki-responds-to-carmen-maria-machados-short-story-a-brief-and-fearful-star .html (accessed August 7, 2023).

Prologue: Flight 191

1. "Aircraft Accident Report Delta Air Lines, Inc., Lockheed L-101 l-385-1, N726DA Dallas/ Fort Worth International Airport, Texas August 2, 1985, NTSB/AAR-86/05," National Transportation Safety Board, August 2, 1985, https://libraryonline.erau.edu/online -full-text/ntsb/aircraft-accident-reports/AAR86-05.pdf (accessed August 7, 2023).
   "Of the 163 persons aboard, 134 passengers and crewmembers were killed; 26 passengers and 3 cabin attendants survived."
   "The aircraft struck the ground about 6,300 feet north of the approach end of runway 17L, hit a car on a highway north of the runway, killing the driver."
2. Ibid.
3. Ibid., Appendix F, page 122.
4. Richard Stimson, "Da Vinci's Aerodynamics," Wright Stories, https://airandspace.si .edu/stories/editorial/leonardo-da-vinci-and-flight (accessed August 7, 2023).
5. "The Wright Brothers: The Invention of the Aerial Age," Smithsonian National Air and Space Museum, https://airandspace.si.edu/exhibitions/wright-brothers/online/ (accessed August 7, 2023).
6. James W. Wilson and Roger M. Wakimoto. "The Discovery of the Downburst: T. T. Fujita's Contribution." *Bulletin of the American Meteorological Society* 82.1 (2001): 49–62, https://journals.ametsoc.org/view/journals/bams/82/1/1520-0477_2001_082_0049 _tdotdt_2_3_co_2.xml (accessed August 7, 2023).

Chapter 1: A Better Business Model

1. "Out Front on Airline Safety: Two Decades of Continuous Evolution," Federal Aviation Administration, August 2, 2018, https://www.faa.gov/newsroom/out-front -airline-safety-two-decades-continuous-evolution#:~:text=Out%20Front%20on%20 Airline%20Safety%3A%20Two%20Decades%20of%20Continuous%20Evolution, -Thursday%2C%20August%202&text=The%20commercial%20aviation%20system%20 in,fatalities%20per%20100%20million%20passengers (accessed August 7, 2023).

2. Often attributed to Henry Russel Sanders, 1953. *Bartlett's Book of Business Quotations* (Grand Central Publishing, 2009).

3. "Read a Selection of Winston Churchill's Most Famous Quotes," International Churchill Society, September 15, 2021, https://winstonchurchill.org/resources/quotes/famous -quotations-and-stories/ (accessed August 7, 2023).

4. "W. C. Fields Quotes," Brainy Quote, https://www.brainyquote.com/search_results?x =0&y=0&q=w.+C.+Fields+don%27t+be+a+damn+fool+about+it (accessed August 7, 2023).

5. Martin A. Makary and Michael Daniel, "Medical Error—The Third Leading Cause of Death in the US," *The BMJ* (May 3, 2016): 353, https://www.bmj.com/content/353/bmj .i2139 (accessed August 7, 2023).

6. "The Emergency Medical Treatment and Active Labor Act (EMTALA): What It Is and What It Means for Physicians," The National Center for Biotechnology Information (NCBI), January 4, 2009, https://www.ncbi.nlm.nih.gov/pmc/articles/PMC1305897/ (accessed August 7, 2023).

7. "W. Edwards Deming," Wikipedia, https://en.wikipedia.org/wiki/W._Edwards_Deming (accessed August 7, 2023).

8. "Festina Lente: Why Slow Is Smooth and Smooth Is Fast," Taylor Pearson webpage, https://taylorpearson.me/interestingtimes/festina-lente-why-slow-is-smooth-and- smooth-is-fast/ (accessed August 7, 2023).

9. "Maslow's Hierarchy of Needs," Wikipedia, https://en.wikipedia.org/wiki /Maslow%27s_hierarchy_of_needs (accessed August 7, 2023).

10. "Murphy's Laws Origin," http://www.murphys-laws.com/murphy/murphy-true .html (accessed March 31, 2020).

11. "Accidents or Unintentional Injuries," Centers for Disease Control and Prevention, updated January 17, 2023, https://www.cdc.gov/nchs/fastats/accidental-injury.htm (accessed August 7, 2023).

12. "Chaos Theory: A Brief Introduction," chrome-extension://efaidnbmnnnibpcajpc glclefindmkaj/https://courses.seas.harvard.edu/climate/eli/Courses/EPS281r/ Sources/Chaos-and-weather-prediction/1-Chaos-Theory-A-Brief-Introduction-IMHO .pdf (accessed August 7, 2023).

13. "Benjamin Franklin Quotes," Goodreads, https://www.goodreads.com/quotes/626466 -for-the-want-of-a-nail-the-shoe-was-lost (accessed August 7, 2023).

    This is a mathematical twist on Ben Franklin's poetic summary of an age-old proverb:
    "For the want of a nail the shoe was lost,
    For the want of a shoe the horse was lost,
    For the want of a horse the rider was lost,
    For the want of a rider the battle was lost,
    For the want of a battle the kingdom was lost,
    And all for the want of a horseshoe-nail."

Chapter 2: Seeing and Understanding Risk

1. Alyssa Newcomb, "A Timeline of Facebook's Privacy Issues—And Its Responses," NBC News, March 24, 2018, https://www.nbcnews.com/tech/social-media/timeline -facebook-s-privacy-issues-its-responses-n859651 (accessed August 7, 2023).

2. Josh Horwitz, "Analysis: Apple Supply Chain Data Shows Receding Exposure to China as Risks Mount," Reuters, November 29, 2022, https://www.reuters.com/technology

/apple-supply-chain-data-shows-receding-exposure-china-risks-mount-2022-11-30/ (accessed August 7, 2023).

3. Seim Mohl, "6 Major Companies That Failed to Innovate in Time," Ground Control, December 9, 2021, https://togroundcontrol.com/blog/6-major-companies-that-failed-to-innovate-in-time/ (accessed August 7, 2023).

4. David A. Graham, "Rumsfeld's Knowns and Unknowns: The Intellectual History of a Quip," *The Atlantic*, March 27, 2014, https://www.theatlantic.com/politics/archive/2014/03/rumsfelds-knowns-and-unknowns-the-intellectual-history-of-a-quip/359719/ (accessed August 7, 2023).

5. "Iraq and Weapons of Mass Destruction," The National Security Archive, updated February 26, 2003, https://nsarchive2.gwu.edu/NSAEBB/NSAEBB80/ (accessed August 7, 2023). As we now know, the presence of weapons of mass destruction used as justification for the invasion of Iraq was never found. As history demonstrated, not seeing and understanding this risk had significant consequences.

6. Ed Young, "Why Do Scorpions Glow in the Dark (and Could Their Whole Bodies be One Big Eye)?" *Discover*, December 23, 2011, https://www.discovermagazine.com/the-sciences/why-do-scorpions-glow-in-the-dark-and-could-their-whole-bodies-be-one-big-eye (accessed August 7, 2023).

7. Pamela Weintraub, "The Doctor Who Drank Infectious Broth, Gave Himself an Ulcer, and Solved a Medical Mystery," *Discover*, April 8, 2010, https://www.discovermagazine.com/health/the-doctor-who-drank-infectious-broth-gave-himself-an-ulcer-and-solved-a-medical-mystery (accessed August 7, 2023).

8. "Rumble Strips and Rumble Stripes." US Department of Transportation Safety, Federal Highway Administration, https://safety.fhwa.dot.gov/roadway_dept/pavement/rumble_strips/ (accessed August 7, 2023).

9. "Antimicrobial Resistance," World Health Organization, http://www.who.int/antimicrobial-resistance/en/ (accessed August 7, 2023).

10. Sabrina Stierwalt, "How Are Seasonal Flu Vaccines Made?" *Scientific American*, February 4, 2016, https://www.scientificamerican.com/article/how-are-seasonal-flu-vaccines-made/ (accessed August 7, 2023).

11. "Vaccine Effectiveness: How Well Do the Flu Vaccines Work?" Centers for Disease Control and Prevention, reviewed on February 8, 2023, https://www.cdc.gov/flu/vaccines-work/vaccineeffect.htm (accessed August 7, 2023).

12. "U.S. Influenza Surveillance System: Purpose and Methods," Centers for Disease Control and Prevention, reviewed on October 15, 2019, https://www.cdc.gov/flu/weekly/overview.htm (accessed August 7, 2023).

13. Maggie Fox, "Why Next Year's Flu Vaccine Will Be Lousy, Too," NBC News, February 23, 2018, https://www.nbcnews.com/health/health-news/why-next-year-s-flu-vaccine-will-be-lousy-too-n850641 (accessed August 7, 2023).

14. "New Surgical Mask Doesn't Just Trap Viruses, It Renders Them Harmless: Innovative Improvement on Surgical Masks Will Make Them Effective by Empowering Them to Kill Viruses," University of Alberta, January 5, 2017, *ScienceDaily*, https://www.sciencedaily.com/releases/2017/01/170105160228.htm (accessed August 7, 2023).

15. W. R. Dowdle, "The Principles of Disease Elimination and Eradication," *Bull World Health Organ* 76 Suppl 2 (1998 2): 22–25, https://www.ncbi.nlm.nih.gov/pmc/articles/PMC2305684/ (accessed August 7, 2023).

16. "Vaccine Safety Basics e-Learning Course," World Health Organization, https://ipc.unicef.org/node/74 (accessed August 7, 2023).

17. Steven H. Woolf, Derek A. Chapman, and Jong Hyung Lee, "COVID-19 as the Leading Cause of Death in the United States," *JAMA*, December 17, 2020, https://jamanetwork .com/journals/jama/fullarticle/2774465 (accessed August 7, 2023).

18. Nassim Nicholas Taleb, *The Black Swan: The Impact of the Highly Improbable* (New York: Random House, 2007).

19. "Antimicrobial," Wikipedia, https://en.wikipedia.org/wiki/Antimicrobial (accessed August 7, 2023).

20. "Stop Antibiotics Before Resistance 'Tipping Point,'" *Science Magazine*, July, 10, 2018, https://scienmag.com/stop-antibiotics-before-resistance-tipping-point/ (accessed August 7, 2023).

21. "Antibiotic," Wikipedia, https://en.wikipedia.org/wiki/Antibiotic (accessed August 7, 2023).

22. Claudio O. Gualerzi, Letizia Brandi, Attilio Fabbretti, and Cynthia L. Pon, *Antibiotics: Targets, Mechanisms and Resistance* (Wiley, 2013), https://onlinelibrary.wiley.com /doi/10.1002/anie.201400593 (accessed August 7, 2023). Abstract: "Millions of lives have been saved by antibiotics since the onset of their use in therapy. However, while the golden era of antibiotic discovery is now over, the need for effective antibiotics is increased as the antibiotics pipelines have dwindled and life-threatening multiresistant pathogenic strains have spread. Finding new anti-infective drugs has become a worldwide emergency, and a more rational approach to antibiotic development is clearly needed to meet the medical need for next-generation antibiotics."

23. Mary Brophy Marcus, "Superbugs Could Kill More People Than Cancer, Report Warns," CBS News, May 19, 2016, https://www.cbsnews.com/news/superbugs-could-kill-more -people-than-cancer-report-warns/; "Tackling Drug-Resistant Infections Globally: Final Report and Recommendations," The Review on Antimicrobial-Resistance, Chaired by Jim O'Neill, published May 2016 (accessed August 7, 2023).

24. S. Gopinath, M. V. Kim, T. Rakib, et al., "Topical Application of Aminoglycoside Antibiotics Enhances Host Resistance to Viral Infections in a Microbiota-Independent Manner," *Nat Microbiol.* 3, no. 5 (2018): 611–621, https://pubmed.ncbi.nlm.nih.gov/29632368/ (accessed August 7, 2023).

25. Gabriel W. Rangel, "Say Goodbye to Antibacterial Soaps: Why the FDA Is Banning a Household Item," *Science in the News*, Harvard University, January 9, 2017, https://sitn .hms.harvard.edu/flash/2017/say-goodbye-antibacterial-soaps-fda-banning-household -item/ (accessed August 7, 2023).

26. Joseph Stromberg, "Five Reasons Why You Should Probably Stop Using Antibacterial Soap," *Smithsonian Magazine*, January 3, 2014, https://www.smithsonianmag.com /science-nature/five-reasons-why-you-should-probably-stop-using-antibacterial -soap-180948078/ (accessed August 7, 2023).

27. "Germs: Understand and Protect Against Bacteria, Viruses and Infection," Mayo Clinic, https://www.mayoclinic.org/diseases-conditions/infectious-diseases/in-depth/germs /art-20045289 (accessed August 7, 2023).

28. "Antimicrobial stewardship is a coordinated program that promotes the appropriate use of antimicrobials (including antibiotics), improves patient outcomes, reduces microbial resistance, and decreases the spread of infections caused by multidrug-resistant organisms," Association for Professionals in Infection Control and Epidemiology (APIC), https://apic.org/Professional-Practice/Practice-Resources/Antimicrobial-Stewardship (accessed August 7, 2023).

29. John L. Rosa, "U.S. Weight Loss Market Worth $66 Billion," WebWire, May 4, 2017, https://www.webwire.com/ViewPressRel.asp?aId=209054 (accessed August 7, 2023).

30. "Dietary Approaches to Stop Hypertension (DASH)," National Institutes of Health, https://www.nhlbi.nih.gov/health-topics/dash-eating-plan (accessed August 7, 2023).

31. "About the State of Childhood Obesity," Robert Wood Johnson Foundation, https://stateofobesity.org/about/ (accessed August 7, 2023).

32. Melissa G. Bublitz, Laura A. Peracchio, and Lauren G. Block, "Why Did I Eat That? Perspectives on Food Decision Making and Dietary Restraint," *Journal of Consumer Psychology* 20, no. 3, July 2010, 239–258, https://myscp.onlinelibrary.wiley.com/doi/abs/10.1016/j.jcps.2010.06.008 (accessed August 7, 2023).

33. James Hamblin, "Science Compared Every Diet, and the Winner Is Real Food," *The Atlantic*, March 24, 2014, https://www.theatlantic.com/health/archive/2014/03/science-compared-every-diet-and-the-winner-is-real-food/284595/ (accessed August 7, 2023).

34. E. J. Rhee "Weight Cycling and Its Cardiometabolic Impact," *J Obes Metab Syndr.* 26, no. 4 (2017): 237–242, https://doi.org/10.7570/jomes.2017.26.4.237 (accessed August 7, 2023).

35. Dominica Sarnecka, "Get the Best Route in Real Time With Help From Fellow Drivers," modified November 13, 2019, *HBS Digital Initiative,* https://d3.harvard.edu/platform-digit/submission/waze-get-the-best-route-in-real-time-with-help-from-fellow-drivers/ (accessed August 7, 2023).

36. Louis Columbus, "10 Charts That Will Change Your Perspective on Artificial Intelligence's Growth," *Forbes*, January 12, 2018, https://www.forbes.com/sites/louiscolumbus/2018/01/12/10-charts-that-will-change-your-perspective-on-artificial-intelligences-growth/#6a1196194758 (accessed August 7, 2023).

37. Similar to Moore's law describing the early growth of transistors and integrated circuits, AI is evolving toward a plateau. Where that plateau leads us is an open question, but autonomous vehicles will demonstrate greater reliability than humans are capable of providing.

38. *Training to proficiency* is an aviation term used to describe training to a performance level that meets or exceeds a qualification standard. The training must include enough repetition and practice to ensure that each individual can perform at the qualification standard level over the entire evaluation period or continuing qualification cycle. "The Advanced Qualification Program," Section 1 Safety Assurance System: Scope, Concepts, and Definitions, General Technical Administration, vol. 3, ch. 21, chrome-extension://efaidnbmnnnibpcajpcglclefindmkaj/https://www.faa.gov/sites/faa.gov/files/2022-11/AC-120-54A%2C%20Chg.1%2C%20AQP.pdf (accessed August 7, 2023).

39. "Neurology Traumatic Brain Injury and Concussion (NTBIC) Program," UCI Health, https://www.ucihealth.org/medical-services/neurology/traumatic-brain-injury-concussion (accessed August 7, 2023).

40. Oscar L. Alves, MD, and Ross Bullock, "Excitotoxic Damage in Traumatic Brain Injury," Department of Neurosurgery, Medical College of Virginia, USA and Faculdade de Me, dicina da Universidade do Porto, Portugal. This is introduced in the book *Brain Injury*, by Robert S. B. Clark and Patrick Kochanek, https://books.google.com/books?id=uRR4jKhF_iUC&pg=PA1#v=onepage&q&f=false (accessed August 7, 2023).

41. "Concussion," Mayo Clinic, https://www.mayoclinic.org/diseases-conditions/concussion/symptoms-causes/syc-20355594 (accessed August 7, 2023).

42. "Answering Questions About Chronic Traumatic Encephalopathy (CTE)," Centers for Disease Control and Prevention, updated January 2019, https://www.cdc.gov/traumaticbraininjury/pdf/CDC-CTE-ProvidersFactSheet-508.pdf (accessed August 7, 2023).

43. Cindy Boren, "A New Study Shows That Hits to the Head, Not Concussions, Cause CTE," *Washington Post*, January 18, 2018, https://www.washingtonpost.com/news /early-lead/wp/2018/01/18/a-new-study-shows-that-hits-to-the-head-not-concussions -cause-cte/ (accessed August 7, 2023).

44. Lisa and Dave are not the real names of the people involved in this true story.

45. Ashley Olivine, Ph.D., MPH, "Everything to Know About Epilepsy Service Dogs," VeryWell Health, https://www.verywellhealth.com/epilepsy-service-dog-7095512 (accessed August 7, 2023).

Chapter 3: System Reliability

1. Bailey Fink, "The Real Reason McDonald's Ice Cream Machines Are Always Broken," Allrecipes, July 15, 2022, https://www.allrecipes.com/article/the-real-reason-mcdonalds -ice-cream-machines-are-always-broken/ (accessed August 7, 2023).

2. "2021 Texas Power Crisis," Wikipedia, https://en.wikipedia.org/wiki/2021_Texas _power_crisis#:~:text=More%20than%204.5%20million%20homes,a%20result%20 of%20the%20crisis (accessed August 7, 2023).

3. "Minneapolis Interstate 35W Bridge Collapse," Minnesota Legislative Reference Library, reviewed October 2022, https://www.lrl.mn.gov/guides/guides?issue=bridges (accessed August 7, 2023).

4. Valerie Strauss, "Class Size Matters a Lot, Research Shows," *Washington Post*, February 24, 2014, https://www.washingtonpost.com/news/answer-sheet/wp/2014/02/24 /class-size-matters-a-lot-research-shows/ (accessed August 7, 2023); "Gladwell on the Effects of Class Size," *MONTROSE42* Blog, January 10, 2015, https://montrose42 .wordpress.com/2015/01/10/gladwell-on-the-effects-of-class-size/ (accessed August 7, 2023).

5. Christopher Lampton, "How Gas Pumps Work," How Stuff Works, July 28, 2009, https://auto.howstuffworks.com/gas-pump.htm (accessed August 7, 2023).

6. "Economic Stimulus Act of 2008," https://en.wikipedia.org/wiki/Economic_Stimulus _Act_of_2008 (accessed August 7, 2023).

Chapter 4: Human Reliability

1. This example is provided by a American Academy of Forensic Sciences member Brian J. Gestring.

2. Michael Burgstahler, "Why Can Computers Complete Some Tasks Exceptionally Well and Others Terribly?" Quora Online Forum, February 18, 2011, https://www.quora .com/Why-can-computers-complete-some-tasks-exceptionally-well-and-others-terribly (accessed August 7, 2023).

3. Nicholas A. Koeppen, "The Influence of Automation on Aviation Accident and Fatality Rates: 2000–2010," Embry-Riddle Aeronautical University, July 15, 2012, https://commons .erau.edu/publication/95/ (accessed August 7, 2023).

4. Applying the scientific method to this experience, then, might lead us to predict the challenges ahead as autonomous vehicles and software make their way onto our nation's roadways. It's easy to predict that drivers will face situations where confusion exists between the autopilot's control versus the driver's control over the car. Two central differences between our aviation example and the future of autonomous vehicles: 1) Most US drivers are not professionally "trained to proficiency," as commercial pilots are, and 2) Auto industry autonomous vehicle software and design criteria have not yet

been standardized, as they have in aviation. Both of these differences point to an early, if debatable, prediction: *Fewer fatalities are likely to result if we can avoid a prolonged period of driver involvement in semi-autonomous driving configurations.* Our provocative conclusion is that once the technology matures to an acceptable level of reliability, the greater the number of lives will be saved the sooner we can remove the human component from the driving system.

5. "Knowledge, Skills and Abilities (KSA): Definitions and Examples," Indeed Career Guide, January 27, 2020, https://www.indeed.com/career-advice/career-development /knowledge-skills-and-abilities (accessed August 7, 2023).

6. Jamie Notter, "No, Culture Does Not Eat Strategy for Breakfast," *Forbes*, May 22, 2018, https://www.forbes.com/sites/forbescoachescouncil/2018/05/22/no-culture-does -not-eat-strategy-for-breakfast/#6f8dc35776be (accessed August 7, 2023).

7. Katie Sullivan, "Peer Pressure May Improve Hand-Hygiene Compliance," Fierce Health-care, September 11, 2014. Studies have shown that healthcare workers' hand hygiene compliance rates improved with the presence and proximity of other healthcare work-ers, https://www.fiercehealthcare.com/healthcare/peer-pressure-may-improve-hand -hygiene-compliance (accessed August 7, 2023).

8. L. T. Kohn, J. M. Corrigan, and M. S. Donaldson, eds., *To Err Is Human: Building a Safer Health System* (Washington, DC: National Academy Press, Institute of Medicine, 1999).

9. Daniel Kahneman, *Thinking, Fast and Slow* (New York : Farrar, Straus and Giroux, 2011).

10. John Medina, *Brain Rules*. In this online video, Medina says: "Multitasking, when it comes to paying attention, is a myth. The brain naturally focuses on concepts sequen-tially, one at a time," http://brainrules.net/brain-rules/ (accessed August 7, 2023).

11. Malcolm Gladwell, *Blink: The Power of Thinking Without Thinking* (New York: Little, Brown, 2005).

12. J. W. Senders and N. P. Moray, *Human Error: Cause, Prediction, and Reduction*. Series in applied psychology (Hillsdale, NJ: Lawrence Erlbaum Associates, Inc., 1991).

13. J. W. Senders and N. P. Moray, *Human Error: Cause, Prediction, and Reduction*. See Reason-Norman definition on p. 27: "An action not in accord with the actor's intention, the result of a good plan but a poor execution."

14. "Act of omission and commission," Stack Exchange, edited December 8, 2017, https:// english.stackexchange.com/questions/207927/act-of-omission-and-commission (accessed August 7, 2023).

15. J. W. Senders and N. P. Moray, *Human Error: Cause, Prediction, and Reduction*, p. 26.

16. I. Wagner, "Total Number of Licensed Drivers in the U.S. in 2018, by State," Statista, February 26, 2020, https://www.statista.com/statistics/198029/total-number-of-us -licensed-drivers-by-state/ (accessed August 7, 2023).

17. Jonah Engel Bromwich, "New Jersey Is Last State to Insist at Gas Stations: Don't Touch That Pump," *New York Times*, January 5, 2018, https://www.nytimes.com/2018/01/05 /nyregion/new-jersey-gas-pump.html (accessed August 7, 2023).

18. "Advanced Driver-Assistance Systems," Wikipedia, https://en.wikipedia.org/wiki /Advanced_driver-assistance_systems (accessed August 7, 2023).

19. "Back to Basics: Multi-factor Authentication (MFA)," NIST, created June 28, 2016, updated December 9, 2019, https://www.nist.gov/itl/applied-cybersecurity/tig/back -basics-multi-factor-authentication (accessed August 7, 2023).

20. David L. Callender and Tonya R. Callender, "The Importance of Being Identified by the Patient Care Team with Two Forms of Identification," UTMB Health Resource Center, https://www.utmb.edu/health-resource-center/partner-in-your-care-patient-safety /two-patient-identifiers-for-every-test-and-procedure (accessed August 7, 2023).

21. Saul McLeod, "Fundamental Attribution Error," *Simply Psychology*, 2018, https://www
.simplypsychology.org/fundamental-attribution.html (accessed August 7, 2023).

22. Jay N. Giedd, "The Amazing Teen Brain," *Scientific American* 312, May 2016, pp. 32–37,
https://www.scientificamerican.com/article/the-amazing-teen-brain/ (accessed
August 7, 2023).

23. Ibid.

24. R. Huey, D. De Leonardis, and M. Freedman, *National Traffic Speeds Survey II: 2009*,
Report no. DOT HS-811-638 (Washington, DC: National Highway Traffic Safety Administration, 2012).

25. "Crocodile Hunter Escapes Charges," CNN, January 5, 2004, http://www.cnn.com
/2004/WORLD/asiapcf/auspac/01/02/australia.crocodileman/ (accessed August 7,
2023).

26. *Larry King Live*, CNN, November 25, 2004, http://edition.cnn.com/TRANSCRIPTS
/0411/25/lkl.01.html (accessed August 7, 2023).

27. "Insanity Is Doing the Same Thing Over and Over Again and Expecting Different Results," Quote Investigator, March 23, 2017, https://quoteinvestigator
.com/2017/03/23/same/ (August 7, 2023).

28. Alice Park, "Why We Take Risks—It's the Dopamine," *Time*, December 30, 2008,
https://content.time.com/time/health/article/0,8599,1869106,00.html (August 7, 2023).

29. John Medina, *Brain Rules: 12 Principles for Surviving and Thriving at Work, Home, and School*
(Seattle: Pear Press, 2008).

30. Ida Kvittingen, "Lower Speed Limits Save Lives," *ScienceNordic*, July 8, 2015, http://
sciencenordic.com/lower-speed-limits-save-lives (accessed August 7, 2023).

31. Seema Singh, "Why Correlation Does Not Imply Causation?" *Towards Data Science*,
August 24, 2018, https://towardsdatascience.com/why-correlation-does-not-imply
-causation-5b99790df07e (accessed August 7, 2023).

    Correlation is a statistical measure (expressed as a number) that describes the size
    and direction of a relationship between two or more variables. A correlation between
    variables, however, does not automatically mean that a change in one variable causes
    a change in the values of the other variable.

    Causation indicates that one event is the result of the occurrence of the other event;
    i.e., there is a causal relationship between the two events. This is also referred to as cause
    and effect.

32. "When and How to Wash Your Hands," Centers for Disease Control and Prevention,
reviewed on April 2, 2020, https://www.cdc.gov/features/handwashing/index.html
(accessed August 7, 2023).

33. "Hand Hygiene in Healthcare Settings," Centers for Disease Control and Prevention,
reviewed on April 29, 2019, https://www.cdc.gov/handhygiene/index.html (accessed
August 7, 2023).

34. Mark Sherman, "As Others See Us," *Psychology Today*, December 4, 2013, https://
https://www.psychologytoday.com/us/blog/real-men-dont-write-blogs/201312/
others-see-us (accessed August 7, 2023).

    Robert Burns, the great eighteenth-century Scottish poet and songwriter, wrote in
    the poem "To a Louse": "O wad some Power the giftie gie us, to see oursels as ithers
    see us!" Or, in modern English, "Oh would some Power the gift give us, to see ourselves
    as others see us."

35. Christopher Mele, "'The Five-Second Rule' for Food on Floor Is Untrue, Study Finds,"
New York Times, September 19, 2016, https://www.nytimes.com/2016/09/20/science

/five-second-rule.html#:~:text=What%20did%20the%20study%20find,fallen%20 food%20escaped%20contamination%20completely (accessed August 7, 2023).

36. Stefan Pfattheicher, Christoph Strauch, Svenja Diefenbacher, and Robert Schnuerch, "A Field Study on Watching Eyes and Hand Hygiene Compliance in a Public Restroom," *Journal of Applied Psychology* 48, no. 4, April 2018, pp. 188–194, https://onlinelibrary .wiley.com/doi/10.1111/jasp.12501 (accessed August 7, 2023); Mauricio N. Monsalve, Sriram V. Pemmaraju, Geb W. Thomas, Ted Herman, Alberto M. Segre, and Philip M. Polgreen, "Do Peer Effects Improve Hand Hygiene Adherence Among Healthcare Workers?" *Infection Control and Hospital Epidemiology* 35, no. 10, 1277–1285, https://doi .org/10.1086/678068 (accessed August 7, 2023).

37. Atul Gwande, "Personal Best," *New Yorker*, September 26, 2011, https://www.newyorker .com/magazine/2011/10/03/personal-best (accessed August 7, 2023).

38. Paul H. Robinson, "An Introduction to the Model Penal Code of the American Law Institute," *SSRN Electronic Journal*, January 2005, https://www.researchgate.net /publication/245550333_An_Introduction_to_the_Model_Penal_Code_of_the_American _Law_Institute (accessed August 7, 2023).

39. *Standing* is a legal term used in connection with lawsuits and a requirement of Article III of the United States Constitution. "If the party cannot show harm, the party does not have standing and is not the right party to be appearing before the court."

Chapter 5: Organizational Reliability

1. Mary Hall, "What Is Insider Trading and Is It Illegal?" *Investopedia*, updated July 31, 2019, https://www.investopedia.com/ask/answers/what-exactly-is-insider-trading/ (accessed August 7, 2023).

2. One online search provided the following result: "Core Values List: Over 500 Core Values Examples," https://www.threadsculture.com/core-values-examples (accessed August 7, 2023).

3. Saul McLeod, "Maslow's Hierarchy of Needs," *Simply Psychology*, updated March 20, 2020, https://www.simplypsychology.org/maslow.html (accessed August 7, 2023).

4. Enron is a cautionary example. In 2006, a jury in Houston, Texas, convicted former chief executive officers Kenneth L. Lay and Jeffrey K. Skilling on charges including conspiracy, securities fraud, wire fraud, and making false statements, eventually leading to the company's bankruptcy, https://en.wikipedia.org/wiki/Enron (accessed August 7, 2023).

5. "Mission, Vision, and Values," Lumen, https://courses.lumenlearning.com/wm -principlesofmanagement/chapter/reading-mission-vision-and-values/ (accessed August 7, 2023).

6. Startup, https://startuptalky.com/uber-story/ (accessed August 7, 2023).

7. Sarah Ashley O'Brien, "Uber's CEO One Year In: The One Thing I Wish I Had Fixed Sooner," CNN Business, August 29, 2018, https://money.cnn.com/2018/08/29/technology /uber-ceo-dara-khosrowshahi-one-year-anniversary/index.html (accessed August 7, 2023).

8. James A. Birchler, et al., "Heterosis," *Plant Cell* 22, no. 7 (2010): 2105–12, https://doi.org /10.1105/tpc.110.076133 (accessed August 7, 2023).

9. Groupthink can be defined as "the practice of thinking or making decisions as a group, resulting typically in unchallenged, poor-quality decision-making."

10. An excerpt from the NTSB Final Report NTSB/RAR-10/01, National Transporta- tion Safety Board PB2010-916301: "Records covering the twenty-eight days before the

accident showed five days with no text messaging and four days with more than one hundred text messages sent or received in a twenty-four-hour period. Activity on the remaining nineteen days averaged about forty messages a day," https://www.ntsb.gov /investigations/AccidentReports/Reports/RAR1001.pdf (accessed August 7, 2023).

11. Tomer Hochma, "The Ultimate List of Cognitive Biases: Why Humans Make Irrational Decisions," Scribd, May 30, 2018, https://www.scribd.com/document/449388077/03 -The-Ultimate-Guide-of-TOK-Theories# (accessed April 2, 2020).

12. "Five Things About Deterrence," National Institutes of Justice, June 5, 2016, Five Things About Deterrence," National Institutes of Justice (accessed August 7, 2023).

13. Norman Vincent Peale, author of *The Power of Positive Thinking*, https://en.wikipedia .org/wiki/The_Power_of_Positive_Thinking (accessed August 7, 2023).

14. Linda and Charlie Bloom, "The Bandwagon Effect," *Psychology Today*, August 11, 2017, https://www.psychologytoday.com/us/blog/stronger-the-broken-places/201708 /the-bandwagon-effect (accessed August 7, 2023).

15. Derek Sivers, "How to Start a Movement," TED2010, https://www.ted.com/talks /derek_sivers_how_to_start_a_movement?language=en (accessed August 7, 2023).

16. Shaunacy Ferro, "Jaywalking Behavior Varies by Culture, Study Confirms," *Mental Floss*, February 21, 2017, https://www.mentalfloss.com/article/92404/jaywalking -behavior-varies-culture-study-confirms (accessed August 7, 2023).

17. Todd Ballowe, "How to Identify Groupthink: An Introduction to the Abilene Paradox," On Strategy, https://onstrategyhq.com/resources/how-to-identify-groupthink-an -introduction-to-the-abilene-paradox/ (accessed August 7, 2023).

18. Disclaimer: In this book, we present general descriptions of adverse events that are known to the public, with open-source information cited wherever possible. In examples where we offer our analyses of these events, our intent is to help the reader manage risk in their everyday lives through an understanding of these accidents. In some cases, our insight into these events may differ from what investigating authorities concluded. It is not our intent to debate those findings where they may differ, but to shed light on how the Sequence of Reliability can help us manage risk more effectively in our daily lives.

19. Tariq Malik, "NASA's Space Shuttle by the Numbers: 30 Years of a Spaceflight Icon," Space.com, July 21, 2011, https://www.space.com/12376-nasa-space-shuttle-program -facts-statistics.html (accessed August 7, 2023).

20. "Richard Feynman (Articulate Scientist) - Space Shuttle Challenger Testimony," You-Tube, https://www.youtube.com/watch?v=MWZs8l2AMps (accessed August 7, 2023).

21. NASA.gov, *Columbia* Accident Investigation Board, Report Volume 1, August 2003.

22. Marie-Elisabeth Paté-Cornell and Robin Dillon, "Probabilistic Risk Analysis for the NASA Space Shuttle: A Brief History and Current Work," *Reliability Engineering & System Safety* 74 (2001), 345–352, https://www.researchgate.net/publication/223386540 _Probabilistic_Risk_Analysis_for_the_NASA_Space_Shuttle_A_Brief_History_and _Current_Work (accessed August 7, 2023).

23. "Space Shuttle Safety Upgrades," Office of the Inspector General, Audit Report, July 1, 2002, https://oig.nasa.gov/docs/ig-02-020.pdf (accessed August 7, 2023).

24. These examples are intended for illustration purposes only, and may not represent all the influences on system, human, and organizational performance.

25. "Predictively" is in the manner of something that tries or succeeds in predicting, antici-pating, or expecting. "Predictably" is in a manner that can be expected or anticipated, https://wikidiff.com/predictively/predictably (accessed August 7, 2023).

Chapter 6: Predictive Reliability

1. In general usage, *effectiveness* and *efficacy* have the same meaning. But in healthcare, clinical trials distinguish between efficacy trials (explanatory trials), which determine whether an intervention produces the expected result under ideal circumstances, and effectiveness trials (pragmatic trials), which measure the degree of beneficial effect under "real-world" clinical settings. Efficacy and effectiveness exist on a continuum, https://www.ncbi.nlm.nih.gov/books/NBK44024/ (accessed on August 7, 2023).

2. "Aviation Safety Action Program," Federal Aviation Administration, https://www.faa.gov/about/initiatives/asap/ (accessed on August 7, 2023).

3. Steve Wolf, "What Does 'Past Is Prologue' Mean: Psychologically Speaking?" http://www.multibriefs.com/briefs/ccapp/prologue.pdf (accessed August 7, 2023).

4. "Abraham Lincoln," Quotemaster, https://www.quotemaster.org/qcobb04f08e008059d8c5512ab8e833d0 (accessed August 7, 2023).

5. James Reason, "A System Approach to Organizational Error," *Ergonomics* 38 (1995): 1708–1721, https://doi.org/10.1080/00140139508925221 (accessed August 7, 2023).

6. James Reason, *Managing the Risks of Organizational Accidents* (Aldershot: Ashgate, 1997).

7. "James Reason HF Model," https://www.skybrary.aero/index.php/James_Reason_HF_Model (accessed August 7, 2023).

8. Adam J. McKee, "Broken Windows Theory," *Britannica*, https://www.britannica.com/topic/broken-windows-theory (accessed August 7, 2023).

9. William Keller and Mohammad Modarres, "A Historical Overview of Probabilistic Risk Assessment Development and Its Use in the Nuclear Power Industry: A Tribute to the Late Professor Norman Carl Rasmussen," *Reliability Engineering & System Safety* 89, no. 3 (September 2005), https://www.sciencedirect.com/science/article/pii/S0951832004002327 (accessed August 7, 2023).

10. "MTBF, MTTR, MTTA, and MTTF: Understanding a Few of the Most Common Incident Metrics," Atlassian Incident Management, https://www.atlassian.com/incident-management/kpis/common-metrics (accessed August 7, 2023).

11. One of the goals of this book is to avoid overly challenging terms and methods beyond the scope of a general readership. The term *mathematical fault trees* is more accurately referred to as Boolean Fault Tree Analysis. But don't be intimidated. Although the mathematics used in performing fault-tree calculations can seem difficult, the statistical formulas are rather straightforward to learn. A simple discussion on this topic can be found at https://en.wikipedia.org/wiki/Fault_tree_analysis (accessed August 7, 2023).

12. "Collision of Metrolink Train 111 with Union Pacific Train LOF65-12," National Transportation Safety Board, January 21, 2010, https://www.ntsb.gov/investigations/AccidentReports/Reports/RAR1001.pdf (accessed August 7, 2023).

    An excerpt from the NTSB Final Report NTSB/RAR-10/01 National Transportation Safety Board PB2010-916301: "Records covering the twenty-eight days before the accident showed five days with no text messaging and four days with more than one hundred text messages sent or received in a twenty-four-hour period. Activity on the remaining nineteen days averaged about forty messages a day."

13. The Associated Press, "California Regulators Ban Cell Phone Use by Train Operators," September 19, 2008, *New York Daily News,* http://www.nydailynews.com/news/world/california-regulators-ban-cell-phone-train-operators-article-1.323507 (accessed August 7, 2023).

14. "Human Error Led to Fatal Train Collision, Spokeswoman Says," CNN, September 14, 2008, http://www.cnn.com/2008/US/09/13/train.collision/ (accessed August 7, 2023).

15. Of course, hindsight bias would lead us to conclude this to be a cause of this accident, which wouldn't be accurate. We could say that the stoplight system was not resilient, and this fact may have contributed to the accident. But to be precisely accurate, we would say that the lack of unidirectional track was *not causal* because it was not a part of the system design at the time of the accident.

16. National Transportation Safety Board, "Collision of Metrolink Train 111 with Union Pacific Train LOF65-12," January 21, 2010, https://www.ntsb.gov/investigations/Accident Reports/Reports/RAR1001.pdf (accessed April 2, 2020).

17. "Positive Train Control," Union Pacific, https://www.up.com/media/media_kit/ptc /index.htm (accessed August 7, 2023); James Rainey, "'Positive Train Control' Ordered by Congress, but Not Yet in Place," NBC News, December 18, 2017, https://www .nbcnews.com/news/us-news/positive-train-control-ordered-congress-not-yet-place -n830961 (accessed August 7, 2023).

18. "Load Shedding: A Valuable Skill for Pilots and Leaders," Flight Level Leadership, June 22, 2011, http://flightlevelleadership.blogspot.com/2011/06/load-shedding-valuable -skill-for-pilots.html (accessed August 7, 2023). The term *load shedding* is an electrical reference to how systems operate. But it applies equally to humans who can become task-saturated under certain conditions. It's an example of the hidden science: Understanding how load shedding happens to systems and people requires a multidisciplinary approach.

19. "The Brain Cannot Multi-Task," YouTube, February 5, 2008, https://www.youtube .com/watch?v=xO_oEGHWSMU (accessed August 7, 2023).

Chapter 7: Big Challenges

1. "Nuremberg Trials," The History Channel, updated June 7, 2010, https://www.history .com/topics/world-war-ii/nuremberg-trials (accessed August 7, 2023).

2. Christina Nunez, January 22, 2019, "What Is Global Warming, Explained," *National Geographic*, https://www.nationalgeographic.com/environment/article/global-warming -overview (accessed August 7, 2023).

3. Paul Hawken, ed., *Drawdown* (New York: Penguin Books, 2017).

4. One Earth home page, https://www.oneearth.org/who-we-fund/media-advocacy -grants/project-drawdown-100-solutions-to-reverse-global-warming/ (accessed August 7, 2023).

5. "DOE National Laboratory Makes History by Achieving Fusion Ignition," Department of Energy, December 13, 2022, https://www.energy.gov/articles/doe-national -laboratory-makes-history-achieving-fusion-ignition (accessed August 7, 2023).

6. Ana M. Soto and Carlos Sonnenschein, "Environmental Causes of Cancer: Endocrine Disruptors as Carcinogens," *Nat Rev Endocrinol.* 6, no. 7 (July 2020): 363–370, https:// pubmed.ncbi.nlm.nih.gov/20498677/ (accessed August 7, 2023).

Chapter 8: Flipping the Iceberg

1. "Flying Quotes of All Kinds," National Poetry Day, https://nationalpoetryday.co.uk /poem/high-flight/ (accessed August 7, 2023).

2. George W. Kattawar, PhD, https://physics.tamu.edu/directory/kattawar/ (accessed August 7, 2023).

3. For an excellent treatment of this general topic, see Craig F. Bohren and Donald R. Huffman, *Absorption and Scattering of Light by Small Particles* (Wiley, 1983).

4. Chris Woodford, "Lidar," Explainthatstuff !, updated January 21, 2019, https://www
.explainthatstuff.com/lidar.html (accessed August 7, 2023).

5. "Doppler Shift," National Aeronautics and Space Administration, https://imagine.gsfc
.nasa.gov/features/yba/M31_velocity/spectrum/doppler_more.html (accessed August
7, 2023).

6. K. Scott Griffith, "Simulated Performance of an Airborne Lidar Wind Shear Detection
System," submitted to the Graduate College of Texas A&M University Physics Depart-
ment in partial fulfillment of the requirement for the degree of Master of Science,
December 1987.

7. Dr. Michael Kavaya, https://lasersdbw.larc.nasa.gov/about-us/profiles/profiles-
michael-j-kavaya/(accessed August 7, 2023); "Russell Targ," Wikipedia, https://
en.wikipedia.org/wiki/Russell_Targ (accessed August 7, 2023); "Dr. Roland Bowles,"
https://www.rmc.edu/news-and-calendar/current-news/2018/03/09/aerospace
-researcher-roland-bowles-58-to-receive-award (accessed August 7, 2023).

8. "The Enhanced Fujita Scale (EF Scale)," NOAA's National Weather Service, https://
www.spc.noaa.gov/efscale/ (accessed August 7, 2023).

9. Yuan-Xiang Li, Qi Hu, and Shi-Qian Liu, "Wind-Shear Prediction with Airport LIDAR
Data," IEEE Explore Digital Library, November 12, 2012, https://ieeexplore.ieee.org/
document/6350611/ (accessed August 7, 2023).

10. Waheed Uddin, principal investigator, "Light Detection and Ranging (LIDAR) Deploy-
ment for Airport Obstructions Surveys," Airport Cooperative Research Program, July
2010, https://www.nap.edu/read/14398/chapter/1 (accessed August 7, 2023).

11. Jamie Condliffe, "This New Lidar Sensor Could Equip Every Autonomous Car in
the World by the End of 2018," *MIT Technology Review*, April 12, 2018, https://www
.technologyreview.com/s/610858/this-new-lidar-sensor-could-equip-every-autonomous
-car-in-the-world-by-the-end-of-2018/ (accessed August 7, 2023).

12. Joe Godfrey, "Profile: Cecil Ewell," AVweb, September 29, 1999, https://www.avweb
.com/features/cecil-ewell/ (accessed August 7, 2023).

13. "Aviation Safety Reporting Program," Federal Aviation Administration, December
16, 2011, https://asrs.arc.nasa.gov/?submit1=Continue (accessed August 7, 2023). The
Aviation Safety Reporting System, or ASRS, is the US Federal Aviation Administration's
(FAA) voluntary confidential reporting system that allows pilots and other aircraft crew
members to confidentially report near misses and close calls in the interest of improving
air safety. The ASRS collects, analyzes, and responds to voluntarily submitted aviation
safety incident reports in order to lessen the likelihood of aviation accidents. The confidential and independent nature of the ASRS is key to its success, since reporters do
not have to worry about any possible negative consequences of coming forward with
safety problems. The ASRS is run by NASA, a neutral party, since it has no power in
enforcement. The success of the system serves as a positive example that is often used
as a model by other industries seeking to make improvements in safety.

14. "Bill Reynard: A Lawyer for All Seasons," *Callback* (NASA's Aviation Safety Reporting System), https://asrs.arc.nasa.gov/publications/callback/cb_204a.htm (accessed
August 7, 2023).

15. "National Air and Space Museum Director Donald Engen Dies in Glider Accident,"
Smithsonian National Air and Space Museum, July 14, 1999, https://airandspace.si.edu
/newsroom/press-releases/national-air-and-space-museum-director-donald-engen-dies
-glider-accident (accessed August 7, 2023).

16. "David R. Hinson," https://peoplepill.com/people/david-r-hinson/ (accessed August
7, 2023).

17. "Aviation Safety Action Program," Federal Aviation Administration, updated August 24, 2017, https://www.faa.gov/about/initiatives/asap/ (accessed August 7, 2023).

18. The Airline Transport Association, or ATA, was renamed Airlines for America, or A4A, in 2011, https://www.prnewswire.com/news-releases/air-transport-association-changes-name-to-airlines-for-america-134819198.html (accessed August 7, 2023).

19. "A Brief History of the FAA," Federal Aviation Administration, https://www.faa.gov/about/history/brief_history (accessed August 7, 2023).

20. Ibid.

21. "History of the National Transportation Safety Board," NTSB, https://www.ntsb.gov/about/history/Pages/default.aspx (accessed August 7, 2023).

22. You've heard of Moore's law, right? In 1965, Gordon Moore, the cofounder of Fairchild Semiconductor and Intel, made the prediction (or actually, extrapolation) that the number of transistors in a dense integrated circuit doubles approximately every two years. This "law" held true until roughly 2015, when Moore himself observed an effect he called "saturation." Rachel Courtland, https://spectrum.ieee.org/gordon-moore-the-man-whose-name-means-progress (accessed August 7, 2023).

23. "Crew Resource Management," Wikipedia, https://en.wikipedia.org/wiki/Crew_resource_management (accessed August 7, 2023); R. L. Helmreich, A. C. Merritt, and J. A. Wilhelm, "The Evolution of Crew Resource Management Training in Commercial Aviation," *International Journal of Aviation Psychology* 9, no. 1 (1999): 19–32, https://www.tandfonline.com/doi/abs/10.1207/s15327108ijap0901_2 (accessed August 7, 2023).

24. The author's observations in CRM classes taught in 1985 at American Airlines.

25. William Langewiesche, "The Human Factor," *Vanity Fair*, October 2014, https://archive.vanityfair.com/article/2014/10/the-human-factor (accessed August 7, 2023).

26. L. Pearce Williams, "The History of Science," *Britannica*, https://www.britannica.com/science/history-of-science (accessed August 7, 2023).

27. "Scientific Method," Wikipedia, https://en.wikipedia.org/wiki/Scientific_method (accessed August 7, 2023).

28. "Richard P. Feynman Quotes," YouTube, https://www.youtube.com/watch?v=p2xhb-SdKog (accessed March 31, 2020).

29. I. A. Walker, S. Reshamwalla, and I. H. Wilson, "Surgical Safety Checklists: Do They Improve Outcomes?" *BJA: British Journal of Anaesthesia* 109, no. 1, July 2012, pp. 47–54, https://doi.org/10.1093/bja/aes175 (accessed August 7, 2023).

30. Qing Li, "'Forest Bathing' Is Great for Your Health. Here's How to Do It," *Time*, May 1, 2018, https://time.com/5259602/japanese-forest-bathing/ (accessed August 7, 2023).

31. "Burn-out an 'Occupational Phenomenon': International Classification of Diseases," World Health Organization, May 28, 2019, https://www.who.int/news/item/28-05-2019-burn-out-an-occupational-phenomenon-international-classification-of-diseases (accessed August 7, 2023).

32. "What Is Data Encryption? Definition, Best Practices & More," Data Insider, November 7, 2022, https://digitalguardian.com/blog/what-data-encryption (accessed August 7, 2023).

33. James Reason, *Managing the Risks of Organizational Accidents* (London: Routledge, 1997).

34. L. T. Kohn, J. M. Corrigan, and M. S. Donaldson, eds., *To Err Is Human: Building a Safer Health System*.

35. Chen Liang, Qi Miao, Hong Kang, Amy Vogelsmeier, Tina Hilmas, Jing Wang, and Yang Gong, "Leveraging Patient Safety Research: Efforts Made Fifteen Years Since *To Err Is Human*," *Studies in Health Technology and Informatics* 264 (2019): 983–987, https://pubmed.ncbi.nlm.nih.gov/31438071/ (accessed August 7, 2023).

36. "ISO 9001 and Related Standards," International Standards Organization, https://www
.iso.org/iso-9001-quality-management.html (accessed August 7, 2023).

37. "Bluetooth," *Britannica*, https://www.britannica.com/technology/Bluetooth (accessed
August 7, 2023).

38. The origin of the "Big Rocks" concept is unknown, but it was popularized by Stephen
Covey in his book *The Seven Habits of Highly Effective People*; Mark Nevins, "What Are
Your Big Rocks?" *Forbes*, January 21, 2020, https://www.forbes.com/sites/hillennevins
/2020/01/21/what-are-your-big-rocks/ (accessed August 7, 2023).

39. David Yaffe-Bellany, Matthew Goldstein, and Emily Flitter, "Prosecutors Say FTX
Was Engaged in a 'Massive, Yearslong Fraud,'" *New York Times*, https://www.nytimes
.com/2022/12/13/business/ftx-sam-bankman-fried-fraud-charges.html (accessed
December 14, 2022).

Epilogue

1. Maria Papageorgiou, "Nick Sabatini: Up Close and Personal," Federal Aviation Administration, chrome-extension://efaidnbmnnnibpcajpcglclefindmkaj/https://www.faa
.gov/sites/faa.gov/files/about/history/people/Sabatini_Up_Close_and_Personal
.pdf (accessed August 7, 2023).

2. Michael Huerta, "Infoshare Works," speech, September 23, 2014, https://www.faa.gov
/air_traffic/environmental_issues (accessed August 7, 2023).

3. Paul LeSage, Jeff T. Dyar, and Bruce Evans, *Crew Resource Management: Principles and
Practice* (Jones and Bartlett, 2011).

4. Richard P. Feynman, *What Do YOU Care What Other People Think?: Further Adventures of
a Curious Character* (New York: W. W. Norton, 1988).

INDEX

ABOUT THE AUTHOR

K. SCOTT GRIFFITH is the founder and managing partner of SG Collaborative Solutions, LLC. He is the originator of the world's first organizational high reliability and just culture standard that is independently audited and certified by a world-leading international accreditation organization. Widely known as the father of the Aviation Safety Action Program, which contributed to a 95 percent reduction in the US fatal accident rate, his work has made high consequence industries more reliable across the globe. In *The Leader's Guide to Managing Risk*, he brings the secrets of his success to any business, organization, or individual striving for sustainable results. An author, speaker, consultant, physicist, captain, and former airline executive, he resides in Westlake, Texas.